Dubai

Richard Plunkett
Lou Callan

LONELY PLANET PUBLICATIONS
Melbourne • Oakland • London • Paris

Dubai
2nd edition – September 2002
First published – April 2000

Published by
Lonely Planet Publications Pty Ltd ABN 36 005 607 983
90 Maribyrnong St, Footscray, Victoria 3011, Australia

Lonely Planet offices
Australia Locked Bag 1, Footscray, Victoria 3011
USA 150 Linden St, Oakland, CA 94607
UK 10a Spring Place, London NW5 3BH
France 1 rue du Dahomey, 75011 Paris

Photographs
Many of the images in this guide are available for licensing from
Lonely Planet Images.
W www.lonelyplanetimages.com

Front cover photograph
Man using mobile phone in front of the Dubai Creek Golf & Yacht Club
(Hugh Sitton, Getty Images)

Map section title page photograph
Aerial view of Dubai (Chris Mellor)

ISBN 1 74059 130 5

Contents – Text

1

PLACES TO STAY 100

PLACES TO EAT 109

ENTERTAINMENT 119

SHOPPING 126

EXCURSIONS 134

LANGUAGE 151

GLOSSARY 159

INDEX 172

METRIC CONVERSION inside back cover

Contents – Maps

The Authors

Richard Plunkett

Richard grew up on a farm and vineyard near Avenel, Australia. He's been a stockmarket reporter, rock concert reviewer (a veteran of no less than three Bon Jovi concerts), farm labourer, sub-editor for *The Big Issue*, and once very briefly had the job of cleaning the mincer at a butchers. Since becoming a travel writer he's visited places like Turkmenistan, the Deccan, Karakalpakstan and Bangladesh. When he's not travelling or travel writing, he writes screenplays.

Lou Callan

After completing a degree in languages, Lou bounced between a variety of jobs while completing further study in publishing and editing. After lots of strenuous book launch parties as Publicity Manager at Oxford University Press Australia, she found work as a contributing editor on *Australian Bookseller & Publisher*. In 1998, after four years at LP as phrasebooks editor, Lou packed up and followed her husband, Tony, to the red dunes of the United Arab Emirates for a very long, hot 2½ years. Here she wrote LP's *Dubai* and, with Gordon Robison, *Oman & the UAE* as well as an update for *Middle East* (3rd edition).

FROM RICHARD

Special thanks to Sophie Morell for her company and sense of humour. Thanks also to Inger Rasmussen at Orient Tours, Siobhan and Adrian at the Sandy Beach Diving Centre, Valerie Upham, Louise Mulshaw and Kathy Mitchell in Dubai, Paul Hofman in Ras al-Khaimah, Peter Deakon and Sohrab Motiwalla at the Victorian Government Export Centre, Colin Richardson, Mohammed Odadi, Marcela Maximova, Samir Ozturk, Ajay Rajguru at the DTCM, Tim Gane, Laetitia Sadier and Mary Hansen. Thanks to Finola Collins in the LP London office for help with flight prices. Thanks also to the author of the 1st edition, Lou Callan (sorry about the mix-up with the *bahoor*) and to Tony Wheeler and Virginia Maxwell for tips and advice. Thanks to all the people who wrote to LP about the last edition.

Back home, thanks to my attorney Justin Wheelahan, long-suffering screenwriting partner Andrew Eather, and most of all to the ever-lovely and charming scientician, Rebecca Ryan.

This Book

The 1st edition of this book was researched and written by Lou Callan; Richard Plunkett revised and updated the text for this 2nd edition.

FROM THE PUBLISHER

The 2nd edition of *Dubai* was edited by Isabelle Young and proofed by Bethune Carmichael. Rodney Zandbergs was responsible for mapping and design. Emma Koch organised the Language chapter; Maria Vallianos designed the cover; Annie Horner from LPI coordinated the photographic images; and Brigitte Ellemor and Meredith Mail were the seniors who oversaw the whole project.

Thanks to author Richard Plunkett for producing a guide that was such a pleasure to work on.

THANKS

Many thanks to the travellers who used the last edition and wrote to us with helpful hints, useful advice and interesting anecdotes:

Micheal Gatto, Gordon Adamson, Temather Al-Rubai, Morten Anthun, Jonathon Aubrey, Elizabeth Bellingham, Marzia Belliami, Michelle Cave, Julia Clark, Ted Cole, Neil Cullen, Marie Dineen, June Egglestone, Tony Fisher, Hetty Fletcher, Alexander Garcia, JK Gill, Vanni Gibertini, Scott Gray, Terje Hagen, John Harrison, Pat Harrison, Brett Havenaar, Shanika Hewa-Geeganage, Derek Holmes, Andrea Hooper, Adrian Jones, James Laidlaw, Vanessa Lawrey, Claire Lessard, Paris Lord, Delyan Manchev, Michael Middleton, C Ng, Vicky Ogilvie, Chris Potts, Jon L Rider, Mike Scales, Ushy Schorno, HJ Small, Carol Stigley, Isabel Van Rompaey, Louisa Walkley, Anja Wildhagen, Michael Wildhagen, Roland Young

THANKS
Many thanks to the travellers who used the last edition and wrote to us with helpful hints, advice and interesting anecdotes. Your names appear in the back of this book.

Foreword

ABOUT LONELY PLANET GUIDEBOOKS

The story begins with a classic travel adventure: Tony and Maureen Wheeler's 1972 journey across Europe and Asia to Australia. There was no useful information about the overland trail then, so Tony and Maureen published the first Lonely Planet guide to meet a growing need.

From a kitchen table, Lonely Planet has grown to become the largest independent travel publisher in the world, with offices in Melbourne (Australia), Oakland (USA), London (UK) and Paris (France). Today Lonely Planet guidebooks cover the globe. There is an ever-growing list of books and information in a variety of media. Some things haven't changed. The main aim is still to make it possible for adventurous travellers to get out there – to explore and better understand the world.

At Lonely Planet we believe travellers can make a positive contribution to the countries they visit if they respect their host communities and spend their money wisely. Since 1986 a percentage of the income from each book has been donated to aid projects and human rights campaigns and, more recently, to wildlife conservation.

Although inclusion in a guidebook usually implies a recommendation we cannot list every good place. Exclusion does not necessarily imply criticism. In fact there are a number of reasons why we might exclude a place – sometimes it is simply inappropriate to encourage an influx of travellers.

UPDATES & READER FEEDBACK

Things change – prices go up, schedules change, good places go bad and bad places go bankrupt. Nothing stays the same. So, if you find things better or worse, recently opened or long-since closed, please tell us and help make the next edition even more accurate and useful.

Lonely Planet thoroughly updates each guidebook as often as possible – usually every two years, although for some destinations the gap can be longer. Between editions, up-to-date information is available in our free, quarterly *Planet Talk* newsletter and monthly email bulletin *Comet*. The *Upgrades* section of our website (W www.lonelyplanet.com) is also regularly updated by Lonely Planet authors, and the site's *Scoop* section covers news and current affairs relevant to travellers. Lastly, the *Thorn Tree* bulletin board and *Postcards* section carry unverified, but fascinating, reports from travellers.

Tell us about it! We genuinely value your feedback. A well-travelled team at Lonely Planet reads and acknowledges every email and letter we receive and ensures that every morsel of information finds its way to the relevant authors, editors and cartographers.

Everyone who writes to us will find their name listed in the next edition of the appropriate guidebook, and will receive the latest issue of *Comet* or *Planet Talk*. The very best contributions will be rewarded with a free guidebook.

We may edit, reproduce and incorporate your comments in Lonely Planet products such as guidebooks, websites and digital products, so let us know if you don't want your comments reproduced or your name acknowledged.

How to contact Lonely Planet:
Online: e talk2us@lonelyplanet.com.au, W www.lonelyplanet.com
Australia: Locked Bag 1, Footscray, Victoria 3011
UK: 10a Spring Place, London NW5 3BH
USA: 150 Linden St, Oakland, CA 94607

Introduction

Aquamarine water, sandy beaches and only five days of rain a year have put Dubai on the map as a holiday destination. Once you have brushed the sand from your toes, there's much more to enjoy and admire. In less than 50 years the city has transformed itself from a sleepy port to a fast-rising global metropolis, built on trade and a quick eye for an opportunity.

One of the best things about Dubai is that you feel you're really in the middle of all this activity. Massive ships loom over Port Rashid, while goods are loaded and off-loaded on hundreds of dhows on the Creek in the heart of the city.

The audacity of the city's rulers is breath-taking. Running out of coastline to build new hotels? Build vast artificial islands with 120km of new beachfront. Need better connections with the world? Build up an award-winning international airline in 15 years. Need some publicity? Stage the world's richest horse race, million-dollar lotteries, international tennis and golf tournaments, and a month-long shopping festival. Need a few landmarks for people to recognise? Up goes the world's tallest and most lavish hotel, built on an artificial platform, and a growing collection of stunning skyscrapers.

The city is a like a particularly success-ful game of SimCity. Once dhows trickled into the city's modest harbour; now Boeings and Airbuses zoom in daily from hundreds of cities to Dubai's ultramodern airport. Bazaars made of mud and palm fronds have made way for vast shopping centres and glittering gold and jewellery shops. Searing summer temperatures and rainless months have been conquered with air-conditioned life and freshwater extracted from the sea, while sun-starved Europeans flock in to soak up Dubai's endless sunny days.

When you first see the glistening, mod-ern buildings lining Dubai Creek and Sheikh Zayed Rd, or sip French wine well into the night at one of the city's many nightclubs, it's hard to believe that this was once an empty, arid desert inhabited by more camels than people.

Nowadays, everyone comes to Dubai for a piece of the action. Pakistani labourers, Indian taxi drivers, Sri Lankan maids, English businessmen, Australian nurses, Jordanian teachers, Filipino waitresses – they're all here, chasing opportunities and a lifestyle unavailable back home. This is what gives the place its polyglot zing and fascinating mix of Arab, Indian, Asian and Western lifestyles and cultures.

It's a go-getting city, ever ready to pounce on an opportunity; whether it's gold for Indians, Swiss watches for Iranians or beach holidays for Europeans, Dubai has the nous to grab a chance when it comes.

Yet Islam is still at the core of Dubai's values. Every neighbourhood in town has its mosque, and the city takes Friday off to de-vote prayers to God. For 11 months of the year you can dance in clubs to the latest trance beats, but not during the fasting month of Ramadan. The sheikhs may drive in shiny new 4WDs and chat on mobile phones, but when the call to prayer wails out from loudspeakers many will pause to pray.

Dubai doesn't believe in any sort of in-tolerant brand of Islam. This is an Islam built on tolerance, honesty and a strong sense of family. Much of the local popula-tion is made up of expats, many of whom are Hindu or Christian, not Muslim.

In architecture Dubai is also a treasure trove of contrasting styles. Rubbing shoul-ders with the postmodern glass, metal and steel skyscrapers sprouting from the sandy coastal flats are traditionally designed mosques, courtyard houses and wind tow-ers. Feast your eyes on the incongruity of these traditional and modern styles, which provide a fascinating portal to the past and the future.

Facts about Dubai

HISTORY
Early Settlement

Less is known about the early history of the area that now forms the United Arab Emirates than about other areas of the Gulf. It is certain, however, that this part of Arabia has been settled for millennia. Archaeological remains found in Al-Qusais, on the northeastern outskirts of present-day Dubai, prove there were humans here as far back as 8000 BC, after the end of the last Ice Age.

Up until 3000 BC the area supported nomadic herders of sheep, goats and cattle. It's thought these early inhabitants camped on the coast and fished during winter, and moved inland with their herds during summer. The first signs of trade emerge with the discovery of pottery from Ubaid (in present-day Iraq) dating back to 5000 BC. Agriculture developed with the cultivation of the date palm around 2500 BC, which not only provided food and a range of materials for building and weaving but also shelter for smaller plants grown for food.

Archaeological evidence also suggests that this area, together with present-day Oman, was closely associated with the Magan civilisation during the Bronze Age. It is thought that the Magans dominated the ancient world's copper trade, exploiting the rich veins of copper in the hills throughout the Hajar Mountains and especially near Sohar (in Oman). It is also likely that they traded pearls in Mesopotamia (now Iraq) and with the Indus Valley civilisation (in present-day Pakistan).

All records of the Magan civilisation cease after the 2nd millennium BC and some historians have speculated that the desertification of the area hastened its demise; others have argued that its importance may have been diminished by the growing reliance on iron over copper for the manufacture of weapons and tools.

The next major occupation of the area does not seem to have occurred for another two millennia. Archaeological excavations at Jumeira, about 10km south of Dubai Creek, have revealed a caravan station dating from the 6th century AD, which is thought to have links with the Sassanid empire. The Sassanids, a dynasty who ruled in Persia from AD 224 to 636, wielded power over the region from about the 3rd century AD until they were uprooted by an Islamic tribe called the Umayyads in the 7th century. Archaeologists believe that the buildings at Jumeira were restored and extended by the Umayyad dynasty, making it the only site in the UAE to span the pre-Islamic and Islamic periods.

The Umayyads brought the Arabic language and joined the region with the Islamic world. Christianity had made a brief appearance in the region in the form of the Nestorian sect, members of which had a monastery on Sir Bani Yas Island west of Abu Dhabi in the 5th century. However, it was the arrival of Islam that shaped the future of the region. The early Islamic period from the 7th century to the 14th century hasn't been well documented in the UAE. It is known that during this period the area was loosely under the control of the Umayyads and their successors the Abbasids. After the Baghdad-based Abbasid dynasty went into decline around AD 1000, the centre of power in the Islamic world shifted to Cairo, leaving the UAE isolated on the periphery. In the absence of centralised control, the tribes of the Arabian Peninsula asserted themselves in the hinterlands, while the coastal regions were dominated by trading ports such as Julfar, near present-day Ras al-Khaimah, and Hormuz, an island in the Strait of Hormuz.

In the early Islamic period, the Gulf experienced a boom in maritime trade due to its location on the major trade routes between the Mediterranean Sea and the Indian Ocean. Trade soon became the backbone of the local economy as ships travelled as far as China, returning laden with silk and porcelain.

Pearling

Memories of the heyday of pearling are laced with romanticism. But for those who went out to collect the pearls, it was a life of hardship as well as pride. For those who dived the depths the rewards were no match for the dangers involved. Most of the divers were slaves from East Africa and the profits of the industry went straight to their master, the owner of the boat.

The only equipment the divers used was a rope tied around the waist, a turtle-shell peg on their nose and leather finger gloves to protect their hands from the sharp coral and shells. At certain times of the year they would wear an all-over muslin bodysuit to protect them from jellyfish stings. The best pearls were found at depths of up to 36m and divers would be under the water for around three minutes. To reach this depth, divers used a rope weighted with a stone that was tied to the boat and thrown overboard.

The pearl-diving season lasted from May until September. On the ship there would be divers, men responsible for hauling up the divers after each dive, a cook, and boys employed to serve food and water and open the oyster shells. Each boat also had a singer, called the *naham*, whose job was to lead the crew in songs or lighten their mood by singing to them. Many of the songs were about lucky men who had become rich through diving, and the joys of returning home after the diving season.

Back on shore, pearl merchants would grade the pearls according to size by using a number of copper sieves, each with different sized holes. The greatest market for pearls was originally India, but in the early 20th century the UK and the US became keen buyers of this fashionable jewel. The discovery of the means to make artificial pearls in the early 20th century triggered the demise of the industry.

The Dubai Museum and the Diving Village feature significant displays on pearling.

The earliest recorded accounts of settlement in Dubai itself came from two Italian explorers: Gasparo Balbi and Marco Polo. In 1580 Marco Polo described Dubai as a prosperous town, largely dependent on pearl fishing.

European Presence

Attracted by the lucrative trade routes with India and the Far East, in the late 16th century Portugal became the first European power to take an interest in this part of the Gulf coast. Its occupation of the area lasted until the 1630s and eventually extended as far north as Bahrain. The arrival of the well-armed Portuguese was a disaster for the Muslim traders. The Portuguese wanted a monopoly on trade routes between Europe and India and they brooked no rivals. Local trade dried up to the extent that many coastal settlements were practically abandoned, and the tribes took refuge in oases far from the coast such as Liwa and Al-Ain. The only evidence of the Portuguese presence today, however, is the two cannons on display at the Dubai Museum.

The area was subsequently infiltrated by the French and the Dutch in the 17th and 18th centuries, both of whom also aspired to control the trading routes to the east. The British were equally intent on ruling the seas in order to protect the sea route to India, and in 1766 the Dutch finally gave way to Britain's East India Company, which had established trading links with the Gulf as early as 1616.

Throughout this time Dubai remained a small fishing and pearling hamlet, perched on a disputed border between two local powers – the seafaring Qawasim of present-day Ras al-Khaimah and Sharjah to the north, and the Bani Yas tribal confederation of what is now Abu Dhabi to the south. The region was also affected by the rivalries between bigger regional powers – the Wahhabi tribes of what is now Saudi Arabia, the Ottoman Empire, the Persians and the British.

The Trucial Coast

At the turn of the 19th century, Dubai was governed by Mohammed bin Hazza who remained ruler of Dubai until the Al Bu Fasalah, a branch of the Bani Yas tribe from Abu Dhabi, came to dominate the town in 1833, severing it from Abu Dhabi. The Bani Yas were the main power among the Bedouin tribes of the interior. Originally based in Liwa, an oasis on the edge of the desert known as the Empty Quarter (Rub al-Khali) in the south of the UAE, they engaged in the traditional Bedouin activities of camel herding, small-scale agriculture, tribal raiding and extracting protection money from merchant caravans passing through their territory. At the end of the 18th century, the leader of the Bani Yas moved from Liwa to the island of Abu Dhabi on the coast.

About 800 people from this tribe settled by the Creek in Bur Dubai under the leadership of Maktoum bin Butti, who established the Al-Maktoum dynasty of Dubai, which still rules the emirate today. For Maktoum bin Butti, good relations with the British authorities in the Gulf were essential to safeguard his new and small sheikhdom against attack from the larger and more powerful sheikhdoms of Sharjah to the north and Abu Dhabi to the south.

In 1841 the Bur Dubai settlement extended to Deira on the northern side of the Creek, though throughout the 19th century Dubai largely remained a tiny enclave of fishermen, pearl divers, Bedouin, and Indian and Persian merchants.

Things began to change, however, around the end of the 19th century. In 1892, the British, keen to impose their authority on the region and protect their empire in India, extended their power through a series of so-called exclusive agreements under which the sheikhs accepted formal British protection and, in exchange, promised to have no dealings with any other foreign power without British permission. (As a result of these treaties or truces, Europeans took to calling the area the Trucial Coast, a title it retained until 1971.)

Meanwhile, at the end of the 19th century, Sharjah, the area's main trading centre, began losing its trade prosperity to Dubai. In 1894 Dubai's ruler, Sheikh Maktoum bin Hasher al-Maktoum, permitted tax exemption for foreign traders and the free port of Dubai was born. Around the same time Lingah (now Bandar-e Langeh) across the Strait of Hormuz in Iran lost its status as a duty-free port, and the Al-Maktoum family made a concerted effort to lure Lingah's disillusioned traders to Dubai while also managing to convince some of Sharjah's merchants to relocate.

At first the Persians who came to Dubai believed that it would just be a temporary move, but by the 1920s, when it became evident that the trade restrictions in southern Iran were there to stay, they took up permanent residence.

More good news for the town came in the early 20th century when the Al-Maktoums, probably with the assistance of the Persian traders, prevailed on a British steamship line to switch its main port of call in the lower Gulf from Lingah to Dubai. This gave Dubai regular links with British India and the ports of the central and northern Gulf (ie, Bahrain, Kuwait, Bushire and Basra). This marked the beginning of Dubai's growth as a trading power, and prosperity soon followed.

The Expanding City

By the turn of the 20th century, Dubai was well established as an independent town with a population of about 10,000. Deira was the most populous area at this time with about 1600 houses, inhabited mainly by Arabs but also by Persians and Baluchis (who came from parts of what are now Pakistan and Afghanistan). By 1908 there were about 350 shops based in Deira and another 50 in Bur Dubai, where the Indian community was concentrated. To this day the Dubai Souq shows a strong Indian influence and is home to the only Hindu temple in Dubai.

The next key event in Dubai's expansion occurred in 1939 when Sheikh Rashid bin Saeed al-Maktoum took over as regent from his father, Sheikh Saeed. (Rashid only formally succeeded to the leadership when his father died in 1958.) He quickly moved to

Returning Fire

The origins of the brief 1940 war between Dubai and Sharjah stem from a complicated struggle within the Al-Maktoum family. Sheikh Saeed al-Maktoum, the ruler of Dubai, was challenged in the 1930s by his cousin, Mani bin Rashid, who at one point practically controlled Deira while Sheikh Saeed held onto Bur Dubai across the Creek. Sheikh Saeed gained the upper hand and sent his cousin into exile in 1939. Mani bin Rashid and his followers then settled in Sharjah, too close to Dubai for Sheikh Saeed's comfort. Sheikh Saeed asked Sheikh Sultan of Sharjah to exile Mani bin Rashid, but Sheikh Sultan refused on the grounds that it compromised the traditions of Arab hospitality. After much fruitless diplomacy, a desultory war broke out in January 1940 between Dubai and Sharjah, all of 23km apart. The British tried to quell the war by restricting the importation of firearms and ammunition. The rival forces then resorted to using ancient muzzle-loading cannons. The soldiers were sometimes able to recover the cannonballs fired at them and to fire them back.

While the war was on, Imperial Airways (a forerunner of British Airways), would still refuel its flying boats on Dubai Creek and send the passengers over to the fort at Sharjah for lunch. For this operation a truce was called, and the passengers would pass through the battlefront without, in most cases, realising anything odd was afoot.

When the ammunition and gunpowder had nearly run out, the rival sheikhs began negotiating again. Mani bin Rashid died peacefully soon after, and the matter was put to rest with him.

bolster the emirate's position as the main trading hub in the lower Gulf. At about the same time, the rulers of Sharjah made the mistake of allowing their harbour to silt up. This mistake cost them dearly because in Dubai Rashid was improving facilities along the Creek. In January 1940, war broke out briefly between Dubai and Sharjah – see the boxed text above for more details.

The development of Dubai as a major trading centre was also spurred on by the collapse, around 1930, of the pearling trade, which had been the mainstay of Dubai's economy for centuries. The pearling trade fell victim both to the worldwide depression of 1929 and to the Japanese discovery, around the same time, of a method by which pearls could be cultured artificially. Sheikh Rashid concluded that the pearling industry was probably finished, and started to look for alternative forms of revenue. This chain of events heralded a new era in Dubai's trade – re-exporting (for more details, see the boxed text 'The Re-Export Trade' under Economy later in this chapter). The rise of this trade was spurred on by WWII and continued to flourish thereafter.

In 1951 the Trucial States Council was founded, bringing the leaders of what would become the UAE together. The council comprised the rulers of the sheikhdoms and was the direct predecessor of the UAE Supreme Council. It met twice a year under the aegis of the British political agent in Dubai.

The end of the war, India's independence and the decline of the British Empire saw the end of Britain's presence in the region and prompted the establishment of the UAE. Before withdrawing from the region, the British set in motion the means by which the borders that now make up the UAE were drawn. Incredibly, this involved a British diplomat spending months riding a camel around the mountains and desert asking village heads, tribal leaders and Bedouin which sheikh they swore allegiance to. The British withdrawal and the discovery of oil accelerated the modernisation of the region (see the boxed text 'Modernisation & Development').

Modern Dubai

When Dubai became one of the seven emirates of the UAE in 1971, the emirs agreed to a formula under which Abu Dhabi and Dubai (in that order) would carry the most weight in the federation but which would leave each emir largely autonomous. Sheikh Zayed bin Sultan al-Nayan of Abu Dhabi became the supreme ruler of the UAE and Sheikh Rashid of Dubai became vice president.

Since 1971, Dubai has been one of the most politically stable cities in the Arab world. This does not mean, however, that political life in the UAE has been devoid of controversy. Border disputes between the emirates continued throughout the 1970s and '80s, and the degree to which 'integration' among the seven sheikhdoms should be pursued has been the subject of constant debate.

In 1979, Sheikh Zayed and Sheikh Rashid sealed a formal compromise under which each gave a little ground on his respective vision of the country. The result was a much stronger federation in which Dubai remained a bastion of free trade while Abu Dhabi imposed a tighter federal structure on the other emirates. Rashid also agreed to take the title of prime minister as a symbol of his commitment to the federation.

Sheikh Rashid, the driving force behind Dubai's phenomenal growth, died in 1990 after a long illness and was succeeded as emir by his son, Sheikh Maktoum. For several years prior to Rashid's death, Maktoum had been regent for his father in all but name, and the new emir has continued to follow in his father's footsteps.

The core of his policies has been to promote Dubai whenever and wherever possible. By the mid-1990s, the Dubai Desert Classic had become a well established stop on the annual Professional Golfer's Association tour, placing the city firmly on the world sporting map. The same logic is behind the staging of world-class tennis tournaments, boat and horse racing, desert rallies and the air show (one of the four largest in the world).

High profile events, such as the Dubai Shopping Festival and Dubai Summer Surprises, attract hoards of tourists mainly from other Gulf countries, and have catapulted Dubai's tourism into the league of the city's other major industries, trade and oil.

Modernisation & Development

Oil was first discovered near Dubai in 1966 and oil exports began three years later. However, a building boom had already begun along the Creek well before Dubai struck oil. Even after oil revenues began coming in, trade remained the foundation of the city's wealth, though oil has contributed to trade profits and encouraged modernisation since its discovery.

The first bank, the British Bank of the Middle East, was established in 1946, and when Al-Maktoum Hospital was built in 1949 it was the only centre for modern medical care on the Trucial Coast until well into the 1950s. When Sheikh Rashid officially came to power in 1958 he set up the first Municipal Council. He also established a police force and basic infrastructure, such as electricity and water supply.

Until the early 1960s the only means of transport in town was donkey or camel. As is still the case today, *abras* (water taxis) were used to transport people across the Creek. Construction of the airport began in 1958 and the British Overseas Airways Corporation (BOAC) and Middle East Airlines (MEA) launched regular flights to Dubai soon after. Roads and bridges appeared in the early 1960s.

The ambitious UK£23 million Port Rashid complex was begun in 1967 after it became obvious that the growing maritime traffic could no longer be managed by the current facilities. It was completed in 1972.

The mid-1970s saw the beginnings of a massive programme of industrialisation that resulted in the construction of Jebel Ali Port, said to be the largest artificial port in the world, and the adjacent industrial centre, which was to become a free trade zone.

All of these developments brought to life Sheikh Rashid's vision of Dubai as one of the Middle East's most important commercial hubs.

The history of Dubai reads like a tale of rags to riches, a chronicle which has witnessed a small coastal hamlet transform into a major commercial hub – a Hong Kong of the Gulf. It is hard to imagine anywhere else in the world that has developed at such a pace and in such a short space of time.

GEOGRAPHY

Dubai sits on the Gulf, in the northwest region of the UAE. This city is the capital of the emirate of the same name, which is the second largest of the seven emirates which comprise the UAE. The emirate of Dubai is 3885 sq km and the constantly expanding city is roughly 35 sq km. Dubai Creek, which extends 12km inland from the coast, divides the city in two.

Prior to settlement, this area was flat sabkha (salt-crusted coastal plain). The sand mostly consists of crushed shell and coral and is fine, clean and white. The sabkha was broken only by clumps of desert grasses and a small area of hardy mangroves at the inland end of the Creek. Photographs of the area from the early 20th century show how strikingly barren the landscape was.

East of the city, the sabkha gives way to north–south running lines of dunes. The farming areas of Al-Khawaneej and Al-Awir, now on the edge of Dubai's suburbia, are fed by wells. Further east the dunes grow larger and are tinged red with iron oxide. The dunes stop abruptly at the gravel fans at the base of the rugged Hajar Mountains, where there are gorges and water holes. A vast sea of sand dunes covers the area south of the city, becoming more and more imposing as it stretches into the desert known as the Empty Quarter that makes up the southern region of the UAE and the western region of Saudi Arabia. North of Dubai, along the coast, the land is tough desert scrub broken by inlets similar to Dubai Creek, until you reach the mountainous northern emirates.

CLIMATE

For most of the year Dubai's weather is warm and humid; the sky is rarely cloudy.

The summer months (May to September) are extremely hot with daytime temperatures in the low to mid-40s (Celsius). July and August are the hottest months, with average temperatures around 43°C with 85% humidity. Sometimes the heat reaches 48°C and the humidity 95%. The sea temperature in the height of summer (June to August) is about 37°C, which provides no relief, and hotel swimming pools have to be cooled during this time so that they don't turn into steaming hot baths.

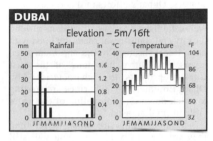

During October, November, March and April the weather is much more bearable, with temperatures in the low to mid-30s. In winter (December to February) Dubai enjoys perfect weather with an average temperature of 24°C, though it can get quite windy. Unlike the desert area inland, Dubai doesn't get too cold on winter nights, the lowest temperature hovering around 15°C. It doesn't rain often, or heavily, but when it does (usually in December or January) getting around can suddenly become difficult as streets turn into rivers and traffic becomes chaotic. Drivers here are not used to wet road conditions, and the city planners decided Dubai didn't need a drainage system, so there are no gutter or storm-water drains. The average annual rainfall is about 6.5cm per year (and it rains only five days a year on average), but rainfall varies widely from one year to the next. In winter there can be fog in the early mornings.

Sandstorms can occur during March and April, although Dubai is protected from the swirling dust and sand to some degree by its many tall buildings.

ECOLOGY & ENVIRONMENT

Other than the wind-blown sand and dust you would expect in an arid desert environment, Dubai is a very clean city, compared with others in the region, though air pollution from the ever-growing traffic is starting to become an issue, and the Creek suffers from marine pollution.

In contrast to Abu Dhabi's emphasis on the 'greening of the desert' regardless of the expense of desalination plants or the effects on the country's limited artesian water resources, Dubai's efforts in this regard have been more modest. There are a number of well-established parks and gardens around the city and some major roads are lined with palm trees, shrubs, flowers and manicured lawns, but Dubai has none of the vast forestry projects that characterise Abu Dhabi Emirate. The authorities are starting to crack down on exploitation of the water table in rural areas.

Although things are much better than they were a few years ago, you will still see rubbish left on beaches, in parks or thrown out of car windows, despite efforts to educate the community about not littering. As a result, an enormous number of workers are employed to make sure that the rubbish on the street doesn't stay around to sully the city's image, and the municipality has slapped a Dh500 fine for littering. Clean-up days are common and advertisements in newspapers alert people to the necessity of recycling and keeping the city clean. Dubai generates one of the highest per capita volumes of waste in the world, and the Emirates Environmental Group has opened a number of recycling centres around the city. One innovative idea being introduced is deploying reverse vending machines, to be trialled at service stations around the city. The machines accept aluminium cans and dispense money or coupons in return.

Additionally, there is a high risk of oil spills off the coast. Over the years the damage caused by these spills has prompted a concerted effort by government agencies to monitor and control marine pollution, not least because they threaten the city's vital desalination plants. Oil companies are required to spend money on the protection of the coast. Dubai is also a member of the Regional Organisation for the Protection of the Marine Environment.

The Real Liquid Gold

Water is without doubt the most precious commodity in Dubai. Most of the water consumed in Dubai comes from the giant Dubai Electricity and Water Authority (DEWA) desalination plants between Al-Mina al-Seyahi and Jebel Ali. Security is tight around the facility, which has a fleet of ships ready to deploy booms in case there's an oil spill offshore. Desalination provides about 95% (and rising) of the city's water supply, the remainder coming from wells.

DEWA is struggling to keep up with demand, and has commissioned the building of the biggest desalination plants in the world. The three units will together produce 180 million litres per day of freshwater from sea water, enough to support 700,000 people, at a cost of US$1 billion. Desalination is an expensive and complicated process, requiring chemical and microbiological analyses to ensure quality. Desalinating water from the Gulf is even more expensive than usual because of the higher salinity levels. Some experts argue that Gulf of Oman water with lower salinity should be pumped in from the east coast. Every year, the demand for water rises by 8% to 10%, and the UAE is said to be the second-biggest per capita consumer of water in the world, after the US.

Dubai's ground water is a fast diminishing resource. In some rural areas the water table is reported to be falling by as much as 1m to 2m each year. With an average rainfall of 6.5cm each year, and scorchingly high temperatures, you can imagine the amount of water required to keep parks, gardens and people alive.

Local Environmental Organisations

The Federal Environmental Agency legislates on environmental issues and encourages communication on these issues between the emirates. There are also a number of NGOs concerned with the environment.

Emirates Environmental Group (☎ 331 8100; ⓦ www.eeg-uae.com) PO Box 7013, Dubai. This group organises educational programmes in schools and businesses as well as community programmes, such as clean-up drives.

Arabian Leopard Trust (☎ 344 4871) PO Box 24444, Sharjah. This is a nonprofit volunteer organisation concerned with protecting endangered species.

Dubai Natural History Group (☎ 349 4816) PO Box 9234, Dubai. This volunteer group organises public lectures and field trips, publishes a newsletter called *The Gazelle* and gives members access to a small lending library of natural history publications. Annual membership of the group costs Dh50.

Emirates Bird Records Committee (☎ 347 2277; ⓔ colinr@emirates.net.ac) This organisation compiles information on all matters ornithological and maintains the UAE's official bird list.

Emirates Diving Association (☎ 393 9390; ⓦ www.emiratesdiving.com) PO Box 33220, Dubai. This association is an active participant in local environmental campaigns, with an emphasis on the marine environment.

FLORA & FAUNA

In Dubai's parks you will see indigenous tree species such as the date palm and the neem, and a large number of imported species, including eucalypts. The sandy desert surrounding the city supports wild grasses and the occasional date-palm oasis.

In the salty scrublands along the coast, the desert hyacinth emerges in all its glory after the rains. It has bright yellow and deep-red dappled flowers. It is not common in the city, but you'll see it a little further out, around the beaches near the Jebel Ali Hotel.

Decorating the flat plains that stretch away from the foothills of the Hajar Mountains, around Hatta, are different species of acacia. These are flat-topped, rather scraggly, incredibly hardy trees. The ghaf also

The Date Palm

If you visit Dubai in early summer, one of the things you will be struck by is the enormous number of date clusters hanging off the huge number of date palms that line many of the streets and parks. The ubiquitous date palm has always held a vital place in the life of Emiratis. For centuries dates were one of the staple foods of the Bedouin, along with fish, camel meat and camel milk. Not a great deal of variety you may say, but consider the fact that there are 80 different kinds of dates in the UAE. Dates are roughly 70% sugar which prevents them from rotting, making them edible for longer than other fruits.

Apart from providing a major foodstuff, the date palm was also used to make all kinds of useful items. Its trunk was used to make columns and ceilings for houses, while its fronds (called *areesh*) were used to make roofs and walls. The date palm provided the only shade available in desert oases. Livestock were fed with its seeds and it was burned as fuel. Palm fronds were, and still are, used to make bags, mats, boats (called *shasha*), shelters, brooms and fans.

grows in this area; this big tree looks a little like a weeping willow. It is able to survive because its roots stretch down for about 80m, allowing it to tap into deep water reserves. The lower foliage of the ghaf is usually trimmed flat by grazing camels and goats.

As in any major city, you don't see much wildlife. Urbanisation, combined with zealous hunting, has brought the virtual extinction of some species. These include the houbara bustard, the Arabian oryx (also called the white oryx), the caracal and the striped hyena. The sand cat and Gordon's wildcat are types of cats that have adapted to desert life and are under threat because of cross-breeding with domestic tabbies.

On the fringes of the city, where the urban sprawl gives way to the desert, you may see a desert fox, sand cat or falcon if you are very lucky. Otherwise, the only animals you are likely to encounter are camels

Falconry

For this traditional Bedouin hunting method a falcon had to be caught and trained in time for the migration season of the houbara bustard. The houbara (now protected) was the preferred prey of the falconer because it was small enough to be caught by the falcon yet big enough to feed a small family. At the end of the migration season in spring, the falcon was let go and another would be caught in autumn to repeat the process. The Bedouin had many ways of catching a falcon; one of these was for a man to be buried in the sand with just his head and arm above the surface. His arm was then hidden within a bush that had a live pigeon tied to it. The fluttering pigeon would attract the falcon and, when the unsuspecting falcon was close enough, the buried man would throw a cloth over its head, immobilising it. It may sound primitive, but it was an effective method that has been passed down through generations of Bedouin.

Local falconers once relied on wild populations of peregrines and sakers, but hybrids between saker falcons and the larger gyr falcons have become more popular in recent years. It's illegal to capture wild falcons in the UAE so falcons are now sourced from special breeding programmes.

The Falcon Hospital in Dubai has treated more than 12,000 birds since it opened in 1983. It has intensive care wards and surgical theatres, and the patients are implanted with microchips to keep track of their medical records. Most injuries result from birds hitting obstacles such as signs, fences and power lines. The hospital also treats conditions that arise from overpampering. Falcon feet become susceptible to infection if they spend too long on padded perches.

and goats. The desert is also home to various reptile species, including the desert monitor lizard (up to a metre long), the sand skink, the spiny tailed agame and several species of gecko. The only poisonous snakes are vipers, such as the sawscaled viper, which can be recognised by their distinctive triangular heads. There are even two remarkably adapted species of toad, which hibernate for years burrowed deep in wadis between floods.

The city is a hot spot for bird-watchers; because of the spread of irrigation and greenery the number and variety of birds is growing. Dubai is on the migration path between Europe, Asia and Africa, and more than 320 migratory species pass through in the spring and autumn, or spend the winter here. The city's parks, gardens and golf courses sustain quite large populations, and on any day up to 80 different species can be spotted. One new urban settler is the common mynah, which arrived in the 1970s from India and now exists in large numbers. Species native to Arabia include the crab plover, the Socotra cormorant, the black-crowned finch lark, and the purple sunbird.

Artificial nests have been built to encourage flamingos to breed at the Khor Dubai Wildlife Sanctuary at the inland end of Dubai Creek. In addition to flamingos, the sanctuary is also home to ducks, marsh harriers, spotted eagles, broad-billed sandpipers and ospreys. Bird-watching tours are available for those who wish to visit (for more details, see Organised Tours in the Getting Around chapter).

The waters off Dubai teem with around 300 different types of fish. Diners will be most familiar with the hamour, a species of grouper, but the Gulf is also home to an extraordinary range of tropical fish and several species of small sharks. Green turtles and hawksbill turtles used to nest in numbers on Dubai's beaches, but today their nesting sites are restricted to islands. Although you won't see them around Dubai, the coastal waters around Abu Dhabi are home to the Gulf's biggest remaining population of dugongs, where they feed off sea grasses in the shallow channels between islands. The Abu Dhabi government is making a concerted effort to preserve their habitat.

[Continued on page 24]

Architecture

TONY WHEELER

CHRIS MELLOR

Title Page: Completed in 2000, the twin Emirates Towers are Dubai's tallest buildings and the ninth tallest in the world (Photo: Clint Lucas)

Top: The distinctive S-shaped construction of the Jumeira Beach Hotel is designed to evoke the image of a breaking wave, with the Gulf as a backdrop

Bottom: Golden afternoon sunlight burnishes Jumeira Mosque, distinguished by its size and elaborate decoration

Any visitor to Dubai will immediately be struck by its stunning architecture. The incongruous blend of traditional Arabian architecture with modern constructions straight out of science fiction make the city an amazing sight. A boat ride along the Creek reveals many of the city's architectural treasures. Moving from the wind-tower houses in the Bastakia Quarter of Bur Dubai to the pointed dhow-like roof of the Dubai Creek Golf & Yacht Club, it's hard to believe it's the same city.

These modern constructions do sit a little awkwardly with the traditional architecture of the city, but the contrast is representative of other clashes in Dubai – Islamic and Western, traditional and modern. It is impossible to compare the traditional and modern architectural styles, simply because they are so different, although some contemporary architecture incorporates traditional elements.

Traditional Architecture

Dubai's traditional architecture was influenced by the demands of the environment, the teachings of Islam and the social structure of the town. There were four categories of buildings – domestic (residential houses), religious (mosques), defensive (forts and watchtowers) and commercial (souqs). Readily available materials, such as gypsum and coral from offshore reefs and from the banks of the Creek, were used. **Sheikh Saeed al-Maktoum House in Shindagha** *(Map 4, #6)* is a fine example of a construction using a mixture of coral and gypsum.

Limestone building blocks were also used and mud served to cement the stones together. However, mud constructions suffered badly in the heat and had a very limited lifespan, sometimes only a few years. The dimensions of buildings were to a degree governed by the use of timber. The length of roof beams, imported from India or East Africa, was determined by the maximum size that could be loaded onto a dhow.

If you wander through the lanes surrounding the Dubai Souq (Map 4) and behind the Al-Ahmadiya School (Map 4, #10) in Deira you will notice that the alleyways are narrow and the buildings are in close proximity. Houses, souqs and mosques were built in this way to provide maximum shade so that inhabitants could move around the town in comfort, protected from the harsh sun.

There were two types of traditional house – the *masayf* was the summer house (incorporating a wind tower) and the *mashait* was the winter house (incorporating a courtyard).

Wind Towers Called *barjeel* in Arabic, wind towers are the Gulf's unique form of nonmechanical air-conditioning. In Dubai, a handful still exist, some atop people's homes and others carefully preserved or reconstructed at museums.

Inset: Detail of the sail-like roof of the Dubai Creek Golf & Yacht Club. (Photo: Chris Mellor)

Traditional wind towers rise 5m or 6m above a house. The tower is open on all four sides and catches any breezes, which are channelled down around a central shaft and into the room below. In the process, the air speeds up and is cooled. The cooler air already in the tower shaft pulls in, and subsequently cools, the hotter air outside through simple convection.

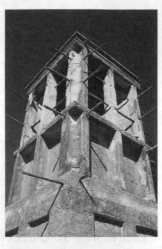

The towers work amazingly well. Sitting beneath a wind tower when it is 40°C and humid, you will notice a distinct drop in temperature and a consistent breeze even when the air outside feels heavy and still.

The wealthy Persian merchants who settled in Dubai around the turn of the 20th century were the first to build a large number of wind towers in the city. You'll find them in the **Bastakia Quarter** *(Map 4)* in Bur Dubai. In some houses the tallest wind tower was above the master bedroom, while smaller wind towers cooled the living rooms. The merchants brought red clay from Iran, which they mixed with manure to make *saruj*. This was baked in a kiln and was used to build the foundations of the wind-tower house. Other materials used included coral rock and limestone (for the walls) and plaster (for decorative work). The walls were built as thick as 60cm, so the house could be extended upwards if the family expanded. Chandel wood from East Africa, palm-frond matting, mud and straw were used to build the roofs.

Courtyards Houses in Dubai were traditionally built around a central courtyard, known as *al-housh* in Arabic, which was considered the heart and lungs of a house. Today they still provide many homes with light, fresh air and the space for a garden. They are also a place for entertaining and somewhere for children to play; if a family owns livestock, this is where the animals usually wander. All the rooms of the house surround the courtyard and all doors and windows open onto it, except those of the guest rooms, which open onto the outside of the house. A veranda provides shade on one or more sides of the house and is usually the place where the women weave their mats or sew their clothes. The veranda also serves to keep sun out of the rooms at certain times of the day.

For a fine example of a courtyard house, visit the **Heritage House** *(Map 4, #9)* in the Al-Ahmadiya district in Deira. In the Bastakia Quarter are several wind-tower houses that have been built around a central courtyard – the **Majlis Gallery** *(Map 4, #54)* near Al-Fahidi Roundabout is another prime example.

Top: Wind towers, such as this one in the Bastakia Quarter of Dubai, are a characteristic feature of traditional Gulf architecture. The tower channels breezes down into the house, functioning as a highly effective form of nonmechanical air-conditioning. (Photo: Chris Mellor)

Barasti The term *barasti* describes both the traditional Arabian method of building a palm-leaf house and the completed house itself. *Barasti* houses consist of a skeleton of wooden poles made from the trunk of the date palm onto which palm leaves *(areesh)* are woven to form a strong structure through which air can still circulate.

They were extremely common throughout the Gulf in the centuries before the oil boom, though few examples of this type of house survive today. Those that do are usually fishermen's shacks and storage buildings in rural and coastal areas of the UAE.

They were relatively easy to build and maintain since, unlike the mud-brick houses you find in the oases around Al-Ain and Buraimi, their construction does not require water. The circulation of air through the palms also made *barasti* houses much cooler than mud-brick structures during the summer.

The courtyard in the **Dubai Museum** *(Map 4, #55)* and the **Heritage Village** *(Map 4, #4)* in Shindagha both contain examples of *barasti* houses. You can also see *barasti* constructions at the **Majlis Ghorfat Um-al-Sheef** *(Map 2, #26)* on Jumeira Rd.

For a detailed description of how a *barasti* house is constructed see Geoffrey Bibby's book *Looking for Dilmun*.

Mosques Fundamentally simple structures, mosques are made up of a few basic elements. The most visible of these is the minaret, the tower from which the call to prayer is issued five times a day. Virtually every mosque in the world has a minaret; many have several. Minarets can be plain or ornate. The first minarets were not built until the early 8th century, some 70 years after the Prophet's death. The idea for minarets may have originated from the bell towers that Muslim armies found attached to some of the churches they converted into mosques during the early years of Islam. The more minarets on a mosque, the more important it is. No mosque has more than seven minarets, the number on the Grand Mosque in Mecca.

A mosque must also have a mihrab, a niche in the wall facing Mecca, indicating the qibla, the direction believers must face while praying. Mihrabs are thought to have been introduced into Islamic architecture around the beginning of the 8th century, and like minarets they can be simple or elaborate.

The *minbar*, a pulpit traditionally reached by three steps, dates from the Prophet's lifetime.

Right: Every neighbourhood in Dubai has a mosque, such as this one in Bur Dubai, the design of which varies according to the ethnic origins of the worshippers. Some follow the Anatolian style, with a massive central dome; others are based on Iranian or Central Asian styles. (Photo: Christine Osborne)

In addition, a mosque needs to have a water supply so that worshippers can perform the *wudu*, or ablutions, that are required before they begin praying.

There are currently around 200 mosques in Dubai. The neighbourhood mosques tend to be used for weekday prayers, with worshippers travelling further afield to the larger mosques for Friday prayers.

The **Jumeira Mosque** *(Map 7, #25)* conforms to the Anatolian style, identified by a massive central dome. Other mosques in Dubai are based on Iranian and Central Asian models, which have more domes covering different areas of the mosque.

Shiite mosques are notable for their stunning green and blue faience tile work covering the facades and main dome. One stunning example is the **Iranian Mosque** *(Map 7, #24)* on Al-Wasl Rd.

The multidomed **Grand Mosque** *(Map 4, #57)* in Bur Dubai is a variation on the Anatolian style. Other mosques, such as the **Bin Suroor Mosque** *(Map 4, #8)* in Shindagha, are small and box-like. Above all they serve the most basic of purposes – to provide a place for people to pray.

Modern Architecture

Dubai's relentless building boom has lured architects from the world over who want to be part of Dubai's metamorphosis into a modern metropolis. This has resulted in an eclectic influence in the design and architecture of the city. There is enough wealth in Dubai to fund the most ambitious of projects and, unlike in Abu Dhabi where all architecture must have Islamic features such as archways, there are no such restrictions on architects in Dubai.

About 90% of Dubai's architecture can be described as 'cosmopolitan' or 'international', and is built using concrete, steel and glass. These materials, more than any others, absorb the heat and transfer it to all parts of the construction, which causes damage over a period of time. Recently, lightweight thermal blocks have been introduced. Although they are expensive, and therefore not widely used, they have great heat resistance. In addition, the final coating on buildings is usually light and contains reflective paint.

Most of the large-scale building projects in Dubai are carried out by foreign architecture firms, usually from Europe.

Emirates Towers (Map 3, #51) Dubai's tallest buildings are also the highest in the Middle East and Europe, and the ninth tallest worldwide. Designed in an ultramodern internationalist style, the twin triangular gun-metal grey towers on Sheikh Zayed Rd soar from an oval base. The taller of the two towers (355m) houses offices, while the second tower (305m) is a hotel. The triangular theme is repeated throughout the building, from the sloped glass roofs to the triangular skylights, as well as in many interior features. This is balanced by the curvilinear base structure, which contains car parks, function rooms and retail space. The curved motif is repeated in the upper storeys of the buildings. The architects were the Toronto-based firm Norr, and the buildings were finished in 2000.

Dusit Dubai (Map 3, #59) Sheikh Zayed Rd has many modern skyscrapers, but none as eye-catching as this one. The 153m-high building has an inverted 'Y' shape; two pillars which join to form a tapering tower. It's supposed to evoke the hands-joined Thai gesture of greeting, appropriate for this Thai hotel chain, although equally you could say it looks like a tuning fork stuck into the ground. Clad in blue glass, the hotel certainly stands out from the crowd on the skyscraper strip.

Burj al-Arab (Map 2, #18) Dubai's rulers wanted a landmark to rival the Eiffel Tower or the Sydney Opera House. What they got was a hotel to outdo anything Las Vegas could even dream of. Designed by UK-based architects WS Atkins & Partners, the Burj al-Arab (Arabian Tower) is like no other building. Completed in 1999, it is set on an artificial island about 300m from the shore, near the southern end of Jumeira Rd in Umm Suqeim. The 60-floor, sail-shaped structure is 321m high, including the thin spire on top. The hotel has 300 two-storey suites, a 200m-high lobby and an underwater restaurant, among other facilities. A restaurant and a helipad extend from either side at the top of the building. A translucent fibreglass wall shields the desert sun during the day, and serves as the screen for a light show at night. Khuan Chew Associates were responsible for the interior design, which has to be seen to be believed. Everything that looks gold is gold, and there's lots of it. The suites have a colour scheme euphemistically described as 'bold'; gold, red, blue and plenty of striped marble producing an almost hallucinatory effect. The design is supposed to evoke

a sail; not the sail of a dhow but of an ultramodern catamaran. Detractors say it looks a bit like an upended cockroach. The cost of the building has never been revealed.

Right: The Burj al-Arab is Dubai's answer to the Eiffel Tower in Paris or the Sydney Opera House. This landmark hotel stands 321m high, on an artificial island just off the shore. Its design evokes the sail of an ultramodern catamaran, which, together with the wave-shaped Jumeira Beach hotel nearby, is supposed to represent Dubai's maritime heritage. A restaurant and helipad extend from either side at the top of the building. (Photo: Neil Setchfield)

Jumeira Beach Hotel (Map 2, #20) This hotel building, on Jumeira Rd, is a long, S-shaped construction, intended to represent a wave, with the Gulf as its backdrop. The glimmering facades of the Jumeira Beach Hotel and its close neighbour the Burj al-Arab are achieved through the use of reflective glass and aluminium. The two structures combined – a huge sail hovering over a breaking wave – symbolise Dubai's maritime heritage. The vast lobby features a mural stretching the full height of the building, with Dubai at the base and the sun at the very top.

Royal Mirage (Map 2, #9)

Built to represent an opulent Arabian fortress, this hotel on Al-Sufouh Rd is just as flamboyant as the Burj al-Arab, yet somehow less over-the-top. It features low-rise mud walls and battlements, protecting an elegant Persian-influenced garden featuring waterways, courtyards and terraces. Outside the hotel 1300 date palms give the illusion of an oasis. The interior references Arabic design elements such as pendant lights and quiet alcoves, with intricate woodwork and mosaic flooring influenced by Islamic geometric designs. Sheikh Mohammed al-Maktoum admired the Sun City complex in South Africa, so he approached Sun City's developers to create something for Dubai. The building was designed by the London firm Wimberley Allison Tong & Co.

National Bank of Dubai (Map 5, #54)

This shimmering golden building, off Baniyas Rd overlooking the Creek in Deira, has become the quintessential symbol of Dubai. Designed by the Swedish firm Carlos Ott and Canadian firm Norr Limited and completed in 1997, it is best described as a long, thin D-shape, with the curved part facing the Creek. The bronze windows reflect the activity on the Creek and at sunset, when the light is just right, it is a beautiful sight.

Dubai Chamber of Commerce & Industry (Map 5, #53)

Next door to the National Bank of Dubai, this triangular building is blanketed in sheets of blue glass. From some angles the building takes on a one-dimensional appearance, like a great featureless monolith.

Dubai Creek Golf & Yacht Club (Map 3, #19)

When you cross either bridge over the Creek, you will probably notice the pointed white roof of this clubhouse set amid acres of lush green lawns and artificial, undulating hillocks. The idea behind this 1993 UK design by Brian Johnson (for Godwin, Austen and Johnson Architects) was to incorporate a traditional element into the design. From the outside, the white clubhouse recalls the sails of a traditional Arab dhow. Inside, it's a temple of modern Western comfort.

Left: The Dubai Creek Golf & Yacht Club is an example of a modern construction that incorporates traditional Arabian design elements. The eye-catching white roof of the clubhouse evokes the sails of a dhow. (Photo: Chris Mellor)

Etisalat Building (Map 5, #59) Recognisable by the giant, sparkling golf ball that perches above this building, the Etisalat headquarters is on the corner of Al-Maktoum and Omar ibn al-Khattab Rds. Designed by the Canadian firm Cansult Ltd and completed in 1990, the building's distinct ball now sits on top of Etisalat's other main buildings in each emirate, enabling Etisalat to be easily recognised wherever you go in the UAE. It represents the world encompassed by the power of global communications. At night the ball appears to sparkle as little lights come on all around it.

Emirates Training Building (Map 3, #17) No, you're not about to get wiped out by an aircraft that's slightly off course. This building, designed by UK architect Brian Johnson (who also designed the Dubai Creek Golf & Yacht Club), is on Al-Garhoud Rd at the Deira entrance to the bridge and is designed to look like the front end of an aeroplane. It's gimmicky, but eye-catching.

Port Rashid Customs Authority (Map 4, #36) There are no prizes for speculating correctly on the concept behind this design. The Port Rashid Customs Authority, on Al-Mina Rd (just south of Khalid bin al-Waleed Rd), looks like the hulls of two enormous dhows from a distance. The bows extend to sit like gargoyles on either side of the entrance to the building. The two hulls run down the side of the building and the offices sit between them.

[Continued from page 16]

GOVERNMENT & POLITICS

Power rests with the ruling family, the Al-Maktoums (see the boxed text). No political parties or general elections are allowed in Dubai. Though the UAE has a federal government, over which Sheikh Zayed of Abu Dhabi presides, each of the rulers is absolutely sovereign within his own emirate. The UAE is, nevertheless, a rare example of Arab unity, a concept much discussed at meetings of Arab rulers but little realised.

The degree of power that the seven emirs cede to the federal government has been one of the hottest topics of debate in government circles since the founding of the UAE in 1971. Over the years, Dubai has fought hardest to preserve as much of its independence as possible and to minimise the power of the country's federal institutions. Along with Ras al-Khaimah, it maintains a legal system separate from the federal judiciary.

Politics in the UAE tends to be rather opaque, but the relative interests of the vari-ous emirs are fairly clear. Abu Dhabi is the largest and wealthiest emirate and has the biggest population. It is, therefore, the dominant member of the federation and is likely to remain so for some time. Dubai is the second largest emirate by population, with an interest in upholding its free-trade policies and a pronounced independent streak. One sign of this is Dubai's relation to OPEC, the cartel of the world's major oil-producing countries. Officially the UAE is a member of OPEC, but in practice Dubai has opted out, while Abu Dhabi has stayed in. Thus, if Abu Dhabi agrees to a cut in production in line with OPEC, there's some tension if Dubai raises its output and Abu Dhabi's has to fall further to compensate. The other emirates are dependent on subsidies from Abu Dhabi, though the extent of this dependence varies widely.

The forum where these issues are discussed is the Supreme Council, the highest legislative body in the country. The council, which tends to meet informally, comprises the seven emirs. New federal laws can be passed with the consent of five of the seven

The Al-Maktoum Dynasty

The ruling family of Dubai has successfully managed to blend its private interests with politics. As in all the Gulf states, the family maintains the Arabian tradition of the *majlis*, in which any Emirati man can approach the ruler to discuss any matter.

The current ruler of Dubai is Sheikh Maktoum bin Rashid al-Maktoum. He's also vice president and prime minister of the UAE. Sheikh Zayed bin Sultan al-Nayan, the ruler of Abu Dhabi, is the supreme ruler of the UAE.

Maktoum's second brother, Sheikh Hamdan, is the deputy ruler of Dubai and the federal minister of finance and industry. Their uncle, Sheikh Ahmed bin Saeed al-Maktoum, is the chairman of Emirates Airlines.

Sheikh Mohammed, the third brother, is the crown prince of Dubai and the defence minister of the UAE. He is probably the best known of all the ruling family, and is constantly in the public eye as a result of his public policies (he's been instrumental in pushing ahead some of the most ambitious projects) and his private pastime, horse racing.

Horse racing is a hobby of all the members of the ruling family and they are well respected in the international equestrian community. Sheikh Maktoum owns the largest racing stables in the world; Sheikh Hamdan is known as a leading breeder of race horses and Sheikh Mohammed owns several champion race horses.

Among the women of the family, Sheikha Hessah bint Maktoum al-Maktoum, the eldest daughter of the ruler, is a well-known artist whose vibrantly coloured abstract paintings have been exhibited in Paris and London.

rulers. The Supreme Council also elects one of the emirs to a five-year term as the country's president. In 1996, Sheikh Zayed was elected to his sixth term as president, a position he seems likely to hold for life. Some commentators see problems ahead when Sheikh Zayed, born in 1915, dies. As he is the UAE's first and only president, the succession issue for the federation has never arisen before.

There is also a cabinet and the posts within it are distributed among the emirates. Most of the federal government's money comes from Abu Dhabi and Dubai so members of these governments hold most of the important cabinet posts.

The cabinet and the Supreme Council are advised, but cannot be overruled, by the Federation Council of Ministers, a 40-member consultative body whose members are appointed by the emirs. Abu Dhabi and Dubai hold almost half of the council's seats, and all the council's members come from leading Emirati merchant families.

Within Dubai, the Dubai Municipality is effectively the local government for the Emirate, handling everything from economic planning to rubbish collection. Above the municipality is Sheikh Maktoum's private office, called the Diwan or the Ruler's Office.

ECONOMY

Oh you who believe! Eat not up your property among yourselves in vanities, but let there be amongst you traffic and trade by mutual goodwill.
Quran 4:29

Dubai is the second richest emirate in the UAE, after Abu Dhabi. It has used its modest oil resources to build a global trading base, with stunning results. About 70% of the UAE's non-oil GDP is generated in Dubai, and about 89.6% of Dubai's GDP is not oil-based. Dubai's reserves of oil and gas were never huge, and while recovery techniques have improved and lengthened the life of its oil and gas fields, Dubai has never been under the illusion that this natural bounty could sustain it indefinitely. It has prudently used its limited oil and gas revenue to create the infrastructure for trade, manufacturing and tourism.

Some analysts believe Dubai has expanded too far, too fast, and that its economy is heading for trouble. Others, including the *Economist* magazine, believe the city has a sufficiently sturdy economic base. Raw data on Dubai's economy is not made public, so it's impossible to know for sure.

Dubai's main exports are oil, natural gas, dates and dried fish; top export destinations are Japan, Taiwan, the UK, the US and India. Imports are primarily minerals and chemicals, base metals (including gold), vehicles and machinery, electronics, textiles and foodstuffs; the main importers into Dubai are the US, China, Japan, the UK, South Korea and India. The re-export trade (see the boxed text 'The Re-Export Trade' on the following page) in Dubai makes up about 80% of the UAE's total re-export business. Dubai's re-exports go mainly to Iran, India, Saudi Arabia, Kuwait and Afghanistan.

Dubai is also the home of a huge dry-dock complex, one of the Middle East's busiest airports and duty-free operations, the best road system in the country, the UAE's biggest airline and large free-trade zones at Jebel Ali, 30 minutes from the city centre, and at Dubai airport. It is the attraction of foreign business to its free-trade zones that has been one of Dubai's greatest economic

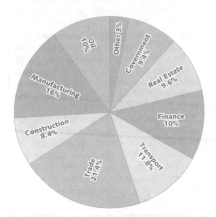

Dubai's economy by sector

achievements in the last 20 years. Companies are enticed with the promise of full foreign ownership, full repatriation of capital and profits, no corporate tax for 15 years, no currency restrictions and no personal income tax for staff. The number of companies setting up business in the free-trade zones increases by about 200 per year, with household names such as Daewoo, Heinz, Reebok and Sony enjoying the benefits.

New projects come up with incredible speed. The Dubai Internet City development near Al-Mina al-Seyahi was predicted to be a flop, but already it has attracted 200 firms employing 4000 people in shiny new offices. All this was achieved in about three years. The neighbouring Dubai Media City complex has been equally successful in adding a new high-tech information stratum to the city's economy.

Dubai's tourism industry has also exploded of late. The city's tolerance of Western habits, profusion of quality hotels, long stretches of beach, warm winter weather, shopping incentives and desert activities have helped it become the leading tourist destination in the Gulf.

For Emirati citizens (or 'nationals' as they are usually referred to locally), all this prosperity translates into the kind of benefits that much of the rest of the world only dreams of: free healthcare, free education, heavily subsidised utilities and, in some cases, free housing.

Dubai's per capita income is estimated to be about Dh60,000 per annum. This is far above the average wage of a professional expat and, when you consider the fact that many unskilled expat labourers earn Dh500 to Dh1000 per month, you get an idea of the kind of salary and benefits that a national takes home.

Still, there is one hurdle in the economy that Dubai is seeking to overcome. Dubai is highly dependent upon expat labour and, at the same time, its citizens spend a great deal of money. The government has made some attempt to 'Emiratise' the economy by placing nationals in the public workforce and imposing local employee quotas on private companies.

However, encouraging people who have never had to work before is problematic. Many private companies are reluctant to hire nationals, believing that it will result in a drop in profits and efficiency. There is no doubt that Dubai will be dependent on foreign labour and expertise for a long time to

The Re-Export Trade

Dubai's economy is built on trade, especially the re-export trade, which started around the time of the collapse of the pearling trade in the 1930s. Its merchants imported goods, which they then sold on to other ports. In practice, this involved smuggling, especially of gold to India. The goods entered and exited Dubai legally; it was the countries at the *other* end of the trade that looked on it as smuggling.

WWII also played a role in the growth of the re-export trade. The war brought much of the trade to a standstill and on top of this there was a shortage of basic food supplies. The British government supplied the Trucial Sheikhdoms with plenty of rice and sugar. Dubai merchants bought these goods cheaply and, finding themselves oversupplied, shipped them off to the black market in Iran.

It was around this time that modern Dubai began to take shape. During the 1950s, Sheikh Rashid became one of the earliest beneficiaries of Kuwait's Fund for Arab Economic Development, which loaned him money to dredge the Creek (it had become badly silted up, reducing the volume of Creek traffic) and to build a new breakwater near its mouth. The project was completed in 1963, and gold smuggling took off like a rocket, using the trade networks built up through the pearling business. India had banned gold imports after 1947 to stabilise its currency, which sent the price of gold in India soaring. In 1967 the price of gold in Dubai was US$35 an ounce, while in India it sold for US$68 an ounce. The gold trade peaked in 1997 when 660 tonnes of gold left Dubai.

Dubai's days as a smuggler's paradise are not over. The trade now supposedly focuses on Iran; dhows take cargo such as VCRs and Levi's jeans to Iranian ports and return laden with caviar and carpets.

The Expat Pecking Order

The expatriate community makes up about 80% of Dubai's population. The majority of expats are from India and the experience for Western and Asian expats is markedly different.

Some of the 45,000 or so Western expats are just here on short-term work contracts; others have entered into long-term relationships with their host country and may well stay here until the end of their working lives. Just look at the benefits. For expats, life in the UAE is a fantasy world of no taxes, often no rent and a free air fare home once or twice a year. Throw in a late model car, and a housemaid or two for the upper professional classes, and you've got a lifestyle few could afford back home. Many expats also report that, despite some frustrations, the work culture in Dubai is less stressful than back home. Friday is always a day off, for example, and relentless long hours aren't as common.

Money is not the only draw card. The crime rate is low, the streets are safe and it's a child-friendly society; many people think it's a great place to raise children. There is also the opportunity to explore Arab culture and enjoy its hospitality and warmth. Ask any Western expat when they're going home for good and you'll find that most won't be able to give you a straight answer.

For the nearly one million or so Asian expats living in Dubai, however, life is very different. Most Indians, Pakistanis, Sri Lankans, Bangladeshis and some Chinese are employed as labourers. Working on building sites without proper safety precautions or digging roads in 45°C heat is hardly the easy life, but for most it's still preferable to unemployment and grinding poverty back home. Even though their salaries are often one-tenth of those earned by Western expats, they still make three or four times as much as they could at home. An Indian man is able to support an extended family back home on his pay packet alone. Many Asian expats stay here for 20 years or more, only seeing their families for one month every two years.

come, which means that much of the money generated in the workforce is leaving the country.

POPULATION & PEOPLE

The best recent estimates are that Dubai's population is around 1.04 million, a giant leap from 183,200 in 1975. These statistics apply to the whole of the Dubai emirate, though most of the population lives in the city of Dubai. The population has been growing by as much as 5% a year, and the authorities are planning for a population of 2 million by 2010. Only about 22% of the total population of Dubai (roughly 220,000 people) are Emiratis; the expatriate community makes up the rest of the population. If you need proof of the fact that there are so many expat workers here, just look at the ratio of men to women. Of the approximately one million people in Dubai only 300,000 are women.

The Emiratis in Dubai stem mainly from the Bani Yas tribe who came from the isolated areas of Al-Ain and Liwa, both oases deep in the desert. There are also a large number of people with Iranian, Indian and Baluchi (from what is now a part of Pakistan and Iran) ancestry. Whether or not these people gain UAE citizenship depends on how long they have been in the country (some sources claim 15 years is required).

The majority of expats (about 60%) are from India, supplying the city with cheap labour, although there are also a large number holding professional positions. Most of the labourers and men in low-prestige positions (taxi drivers, hotel cleaners etc) come from the southern Indian state of Kerala, and many are Muslims. There are also lots of workers from the Indian states of Tamil Nadu and Goa. In contrast, most of the Indians in office jobs or managerial positions are recruited by agencies based in Mumbai, and many come from that city. In addition, all of the leading Indian mercantile communities – Jains, Sindhis, Sikhs and Marwaris – are represented here. These communities are sometimes collectively called the Banians or Traders.

Dubai is also something of a refuge for the wealthy and well connected of the subcontinent. The former prime minister of Pakistan, Benazir Bhutto, is a resident. In the 1980s Dubai earned notoriety as a base for Indian underworld figures, such as the Al Capone of Mumbai, Dawood Ibrahim.

About 12% are from other Arab countries (mainly Lebanon, Syria, Jordan and Egypt). There's also a substantial Iranian community. The first wave of Iranians built the Bastakia neighbourhood in the 1930s. They were mostly religiously conservative Sunnis and Shiites from southern Iran. After the 1980 Islamic revolution, a more affluent, often Western-educated, group of Iranians settled in Dubai. There is also a growing community of Filipino expatriates, as well as some Chinese, Indonesian and Vietnamese residents. Western expats make up about 3% of the population, once predominantly British but now also strongly represented by people from Ireland, Germany and France.

EDUCATION

Universal education in Dubai has made great strides in the last 20 to 30 years. As recently as 1952, there were no schools in Dubai, and only a handful of *kuttab* (religious schools) where boys and girls learned the Quran by rote and some learned to read and write. A school-building programme began in the 1960s and by 1972 there were 16 boys' schools and 12 girls' schools. The teachers were recruited mainly from other Arab nations.

Primary education is now compulsory in Dubai and secondary education is available to all. It is estimated that there are around 80 government schools in Dubai, from kindergarten to secondary, with a total of 45,000 students, a little over half of whom are girls. There are also about 100 private schools with a total enrolment of around 80,000.

Since Dubai is a multi-ethnic society, there are a large number of schools that cater specifically to the different nationalities of expat families, offering curriculums from the UK, US and India.

Not long ago, Dubai residents had to go abroad, usually to the UK or Pakistan, with the help of government grants, to seek tertiary education. This changed in 1977 with the establishment of the UAE University in Al-Ain, about 1½ hours from Dubai. In 1988 a system of Higher Colleges of Technology was set up to offer more technically oriented courses. Today Dubai also has two private universities: the American University in Dubai (Map 2, #13) on Sheikh Zayed Rd, and the University of Wollongong Dubai Campus on Jumeira Road in Jumeira. Both offer courses in business administration, technology and computer science. Apart from these universities, all tertiary education is free. As a way of encouraging nationals to contribute to the workforce, those who go on to tertiary education are given a very generous monthly salary simply for attending their course. The federal government is also willing to pay the cost of overseas study for UAE citizens.

ARTS
Song & Dance

Traditional songs and dances are inspired by the environment – the sea, desert and mountains. Contact with other cultures through Dubai's trading history has brought many other influences. Traditional song and dance displays are generally confined to special events and celebrations such as weddings, or heritage displays during the Dubai Shopping Festival and Dubai Summer Surprises. It is unlikely that you will come across a spontaneous music or dance performance in Dubai.

One of the most popular dances is the *liwa*, which is performed to a rapid tempo and loud drum beat. It was most likely brought to the Gulf by East African slaves and it is traditionally sung in Swahili.

Another dance, the *ayyalah*, is a typical Bedouin dance, celebrating courage and strength. The *ayyalah* is performed throughout the Gulf, but the UAE has its own variation, which is performed to a simple drum beat. Anywhere between 25 and 200 men stand with their arms linked in two rows facing each other. They wave walking sticks or swords in front of them and sway back and forth, the two rows taking it in turn to sing. It is a war dance and the words expound the virtues of courage and bravery in battle. There is a display on video of this dance in the Dubai Museum.

Music

The instruments used at traditional musical celebrations in Dubai are the same as those used in much of the rest of the Gulf. The *tamboura*, a harp-like instrument, has five strings made of horse gut, which are stretched between a wooden base and a bow-shaped neck. The base is covered with camel skin and the strings are plucked with sheep horns. It has a deep and resonant sound, a little like a bass violin.

A much less sophisticated instrument is the *manior*, a percussion instrument that is played with the body. It is a belt made of cotton and decorated with dried goats' hooves. It is wrapped around the player who keeps time with the beat of the tamboura while dancing.

The *mimzar* is a wooden instrument a little like a small oboe, but it delivers a higher pitched sound, which is haunting and undeniably Middle Eastern.

An unusual instrument and one that you'll often see at song and dance displays is the *habban*, the Arabian bagpipes. This instrument is made from a goatskin sack that has two pipes attached. The sack retains its goat shape and the pipes resemble its front legs. One pipe is used to blow air into the sack and the other produces the sound. The *habban* sounds much the same as the Scottish bagpipes, but is shriller in tone.

The *tabl* is a drum, and has a number of different shapes. It can resemble a bongo drum that is placed on the floor, or a *jaser*, a drum with goatskin at both ends, which is slung around the neck and hit with sticks.

Literature

You will have trouble digging up many published Emirati authors in Dubai. The best known writer is perhaps US-educated Mohammed al-Murr, whose books have been translated into English. One of these is

Poetry

Nothing touches the heart of a Gulf Arab quite like poetry. It dominates Arabian literature, and some argue that the passion and images of Arabic poetry are a dominant influence on Arab intellectual life. The Quran is regarded as divine poetry, but even before Islam the shrine of the Kaaba was bedecked with banners embroidered with poems. These poems, the *Muallaqat* (Hung Ones), are still studied at schools today.

In Bedouin culture a facility with poetry and language was greatly prized. A poet who could eloquently praise his own people while pointing out the failures of other tribes was considered a great asset. Modern poets of note from the UAE include Sultan al-Owais, some of whose poems have been translated into English, and Dr Ahmed al-Madani who wrote in the romantic *baiti* style. Palestinian resistance poets such as Mahmood Darwish and Samih al-Qasim are popular, though traditionalists complain that they have broken with the 16 classical meters of poetry developed by the 8th-century Gulf Arab scholar Al-Khalil bin Ahmed.

Nabati or vernacular poetry is especially popular. Sheikhs such as Sheikh Zayed, the president of the UAE, and Sheikh Mohammed bin Rashid al-Maktoum, Dubai's crown prince, are keen writers in this tradition. Many Arabic-language newspapers and magazines publish a page of *nabati* poetry.

There are about 50 well-known male poets in the UAE who still use the forms of classical Arabic poetry, though they often experiment with combining it with other styles. There are also some well-known female poets, most of whom write in the *tafila* or prose style.

Dubai Tales, a collection of 12 short stories exploring aspects of the traditional lives and values of the people of Dubai. The other is called *The Wink of the Mona Lisa*. Al-Murr's popularity could be attributed to the presentation of his characters: they all have great pride in their origins and tradition, which seems to strike a chord with readers looking for literature they can empathise with.

Painting

The encouragement of artists is still a relatively new concept in Dubai, though gallery owners agree that there has been an increase in patronage over the last five years. Patronage generally takes the form of commissions from government offices and hotels as well as from sheikhs and other wealthy Emiratis.

A few Emirati artists have gained well-deserved attention from the international art community. Sheikha Hessah, the eldest child of Sheikh Maktoum, was trained by renowned Bangladeshi artist Tina Ahmed.

Abdul Qader al-Rais is considered to be a torchbearer of the artistic movement in the Emirates. Abdul Rahim Salem, chairman of the Emirates Fine Arts Society, is also a successful artist who was born and bred in Dubai. His work is unusual in that he doesn't resort to the stereotypical Arabian themes that are so common in the work of other Dubai artists. His strikingly modern paintings use colour boldly to evoke a strong emotional reaction.

Other Emirati artists are Azza al-Qasimi, Sawsan al-Qasimi (of the ruling family of Ras al-Khaimah), Safia Mohammed Khalfan and Khulood Mohammed Ali.

Most of the art you will see in the galleries and shops is by resident expatriates. Many of the themes adopted by expatriate artists reflect the history and tradition of Dubai: family life, traditional pastimes, souq life, Bedouin heritage and seafaring.

The Sharjah Art Museum (see Sharjah in the Excursions chapter), which is headed by the painter Abdul Rahim Salem, exhibits some work by local artists although the bulk of its collection comes from overseas. There has been a concerted effort by the Sharjah Ministry of Culture to encourage local artists, both Emiratis and resident expatriates, to come together and practice their art at the Bait Obeid al-Sharasi artists' studios in Sharjah.

Crafts

On the whole, traditional crafts are confined to Dubai's museums and to exhibitions in hotel lobbies during events such as Dubai Summer Surprises or the Dubai Shopping Festival. You will occasionally see local crafts in the Dubai Souq in Bur Dubai.

Most of the pottery you will see in souqs is made outside Dubai in the mountainous areas of Ras al-Khaimah, Fujairah and Dibba where the clay is more suitable. Traditional pots of various shapes and sizes have different uses. A *khir* is used to preserve dates. Milk is stored in a *birnah* and a *hibb* keeps water cold. Pots are also used as cooking vessels.

For centuries the Bedouin have used date-palm fronds to weave various household items. The cone-shaped mat used to cover food is called a *surood* while the large, round floor mat on which food is placed is called a *semma*. A *jefeer* is a shopping basket and a *mehaffa* is a hand-held fan. Camel bags or cushion covers woven from camel hair are another traditional craft, as is *talli* work. *Talli* is the interweaving of different coloured cotton threads with silver or gold threads to make decorative ankle, wrist and neck bands which are worn by women at special events such as weddings.

Arabic perfumes and incenses are still concocted in small workshops near the perfume souq in Deira. The most common type of Arabic perfume is *attar*, a heavily scented, oil-based fragrance. Another form is *bahoor* (incense) which comes in a compressed powder form. Then there is frankincense (*luban* in Arabic). Traditionally used to perfume a room, incense was also used by men and women to keep themselves and their clothes smelling nice.

SOCIETY & CONDUCT
Traditional Culture

Dubai is a tolerant and relaxed society, with its cultural life firmly rooted in Islam. Day-to-day activities, relationships, diet and dress are dictated very much by religion. Gender roles are still pretty strictly adhered to; men engage with the outside world, and women rule the roost in domestic life.

In Dubai very little traditional Arabic and Bedouin culture remains. The skeletons of this past life still exist in the form of the old buildings in Bur Dubai (Map 4) along the waterfront near the souq and in Deira around Al-Ahmadiya School (Map 4, #10). To get an idea of traditional culture, you need to visit the Dubai Museum or venture out of Dubai to some of the villages around the east coast and to Al-Ain where life appears not to be too far removed from the way it was before federation.

Emirati society is highly stratified. For example, when student elections are held on campuses, there is no campaigning among candidates. The usual method is that the students get together and decide who among them comes from the highest-ranking family. They feel there's no point choosing a student from a goatherder's family, because the goatherder's son won't be taken seriously if he had to represent the students at a high-level meeting.

Of the traditional Bedouin activities, boat building is still practised, but only on a small scale. Date cultivation is still an important part of life, though it is no longer as necessary to survival as it once was. Pearling was once the livelihood of many coastal inhabitants, but you will have to visit the museum to learn about it now.

Dubai has been very active over the last few years in trying to revive and preserve many of the traditions that have diminished in the wake of modernity, wealth and the influx of foreigners. The Dubai Museum and the Heritage Village in Shindagha (see the Things to See & Do chapter) display traditional village life, as does the Heritage Village in Hatta (see the Excursions chapter). Expensive restoration work is being carried out on traditional turn-of-the-century houses in the Al-Ahmadiya district of Deira and in the Bastakia Quarter and the Shindagha area of Bur Dubai. The aim of such work is not just to attract and entertain tourists, it is also designed to educate young Emiratis about their culture and heritage.

Festivals such as the Dubai Shopping Festival and Dubai Summer Surprises usually feature displays of traditional song and dance as well as food and craft.

One matter of great concern to the authorities is the trend for Emirati men to marry foreign women. One reason for this is believed to be the prohibitive cost of a traditional wedding, plus the dowry that the groom must provide – it's cheaper and easier to marry a foreign woman. There's also a suggestion that as Emirati women have become better educated, they are less willing to settle down in the traditional role of an Emirati wife. This issue is discussed in great depth in the Arabic press. In a culture where women who are unmarried by the age of 24 are perceived as being 'on the shelf', or even as a slight on the family's honour, the growing numbers of single women is a hot topic indeed. The rising divorce rate is another topic that attracts considerable concern.

The UAE Marriage Fund, set up in 1994 by the federal government to facilitate marriages between UAE nationals, grants Dh70,000 to each couple to pay for the exorbitant cost of the wedding and dowry. It also promotes mass weddings, which allow nationals to save most of the marriage grant for a down payment on a house and other living costs. These have reduced

Henna Night

A few nights before their wedding night, brides-to-be are honoured with *layyat al-henna*, henna night. This is a women-only affair, part of a week of festivities and events before the wedding ceremony. At this party, the bride-to-be is anointed from head to toe with expensive perfumes and oils, her hair is washed with jasmine and frankincense perfumes, and her hands, wrists, ankles and feet are decorated with henna. How well the henna pattern lasts is said to be an indication to the mother-in-law of what kind of wife the bride will make. If she's been a hard worker, the henna will penetrate deeper into the roughened skin of her hands, and remain longer. The henna is applied in intricate, often floral patterns. On henna night, the female friends and relatives of the bride-to-be share a feast of special foods, and sing and dance. It's also a night for the trousseau – silks, jewellery and perfumes given as gifts by her fiance – to be displayed.

the rate of intermarriages between Emirati men and foreign women to a degree, but not sufficiently to see that every Emirati woman has a husband.

Traditional Dress

Almost all Emiratis wear traditional dress. Men wear the 'I-don't-know-how-they-keep-it-so-clean' ankle-length, white *dishdasha*. The *gutra* is the white head cloth which is held on the head by a black coil called an *agal*. Sometimes men wear a red-and-white checked *gutra* although they are usually not Emirati. Underneath the *gutra* men wear a lace skullcap called a *taqia*; sometimes they will just wear the *taqia* on its own. On special occasions, sheikhs and other important men wear a black or gold cloak, called an *abba*, over their *dishdasha*. You will see a picture in the newspaper almost every day of Sheikh Zayed or Sheikh Maktoum wearing their *abba*s for important diplomatic meetings.

Women wear a long, black cloak, called an *abeyya*, which covers everything from head to foot. In addition, a black head cloth called the *shayla* is usually worn over the top to cover the face. In rural areas, women also wear a *burqa*, a stiff mask made of gold-coloured material that covers the eyebrows, nose and mouth. Sometimes, however, the *burqa* is just a simple piece of black chiffon tied around the head, which covers the face from under the eyes down.

Underneath their *abeyyas* women wear whatever they want. Among the younger women in Dubai this may be tight trousers and tops; however, the traditional costume is a simple floral dress called a *kandoura*. Men also wear a *kandoura* that is like a short-sleeved kaftan. On special occasions women wear *sirwal* under their *kandoura*s. These are loose trousers that come in tight from the knee down and are often decorated around the ankles with an embroidered band, called *talli*, made from gold and coloured thread.

Dos & Don'ts

Alcohol This is legal in Dubai (but not in Sharjah) if consumed in private or in a li-

censed venue. You should never, ever drive while you're drunk. Apart from the obvious dangers, if you are caught doing so there will be, at the very least, a steep fine to pay and you may wind up spending a month or more in jail.

Mosques If you are not a Muslim you are not permitted to enter mosques in the UAE.

What to Wear Women will find it best to wear loose-fitting clothing that is not too revealing. Although you'll see women with exposed midriffs, short skirts and tight trousers in Dubai, you'll attract less attention if you dress conservatively – it's worth considering the impression you are making. Bathing suits are acceptable for the beach, though women may want to cover up more at public beaches to avoid the ogling of men.

It's best for men not to appear bare-chested in public except when at the beach or at a swimming pool. Emiratis in Dubai are used to seeing Western men in shorts and they are seen as something comical rather than offensive. If you do wear shorts they should be relatively long – all the way to the knee if possible – but don't wear them into someone's home.

Social Etiquette Although Dubai is very used to the habits of a wide variety of nationalities and is particularly forgiving of Westerners and their faux pas, etiquette is still very important. You will generate more respect for yourself if you remember a few basic rules.

As is the case anywhere, it is impolite to photograph people without asking their permission and you should never photograph women. Avoid pointing your camera at police stations, airports and palaces.

You should always stand when someone enters the room. Upon entering a room yourself shake hands with everyone, touching your heart with the palm of the right hand after each handshake. This goes for both Arab men and women, though men finding themselves in the presence of Arab women should not offer to shake hands unless the

A lifeguard watches over Jumeira Beach

The Burj al-Arab makes a stunning beach backdrop

The past meets the future on Dubai's waterfront, where glittering skyscrapers overlook wooden dhows

Abra passengers

*Abra*s (water taxis) link the historic souqs of Deira and Bur Dubai

A fresh catch from the Gulf

Trade is Dubai's lifeblood and the wharves bustle with activity as goods are loaded and offloaded

woman takes the lead by extending her hand first. Western women will occasionally find that a man may not extend his hand to shake theirs, or he will cover his hand with his *dishdasha* first and extend his fist. This is because some stricter Muslims will not touch a woman who is not part of their family. When two men meet it is considered polite for them to inquire after each other's families but *not* each other's wives.

It is common to attach forms of address to people's given names. Just as Arabs refer to each other as 'Mr Mohammed' or 'Mr Abdullah', they will refer to you as 'Mr John', 'Miss Simone' or 'Mrs Susan'. Often women will be referred to by their husband's name, for instance 'Mrs Tony'.

The word 'sheikh' applies *only* to members of the ruling family. The rulers themselves carry the formal title of 'emir' (prince), but are usually referred to as 'sheikhs', as in 'Sheikh Mohammed bin Rashid al-Maktoum'. The feminine form of sheikh is 'sheikha'. It applies to all female members of the ruling family.

If you are in a frustrating situation, be patient, friendly and sensitive. Never lose your temper. A confrontational attitude doesn't go well with the Arab personality and loss of face is a sensitive issue. If you have a problem with someone, be firm, calm and persistent.

You'll notice that people do not use the term 'thank you' as much as in the West. This is because one is expected to repay significant favours by actions – words alone are not enough. For a service that is paid for or expected, such as the bell-boy bringing luggage to a room, thanks are not considered necessary.

Treatment of Animals

Compared with Western society, Arab culture has a different relationship with some animals. Dogs, for example, have a status on a level with rats in the Quran, so very few Emiratis keep dogs as pets. Pigs are equally reviled. Camels and falcons, on the other hand, are greatly loved, as are horses. Some expatriates and visitors have been disturbed by the condition of the local stray cat and

dog populations. Two local volunteer expat groups that care for strays are **Feline Friends** (☎ 050-451 0058) and **K9 Friends** (☎ 342 1081; Ⓦ www.k9friends@freeserve.co.uk).

RELIGION

Though other religions are tolerated in Dubai, the official religion in town is Islam. As with any religion embracing about one billion people, Islam has produced many sects, movements and offshoots.

Most of Dubai's Muslim population are Sunni Muslims subscribing to the Maliki or Hanbali schools of Islamic law. Many of the latter are Wahhabis, though UAE Wahhabis are not nearly as strict and puritanical as the Wahhabis of Saudi Arabia. There is also a smaller community of Shiite Muslims, descendants mainly from merchants and workers who crossed to the Trucial Coast from Persia in the late 19th or early 20th century. Shiite mosques are distinguished by their dazzling tilework, in swirling patterns of blue and green.

Islam

Muslims believe the religion preached by the Prophet Mohammed to be God's final revelation to humanity. For them the Quran (meaning 'the Recitation' in Arabic) represents God's words revealed through the Prophet. It supplements and completes the earlier revelations around which the Christian and Jewish faiths were built, and corrects misinterpretations of those earlier revelations.

For example, Muslims believe that Jesus was a prophet second only to Mohammed in importance, but that his followers later introduced into Christianity the heretical idea that Jesus was divine (the son of God). Adam, Abraham, Moses and a number of other Christian and Jewish holy men are regarded as prophets by Muslims. Mohammed, however, was the 'Seal of the Prophets' – the last one who has, or will, come.

The essence of Islam is the belief that there is only one God and that it is the people's duty to believe in and serve Him in the manner which He has laid out in the

The Five Pillars of Islam

Shahadah The profession of faith: 'There is no god but God, and Mohammed is the messenger of God'.

Salat Muslims are required to pray five times every day: at dawn, noon, mid-afternoon, sunset and twilight. During prayers a Muslim must perform a series of prostrations while facing the Kaaba, the ancient shrine at the centre of the Grand Mosque in Mecca. Before a Muslim can pray, however, he or she must perform a series of ritual ablutions, and if no water is available for this purpose, sand or soil may be substituted.

Zakat Muslims must give a portion of their income to help the poor. How this has operated in practice has varied over the centuries: either it was seen as an individual duty or the state collected it as a form of income tax to be redistributed through mosques or religious charities.

Sawm It was during the month of Ramadan that Mohammed received his first revelation in AD 610. Muslims mark this event by fasting from sunrise until sunset throughout Ramadan. During the fast a Muslim may not take anything into his or her body. Food, drink, smoking and sex are banned. Young children, travellers and those whose health will not permit it are exempt from the fast, though those who are able to do so are supposed to make up the days they missed at a later time.

Haj All able Muslims are required to make the pilgrimage to Mecca at least once, if possible during a specific few days in the first and second weeks of the Muslim month of Dhul Hijja. Visiting Mecca and performing the prescribed rituals at any other time of the year is considered spiritually desirable. Such visits are referred to as *umrah*, or 'little pilgrimages'.

Quran. In Arabic, *islam* means 'submission' and a Muslim is one who submits to God's will.

Muslims must observe five central tenets of the faith (see the boxed text 'The Five Pillars of Islam'). Beyond these five pillars there are many other duties incumbent on Muslims.

In the West the best known and least understood of these is jihad. The word is usually translated into English as 'holy war', but jihad literally means 'striving in the way of the faith'. Exactly what this means has been the subject of keen debate among Muslim scholars for the last 1400 years. Some scholars see jihad in spiritual, as opposed to martial, terms. The idea of a crusade, in the sense of both a religious war and a personal crusade against whatever ails yourself or society, is a close equivalent to the concept of jihad.

Muslims are forbidden to eat or drink anything containing pork or alcohol, and the meat (or blood) of any animal that died of natural causes (as opposed to having been slaughtered in the prescribed manner). Muslim women may not marry non-Muslim men, though Muslim men are permitted to marry Christian or Jewish women (but not, for example, Hindus or Buddhists).

Sunnis & Shiites

The schism that divided the Muslim world into two broad camps took place a few years after the death of the Prophet. When Mohammed died in 632, he left no clear instructions either designating a successor or setting up a system by which subsequent leaders could be chosen. Some Muslims felt that leadership of the community should remain within the Prophet's family, and supported the claim of Ali bin Abi Taleb, Mohammed's cousin and son-in-law and one of the first converts to Islam, to become the caliph, or leader. But the rest of the community chose Abu Bakr, the Prophet's closest companion, as leader, and Ali was passed over in two subsequent leadership contests.

This split the Muslim community into two competing factions. Those who took Ali's side became known as the *shiat Ali*, or 'partisans of Ali'. Because Shiites have rarely held power over long periods of time, their doctrine came to emphasise the spiritual position of their religious leaders, the imams. The Sunnis followed their political leaders, such as the Caliphs, while the Shiites followed their imams, and developed a hierarchy of clerics culminating in the Velayet-e Faqih, the most senior of the grand ayatollahs.

Wahhabism

This form of Islam takes its name from Mohammed bin Abdul Wahhab (1703–92), a preacher and judge who, after seeing an increasing lack of respect for Islam among the Bedouin tribes of central Arabia, preached a return to Islam's origins and traditions as interpreted by the Hanbali school of Islamic jurisprudence. This meant strict adherence to the Quran and the Hadith (accounts of the Prophet's words and actions).

Wahhabism is a rather austere form of Islam. Wahhabis reject such concepts as sainthood and forbid the observance of holidays such as the Prophet's birthday. Even the term Wahhabi makes strict followers of the sect uncomfortable because it appears to exalt Mohammed bin Abdul Wahhab over the Prophet. Strict Wahhabis prefer the term *muwahidin*, which translates as 'unitarian', because they profess only the unity of God.

Islamic Law

The Arabic word Sharia'a is usually translated as 'Islamic Law'. This is misleading. The Sharia'a is not a legal code in the Western sense of the term. It refers to the general body of Islamic legal thought. Where the Quran does not provide guidance on a particular subject, Muslim scholars turn to the Sunna, a body of works recording the sayings and doings of the Prophet and, to a lesser extent, his companions, as reported by a string of scholarly authorities.

The Quran and Sunna together make up the basis of Sharia'a. In some instances the Sharia'a is quite specific (eg, inheritance law and punishments for certain offences). In many other cases it acts as a series of guidelines. Islam does not recognise a distinction between the secular and religious lives of believers. Thus, a scholar or judge can, with enough research through use of analogy, determine the proper 'Islamic' position on any problem.

There are many Sunna authorities and their reliability is determined by the school of Islamic jurisprudence to which one subscribes. There are four main Sunni and two principal Shiite schools of Islamic jurisprudence. The orthodox Sunni schools of jurisprudence are the Shafi'i, Hanbali, Hanafi and Maliki. All but the first of these schools are found widely in the Gulf, though Hanbali is the largest in Dubai. Hanbali Islam is generally regarded as the sternest of the four orthodox Sunni rites. Hanafi jurisprudence has particular influence over commercial affairs. Mohammed Shaibani, one of the founders of the Hanafi school, was also the author of a business manual called the Kitab al-Kasb (Book of Profit). This book emphasised that making a decent living was not just permissible under Islam, but a religious duty. The largest schools of Shiite jurisprudence are the Jafari and the Akhbari.

LANGUAGE

Arabic is the official language of Dubai while English is the language of business, though it competes with Hindi and Urdu as the lingua franca. You will have little trouble making yourself understood, although when you venture out into rural areas you will find that English is not as widely spoken or understood there. Knowing the Iranian language, Farsi, will help you get by. Hindi, Urdu and Malayalam (the language of Kerala in India) can all be reasonably useful because of the large number of Indian and Pakistani expats. For some useful words in Arabic see the Language chapter.

Facts for the Visitor

ORIENTATION

Dubai is really two towns merged into one and divided by Dubai Creek (Khor Dubai): Deira is to the north of the Creek and Bur Dubai to the south. Both districts are home to Dubai's traditional architecture and souqs. The modern city is growing at an extraordinary rate, stretching 35km down the coast to Jebel Ali Port as well as eastwards into the desert past the airport, and nearly joining with Sharjah further up the coast. The city is poised to become the centre of a continuous urban sprawl stretching for 60km along the shores of the Gulf, from Jebel Ali to Ajman.

Although Deira and Bur Dubai are actually only small districts on either side of the Creek near its mouth, locals often use these

When to Go		
month	**advantages**	**disadvantages**
January	Temperatures range from 24°C to 30°C, with some overcast cool days.	There is the occasional rain shower although this can hardly be seen as a disadvantage as rain is such a treat in this part of the world.
February	This is probably the nicest month of the year weather-wise, with clear sunny days and less chance of windy or overcast spells than in January. Although many tourists come in February, it is not as busy as January. Be prepared for some cool evenings.	None to speak of.
March & April	The Dubai Shopping Festival is on (although any month is a good month to shop in Dubai). The hot weather begins its gradual return, with average day temperatures of 28°C in March and 32°C in April. On the other hand, humidity is relatively low.	The hordes of shoppers can be a disincentive to travel to Dubai at this time of year. You'll need to book hotels ahead as they get very full and prices rise somewhat as proprietors look to cash in on the shopping season, and the traffic can be chaotic. The occasional dust storm sweeps into town and creates momentary havoc.
May	The tourist season is petering out and although it's hot (mid- to high 30s), it's not too hot to walk around in the early morning and evening. Hotels begin offering summer discounts (up to 70%) from mid- to late May.	The heat will be too much for most people, so you may find yourself restricted to indoor activities.
June	Hotel prices dive.	It's too darn hot.

terms to refer generally to the areas north and south of the Creek.

Deira is the old city centre, supplanted by the skyscrapers springing up along Sheikh Zayed Rd. Activity in Deira focuses on Baniyas Rd, which runs along the Creek, Baniyas Square (which used to be called Al-Nasr Square and is still generally known by that name), Al-Maktoum Rd, Al-Maktoum Hospital Rd and Naif Rd. The Deira souqs, around which many of the cheap hotels are located, occupy most of the area west of Baniyas Square and south of Naif Rd.

On the Bur Dubai side, the old souq area runs from Al-Ghubaiba Rd (where the bus station is) to the Diwan (Ruler's Office) and inland as far as Khalid bin al-Waleed Rd. Running at right angles to Khalid bin al-Waleed is Sheikh Khalifa bin Zayed Rd, a vital arterial known to everyone as Trade Centre Rd. This road is Dubai's real centre of gravity, cutting between the new apartment blocks of the Golden Sands area and the bustling Asian expatriate suburb of Karama.

New suburbs are being built all the time. Many Western expatriates have found areas

When to Go

month	advantages	disadvantages
July & August	The hotels are still remarkably cheap. Dubai Summer Surprises is held, mainly to attract visitors to the shopping centres. (It's too hot to be anywhere else.) This is a series of events and promotions when you can see traditional dancing and music displays, crafts and exhibitions of local artworks.	The heat and humidity are so extreme that you can only be outdoors for a few minutes at a time. Even at night, just walking along the street can be an exhausting and sweaty experience.
September	Most hotels have discounted summer rates until mid-September.	It's still too hot (about 39°C) though there is the occasional downpour that can entirely flood the roads.
October & November	For some of the time it will be Ramadan which means that some hotels offer up to 70% off their normal rates. You'll have the city to yourself as most tourists stay away during Ramadan. The breaking of the fast (iftar) each evening is a big event and the streets tend to come alive after dark. It's an exciting time. Except for restrictions on eating and smoking in public, and a ban on live music and discos, life goes on. The weather is tropical and it's the perfect time for a beach holiday.	The weather may still be too hot for some. If it's Ramadan you can't eat, drink or smoke in public during daylight hours. Often the only place you can eat during the day is in your hotel room although most hotels will serve breakfast and lunch in their restaurants. Shops are shut for the afternoon, even in the shopping centres, and they don't open until about 7pm. Some tour companies reduce the number of tours on offer at this time of year.
December	Delicious, wonderful winter: warm days and cool evenings.	It could rain, but don't bet on it.

such as the beachside suburbs of Jumeira and Umm Suqeim to be too expensive, so they've relocated to Mirdif and Rashidiya past the airport, east of the city.

There are four ways of crossing the Creek: Al-Shindagha Tunnel runs under the Creek at the western end, near its mouth (there is also a pedestrian tunnel here); Al-Maktoum Bridge, on the eastern edge of the centre, is the main traffic artery across the waterway; further east, Al-Garhoud Bridge is used mostly by traffic trying to bypass the centre; and *abras*, small, flat-decked water taxis crisscross the waterway throughout the day.

Street addresses are only now being introduced to Dubai, in preparation for a postal delivery service. People usually refer to the main roads by name, but few people know the names of the smaller, numbered streets. You'll find that addresses are given as 'the green Emirates building at the Falcon Roundabout' or 'the white villa, next to the big tree, across from the Avari Hotel'. Of course, these instructions assume that you know the Falcon Roundabout or the Avari Hotel. Don't worry if you don't know them because a taxi driver most likely will.

Dubai has been growing so fast that the municipality hasn't got around to naming all the roads. Many are just given numbers, but there's a new campaign to rename roads after Arab capital cities. Many main streets are known by more familiar names, which can become confusing. It helps to be aware of the following alternative names:

official name	other names
Al-Esbij St	Astoria Hotel Rd
Al-Wasl Rd	Iranian Hospital Rd
Baniyas Square	Al-Nasr Square
Jumeira Rd	Jumeira Beach Rd or Beach Rd
Khalid bin al-Waleed Rd	Bank St (from Za'abeel Rd to Al-Mankhool Rd)
Khalid bin al-Waleed Rd	Computer St (from Al-Mankhool Rd to Al-Mina Rd)
Sheikh Khalifa bin Zayed Rd	Trade Centre Rd
Sheikh Zayed Rd	Abu Dhabi Rd

MAPS

Maps of Dubai are available from the bigger bookshops around town (see Bookshops in the Shopping chapter for location details). All the maps mentioned here should also be available in the bookshops at five-star hotels, though there can be shortages at times. The Dubai Municipality wasn't planning to print new maps until the next bout of road building had been authorised.

The *Dubai Tourist Map* (Dh45), published by the municipality, is the best of the local maps though completely unwieldy for unfolding in a car. It has a montage of modern buildings and horse racing on the front.

Geoprojects publishes a map of Dubai which is not bad, but it's becoming increasingly outdated and it doesn't include the names of all the minor streets. It is available from most bookshops and hotels for Dh30.

There is also the *Dubai 3D Tourist Map*, which is fairly up-to-date and useful for locating landmarks such as hotels, souqs and banks around town. It costs Dh20.

RESPONSIBLE TOURISM

Although tourism in Dubai has not reached the heights it has in other cities in the region, it does have an impact on the environment. There are a number of things you can do to be a responsible tourist:

- Preserve natural resources. Try not to waste water. Switch off lights and air-con when you go out, though in midsummer you will need to leave the air-con on.
- Ask before taking photographs of people, especially women. Don't worry if you don't speak Arabic. A smile and gesture will be understood and appreciated.
- Remember that the UAE is a Muslim country and although Dubai is the most international and cosmopolitan city of the Gulf, revealing clothes will still cause offence to most people.
- Similarly, public displays of affection between members of the opposite sex are inappropriate.
- Learning something about Dubai's history and culture helps prevent misunderstandings and frustrations.

Be aware of environmental issues. The invention of the jet ski was an environmental mistake that would cheer Satan. Before you hire a jet ski remember that they pollute the water, make an awful noise and are just plain dangerous when there are swimmers and other watercraft around.

Desert safaris in a 4WD make for a popular day excursion for visitors, but they are not environmentally sound activities. Expats are just as guilty of 'dune-bashing' the environment as tourists are, as the sport is becoming an increasingly popular weekend pastime. If you are taking part in any desert activities bear in mind the following guidelines:

- To minimise your impact on the land, stick to the tracks and avoid damaging the all-too-rare vegetation that is such an important part of the fragile desert ecosystem.
- Driving in wadis (seasonal rivers) should be avoided to ensure that they are not polluted with oil and grease. They are sometimes important sources of irrigation and drinking water.
- When diving or snorkelling, avoid touching or removing any marine life, especially coral.
- If you plan to camp out, remember to take your own wood – don't pull limbs from trees or up-root shrubs. Plants may look dead but usually they are not.

TOURIST OFFICES
Local Tourist Offices
The **Department of Tourism & Commerce Marketing** (DTCM; ☎ 223 0000, fax 223 0022; e info@dubaitourism.co.ae, w www .dubaitourism.co.ae) is the official tourism board of the Dubai government. It is also the sole regulating, planning and licensing authority for the tourist industry in Dubai. It has three welcome bureaus you can call for information or for help in booking hotels, tours and car hire; these are at the airport arrivals area (☎ 224 5252; open 24 hrs); in Baniyas Square in Deira (Map 4, #77; ☎ 228 5000; open 9am-11pm daily); and about 40km out of town on Sheikh Zayed Rd on the way into Dubai from Abu Dhabi (☎ 884 6827; open 9am-9pm daily). The quality of information they give depends largely on whether the person behind the desk could give a damn. On a bad day, all they'll give you are a few glossy pamphlets and some not very useful maps. You can generally get better information, however, from tour operators, such as those listed under Organised

Tours in the Getting Around chapter, and some of the larger hotels.

Dubai National Travel & Tourist Authority (DNATA) is the quasi-official travel agency in Dubai; it has the monopoly on travel services at wholesale level. The **DNATA head office** (Map 5, #19; ☎ 295 1111; Al-Maktoum Rd, Deira) is at the DNATA Airline Centre.

Tourist Offices Abroad
The DTCM has a number of branches overseas that are vigorously promoting Dubai as an upmarket tourist destination. These branches go by the name of the Dubai Tourism & Commerce Promotion Board and include the following:

Australia & New Zealand (☎ 02-9956 6620, fax 9929 8493; e dtcm_aus@dubaitourism.co .ae) Level 6, 75 Miller St, North Sydney 2060
France (☎ 01 44 95 85 00, fax 01 45 63 13 14; e dtcm-france@wanadoo.fr) 15 bis rue de Marignan, 75008 Paris
Germany (☎ 069-710 00 20, fax 710 02 34; e dtcm_ge@dubaitourism.co.ae) Bockenheimer Landstrasse 23, D-60325, Frankfurt-am-Main
India (☎ 022-283 3497, fax 283 3510; e dtcm_in@dubaitourism.co.ae) 51 Bajaj Bhavan, 5th floor, Nariman Point, Mumbai 400 021
Italy (☎ 02-72 02 24 66, fax 72 02 01 62; e dtcm_it@dubaitourism.co.ae) Piazza Bertarelli 1, 20122 Milan
Japan (☎ 03-3379 9311, fax 3379 9313; e dtcm_ja@dubaitourism.co.ae) One-Win Yoyogi Bldg, 4th floor, 3-35-10 Yoyogi, Shibuya-ku, Tokyo 151-0053
Russia, CIS & Baltic States (☎ 095-745 8700, fax 745 8706; e dtcm@pbn.ru) Krasina St, 14, Bldg 2, 1st floor, 123056 Moscow
Scandinavia (☎ 08-411 1135, fax 411 1138; e dtcm_sca@dubaitourism.co.ae) Skeppsbron 22, SE-111 30 Stockholm
South Africa (☎ 011-785 4600, fax 785 4601; e dtcm_sa@dubaitourism.co.ae) 1 Orchard Lane, Rivonia, PO Box 698, Johannesburg 2128
UK & Ireland (☎ 020-7839 0580, 24-hr brochure line ☎ 7839 0581, fax 7839 0582; e dtcm_uk@dubaitourism.co.ae) 125 Pall Mall, London SW1Y 5EA
USA (☎ 215-751 9750, fax 751 9551; e dtcm_usa@dubaitourism.co.ae) 8 Penn Centre, Philadelphia, PA 19103 ● (☎ 310-752 4488, fax 752 4444; e dubaiusa@aol.com) 901 Wilshire Blvd, Santa Monica, CA 90401

TRAVEL AGENCIES

Some recommended travel agencies include:

Al-Ghaith & Al-Moosa Travel Agency (Map 5, #42; ☎ 294 5666, fax 295 7555) Al-Maktoum Rd, Deira

Al-Rais Travels (Map 6, #1; ☎ 352 0123, fax 351 9478) Al-Rais Centre, Al-Mankhool Rd, Mankhool

Team Travel & Tours (Map 4, #18; ☎ 353 3000) Bank of Baroda Bldg, 34 St, Bur Dubai

The Travel Market (Map 5, #13; ☎ 266 4455, fax 268 2111) cnr Al-Muraqqabat & Abu Baker al-Siddiq Rds, Deira

Thomas Cook Al-Rostamani (Map 3, #54; ☎ 223 6060, fax 228 3318) Al-Rostamani Towers, Sheikh Zayed Rd

DOCUMENTS
Visas

To visit Dubai your passport must have at least two months validity left from your date of arrival. Visit visas valid for 60 days are available on arrival in the UAE at approved ports of entry, including all airports and ports, for citizens of most developed countries. These include all Western European countries (except Malta and Cyprus), Australia, Brunei, Canada, Hong Kong, Japan, Malaysia, New Zealand, Singapore, South Korea and the USA. Tourist visas are valid for 60 days despite the fact that the stamp on your passport, which is in Arabic, says it is valid for 30 days. Perhaps this will change when immigration officials are issued with the new stamps. No fee is charged for tourist visas.

Citizens of other Gulf Cooperative Council (GCC) countries do not need visas to enter the UAE, and can stay pretty much as long as they want. For citizens of other countries, a transit or tourist visa must be arranged through a sponsor. This can be a hotel, a company or a resident of the UAE. Most hotels charge a fee for arranging a visa of around Dh100.

Officially, you will be denied entry if your passport shows any evidence of travel to Israel, although we've heard from several travellers who report that in practice this isn't an issue.

Visa Extensions Visit visas can be extended once for 30 days by the **Department of Immigration and Naturalisation** *(Map 7; ☎ 398 000; Sheikh Khalifa bin Zayed Rd)*, near the Za'abeel Roundabout, for Dh500 and a fair amount of paperwork. You may be asked to provide proof of funds.

For longer periods, you have to leave the country and come back to get a new stamp. People have been known to stay in Dubai for a year or more simply by flying out to Bahrain, Doha or Kish (an island off the Iranian coast) every two months and picking up a new visa on their return at a total cost of about Dh400 per trip.

Visas can only be extended in the city or emirate you arrived in, so if you landed in Sharjah you can't get your visa extended in Dubai.

Travel Insurance

A travel insurance policy to cover theft, loss and medical problems is a good idea. Some policies offer lower and higher medical-expense options; the higher ones are chiefly for countries such as the USA, which have extremely high medical costs. There are a wide variety of policies available, so check the small print. Some policies specifically exclude 'dangerous activities', which can include scuba diving and motorcycling.

Wusta

This translates loosely as 'influence high up'. Never underestimate the power of *wusta*. It is a very desirable thing to have. It can be especially useful when you're trying to get through tedious and protracted administrative procedures, such as registering a car. A little *wusta* at the traffic police is very handy indeed. Many businesses employ agents whose role is to speak to the right people in the bureaucracy to get paperwork processed in a trouble-free manner. Most Westerners get a little outraged at the thought of a select few receiving favours and special treatment because of powerful contacts. While *wusta* is an accepted part of life in Dubai, in the West it's given other names: 'favouritism', 'bias', 'nepotism' and often just plain 'luck'.

Visas for Other Countries

You may want to apply for a visa for further travel in the Middle East while you are in Dubai. Remember that it is not possible to get visas to some countries in the region from consulates in Dubai. You may have to arrange them before you leave home. Also, if you are a resident in Dubai the requirements are sometimes different to those that apply if you are here on a tourist visa. Two popular onward destinations are Iran and Oman.

Iran

Tourists and GCC residents need one photo and one photocopy of their passport. The fee for most nationalities is Dh185; for British passport holders it is Dh220. One-month visas typically take one week to issue. The process may be more difficult for US citizens, who might be required to visit as part of an organised tour.

Oman

There has been talk of a joint visa arrangement between Oman and the UAE, that is, the visa given on arrival in Dubai would be valid for Oman as well. Unfortunately this idea seems to have been passed over, but there is still much confusion among Omani officials about it. However, it is now possible for many foreign nationals (including those from the EU, North America, Australia and New Zealand) to obtain a visa on arrival at Sceb airport in Muscat or at border posts. These on-arrival visas cost OR5 and are valid for two weeks. If you are crossing to the Musandam Peninsula, the fee is just OR1.

FACTS FOR THE VISITOR

You may prefer a policy that pays doctors or hospitals directly rather than you having to pay on the spot and claim later. If you have to claim later make sure you keep all documentation. Some policies ask you to call back (reverse charges) to a centre in your home country where an immediate assessment of your problem is made.

Check that the policy covers ambulances or an emergency flight home.

Driving Licence & Permits

If you are visiting Dubai, you can drive with most foreign driving licences in Dubai so long as you are either a citizen or a resident of the country that issued the licence. Some car-rental companies insist on an international licence, however, so it's a good idea to get one of these before you leave home.

If you are resident in Dubai, you'll need to get a permanent UAE licence. For most Western nationalities this means just swapping your own driving licence for a UAE one. For other nationalities, it's necessary to sit a test.

Other Documents

International Student Identity Cards and Seniors' Cards are not recognised in the UAE and having one will not grant you discounts at hotels or tourist sites.

Copies

All important documents (passport data page and visa page, credit cards, travel insurance policy, air/bus/train tickets, driving licence etc) should be photocopied before you leave home. Leave one copy with someone at home and keep another with you, separate from the originals.

You could also store details of your travel documents in Lonely Planet's free online Travel Vault in case you lose the photocopies or can't be bothered with them. Your password-protected Travel Vault is accessible online anywhere in the world; you can create it at W www.ekno.lonelyplanet.com.

If you need to make photocopies while in Dubai, there are hundreds of small Typing & Photocopy shops around Bur Dubai and Deira, which charge 10 to 25 fils a copy. If you have more complex photocopying to do, there's a 24-hour **Kinko's copying centre** *(Map 6, #13; Khalid bin al-Waleed Rd)* opposite the Bur Juman Centre, near the intersection with Sheikh Khalifa bin Zayed Rd.

EMBASSIES & CONSULATES

It's important to realise what your own embassy can and can't do to help you if you get into trouble.

Generally speaking, it won't be much help in emergencies if the trouble you're in is remotely your own fault. Remember that you are bound by the laws of the UAE. Your embassy will not be sympathetic if you end up in jail after committing a crime locally, even if such actions are legal in your own country.

In genuine emergencies you might get some assistance, but only if other channels have been exhausted. For example, if you need to get home urgently, a free ticket home is exceedingly unlikely – the embassy would expect you to have insurance. If you have all your money and documents stolen, it might assist with getting a new passport, but a loan for onward travel is out of the question.

Some embassies used to keep travellers' letters and stock home newspapers, but the mail-holding service has usually been stopped and newspapers tend to be out of date.

UAE Embassies & Consulates

Contact details for UAE diplomatic missions include the following:

Australia (☎ 02-6286 8802, fax 6286 8804) 36 Culgoa Circuit, O'Malley, ACT 2606
Bahrain (☎ 723 737, fax 727 343) House No 221, Rd 4007 – Complex 340, Manama
Egypt (☎ 02-360 9722, fax 570 0844) 4 Ibn Seena Street, Giza, Cairo
France (☎ 01 45 53 94 04, fax 01 47 55 61 04) 3 Rue de Lota, 75116 Paris
Germany (☎ 0228-267 070, fax 267 0714) Erste Fahrgasse, D-54113, Bonn
India (☎ 022-687 2822, fax 687 3272) EP 12 Chandra Gupta Marg, Chanakyapuri, New Delhi 11002
Iran (☎ 021-295 027, fax 878 9084) Wali Asr St, Shaheed Waheed Dastakaardi St No 355, Tehran
Kuwait (☎ 252 1427, fax 252 6382) Al-Istiqlal St, Qaseema 7, Al-Assaffa, PO Box 1828, Kuwait 13019

Oman (☎ 600 302, fax 602 584) Al-Khuwair, PO Box 551 code 111, Muscat
Qatar (☎ 885 111, fax 822 837) 22 Al-Markhiyah St, Khalifa Northern Town, PO Box 3099, Doha
Saudi Arabia (☎ 01-482 6803, fax 482 7504) Abu Bakr al-Karkhi Zone, Amr bin Omayad St, PO Box 94385, Riyadh 11693
UK (☎ 020-7581 1281/4113) 30 Princes Gate, London SW1
USA (☎ 202-338 6500, fax 337 7029) 3000 K St NW, Suite 600, Washington DC 20007

Embassies & Consulates in Dubai

Most countries have diplomatic representation in the UAE. Dubai is home to the consulates and one embassy, the British embassy; other embassies are in Abu Dhabi and are listed in the front pages of the Dubai phone book. The telephone area code for Dubai is ☎ 04.

Australia (Map 7, #19; ☎ 331 3444, fax 331 4812) 6th floor, Dubai World Trade Centre, Sheikh Zayed Rd, Za'abeel; open 8am-3.30pm Sat-Tues, 8am-2.45pm Wed
Canada (Map 6, #10; ☎ 352 1717, fax 351 7722; @ dubai@dfait-maeci.gc.ca) 7th floor, United Bank Bldg, Khalid bin al-Waleed Rd, Bur Dubai; open 8am-11.30am Sat-Wed
Egypt (Map 6, #16; ☎ 397 1122, fax 397 1033) 11 St, Bur Dubai; open 9am-noon Sat-Wed
France (Map 7, #22; ☎ 332 9040, fax 332 8033; @ fransula@emirates.net.ae) 18th floor, API World Tower, Sheikh Zayed Rd, Za'abeel; open 8.30am-1pm Sat-Wed
Germany (Map 6, #14; ☎ 379 0002, fax 397 0003; @ aadubai@emirates.net.ae) 1st floor, Sharaf Bldg, Khalid bin al-Waleed Rd, near Bur Juman Centre, Bur Dubai; open 9am-noon Sat-Wed
India (Map 6, #19; ☎ 397 1222, fax 397 0453; @ cgidubai@emirates.net.ae) 7B St, Bur Dubai; open 8am-4.30pm Sun-Thur
Iran (Map 7, #34; ☎ 344 4717, fax 344 9499; @ irancons@emirates.net.ae) cnr Al-Wasl Rd & 33 St, Jumeira; open 8am-1pm Sat-Wed
Italy (Map 7, #19; ☎ 331 4167, fax 331 7469; @ consulit@emirates.net.ae) 17th floor, Dubai World Trade Centre, Sheikh Zayed Rd, Za'abeel; open 9am-1pm Sat-Wed
Jordan (Map 6, #21; ☎ 397 0500, fax 397 1675; @ jorconslt@emirates.net.ae) 11 St, Bur Dubai; open 8am-12.30pm Sat-Wed
Kuwait (Map 5, #58; ☎ 228 4111, fax 223 2024; @ kuwait@emirates.net.ae) Baniyas Rd, Deira; open 8.30am-2.30pm Sat-Wed

Lebanon (Map 6, #18; ☎ 397 7450, fax 397 7431; e lebconsd@emirates.net.ae) 3 St, Bur Dubai; open 9am-noon Sat-Wed

Netherlands (Map 4, #48; ☎ 352 8700, fax 351 0502; e nlgovdba@emirates.net.ae) 5th floor, ABN-Amro Bank Bldg, Khalid bin al-Waleed Rd, Bur Dubai; open 9am-3pm Sat-Wed

Oman (Map 6, #20; ☎ 397 1000, fax 397 7688; e general@ocodubai.com) 11 St, Bur Dubai; open 8am-2pm Sat-Wed

Pakistan (Map 6, #15; ☎ 397 0412, fax 397 1975; e parepdub@emirates.net.ae) 11 St, Bur Dubai; open 8am-noon Sat-Wed

Qatar (Map 6, #39; ☎ 398 2888, fax 398 3555, e qatar98@emirates.net.ae) cnr Al-Adhid Rd & 52 St, Al-Jafiliya; open 8am-11.30am Sat-Wed

Saudi Arabia (Map 3, #4; ☎ 266 3383, fax 266 2524) 28 St, Hor al-Anz; open 8.30am-11.30am Sat-Wed

South Africa (Map 6, #14; ☎ 397 5222, fax 397 9602; e sacons@emirates.net.ae) 3rd floor, Sharaf Bldg, Khalid bin al-Waleed Rd, near Bur Juman Centre, Bur Dubai; open 8.30am-12.30pm Sat-Wed

Syria (Map 2, #34; ☎ 266 3354, fax 265 3393) cnr 15 & 10C Sts, Al-Wuheida, Deira; open 8.30am-2.30pm Sat-Wed

Turkey (Map 7, #19; ☎ 331 4788, fax 331 7317; e tcdubkon@emirates.net.ae) 11th floor, Dubai World Trade Centre, Sheikh Zayed Rd, Za'abeel; open 9am-noon Sat-Thur

UK (Map 4, #52; ☎ 397 1070, fax 397 2153; e britemb@emirates.net.ae) Al-Seef Rd, Bur Dubai; open 8am-1pm Sat-Wed

USA (Map 7, #19; ☎ 311 6000, fax 311 6166) 21st floor, Dubai World Trade Centre, Sheikh Zayed Rd, Za'abeel; open 8.30am-5pm Sat-Wed

Yemen (Map 6, #17; ☎ 397 0131, fax 397 2901) 7B St, Bur Dubai; open 8.30am-11.30am Sat-Wed

CUSTOMS

The duty-free allowances for tobacco are huge: 2000 cigarettes, 400 cigars or 2kg of loose tobacco (this is *not* a country cracking down on smoking). Non-Muslims are allowed to import 2L of wine and 2L of spirits. Note that if you are entering the UAE through Sharjah, where alcohol is prohibited, you won't be able to bring any in. You are generally not allowed to bring in alcohol if you cross into the UAE by land. No customs duties are applied to personal belongings. If videos and magazines are sent to you by post they will probably be confiscated for about a month while they are inspected for any offensive content. If you bring them in as luggage, they are unlikely to be checked. It is also illegal to bring in materials which insult Islam (this includes Salman Rushdie's *The Satanic Verses*) or materials which might be used to convert Muslims to another religion. However, unless you're drunk and rowdy or are otherwise acting suspiciously, it's very unlikely your possessions will be searched.

MONEY
Currency
The UAE dirham (Dh) is divided into 100 fils. Notes come in denominations of Dh5, 10, 20, 50, 100, 200, 500 and 1000. There are Dh1, 50 fils, 25 fils, 10 fils and 5 fils coins (although the latter two are rarely used today). A few years ago the government issued new coins, which are smaller than the old ones. Both types remain legal tender, but you should look at your change closely as the new Dh1 coins are only slightly smaller than the old 50 fils coins.

Exchange Rates
The UAE dirham is fully convertible and is pegged to the US dollar. Exchange rates, at the time of writing, were as follows:

country	unit		dirhams
Australia	A$1	=	2.04
Canada	C$1	=	2.39
euro zone	€1	=	3.38
Japan	¥100	=	2.94
New Zealand	NZ$1	=	1.74
Oman	OR1	=	9.56
UK	UK£1	=	5.35
USA	US$1	=	3.67

Exchanging Money
Don't be tempted to exchange money at the airport; the rates are terrible. Once in the city, there is no shortage of banks and exchange houses. In central Deira, especially along Sikkat al-Khail St, and around Baniyas Square, every other building seems to contain a bank or a moneychanger. In Bur Dubai there are plenty of moneychangers (though most of them only take cash and

not travellers cheques) around the *abra* dock. **Thomas Cook Al-Rostamani** has a number of branches around the city, including one on Sheikh Zayed Rd *(Map 3, #54)*, south of the Crowne Plaza Hotel; on Al-Fahidi Rd *(Map 4, #21)* in Bur Dubai; and on Road 14 *(Map 4, #80)* in Deira, near Al-Khaleej Hotel.

If you are changing more than US$250 it might pay to do a little shopping around. Moneychangers sometimes have better rates than banks, and some don't charge a commission. The problem with moneychangers is that some of them either will not take travellers cheques or will take one type only. Some places will only exchange trav-ellers cheques if you can produce your original purchase receipt. If you don't have the receipt try asking for the manager.

Currencies of neighbouring countries are all recognised and easily changed with the exception of the Yemeni rial.

American Express (AmEx) is represented in Dubai by **Kanoo Travel** *(Map 6, #33; ☎ 336 5000, fax 336 6006; Za'abeel Rd, Karama; open 8.30am-1pm & 3pm-6.30pm Sat-Thur)*. The office is on the 1st floor of the Hermitage Building, next to the main post office. It won't cash travellers cheques but will hold mail for AmEx clients. Address mail to: c/o American Express, Client's Mail, PO Box 290, Dubai, UAE.

Hawala: the Business of Trust

Imagine a money transfer system with minimal or no fees, quick delivery, and which is available to people in the poorest countries in the world. This is *hawala*, and Dubai is one of its key centres.

Hawala is an Arabic term for a written order of payment. It works like this. You hand over your dirhams and the contact details of the recipient to your neighbourhood hawala trader. In return you get a code – say, a letter and four numbers. Then you ring up the recipient and give them the code. The trader contacts the people in his network. The next day, maybe two days later, the *hawala* trader's partner hands over the money, sometimes delivering it to the door of the recipient. The commission taken by the *hawala* traders might be as little as 1% or 2%, even zero if they can make a little profit on exchange-rate differences.

Some newspaper reports say as much of 90% of wages remitted to developing countries from the UAE were sent via this system until recently. Sending Dh100 to India via a bank would yield Rs1200, while via a *hawala* trader it yields Rs1280. The smaller the amount to be sent, the bigger the difference is between bank rates and *hawala* rates. It's a huge benefit to workers who can only afford to send home small amounts.

The *hawala* system has existed among Arab and Muslim traders for centuries as a defence against theft. It's a uniquely Islamic system, completely dependent on trust and honour. *Hawala* traders hardly ever cheat their customers, but if they do the punishments are said to be abrupt and severe. Their reputation is crucial to their business.

The *hawala* system developed in Dubai through the gold smuggling business in the 1960s. Once the gold was sold in India or Pakistan, the traders couldn't get the money back to Dubai. They found their solution in the growing numbers of expatriate workers. The workers gave their wages to the gold traders in Dubai, and the gold traders in India paid their relatives. Thus the books balanced.

Today the system is under pressure. The US claims *hawala* is being used to transfer money to terrorists. What they don't say is that *hawala* is also used to transfer money to people who would find it impossible to receive it any other way, because they're illiterate, they don't have a bank account, or don't live in a village with a bank. In Dubai's open economy there used to be no restrictions on currency trading and no specific laws against *hawala* trading, but the authorities have moved to shut down some of the *hawala* networks allegedly linked to terrorist groups. The future of this remarkable system in Dubai is uncertain, and there are reports that the hub of the *hawala* business may shift to another country, perhaps Nepal.

ATMs & Credit Cards There are globally linked ATMs all over Dubai, at banks, shopping centres and at some of the hotels and hotel 'residences'. If you need an ATM in central Deira look for **Emirates Bank International**, which has a branch on Baniyas Rd *(Map 4, #84)*, near Al-Khaleej Hotel; another on Al-Maktoum Rd *(Map 5, #36)*, near the Metropolitan Palace Hotel; and another on Al-Souq St *(Map 4, #16)* in Bur Dubai. Its ATMs are tied into the Electron, Cirrus, Switch and Global Access systems. ATMs at branches of **HSBC** are linked to the Global Access system. You'll find one on Baniyas Square *(Map 4, #79)* and another in Bur Dubai, near the Moneychangers Souq *(Map 4, #15)*. The highest concentration of international banks is along Khalid bin al-Waleed Rd in Bur Dubai, east of Al-Mankhool Rd.

All major credit cards (Visa, MasterCard, Diners Club) are widely accepted at shops, hotels and restaurants throughout Dubai.

Costs

Dubai is not a low-budget city, such as Cairo or Bangkok, but it is possible to keep costs under control. Basic but decent hotels can be found for Dh100 to Dh150, and eating well for Dh15 to Dh25 is rarely a problem, though alcohol will add considerably to your bill. Taxis around the centre cost from Dh5 to Dh12, and admission to museums and other tourist sites is either very cheap or free.

Plan on spending Dh150 to Dh200 per day for budget travel. If you stay in the youth hostel you might be able to keep your budget down to half that. For mid-range to top-end travel you'll spend from Dh300 (if you eat cheaply) to whatever your pocket allows.

Tipping & Bargaining

Tips are not generally expected since a service charge is added to your bill (this goes to the restaurant, not the waiter, however). If you want to leave a tip, 10% is sufficient.

Bargaining in souqs can be exhausting. Hang in there, be firm and be prepared to spend some time at it. In Dubai, prices probably won't come down by more than about 20%, but if you are at a souq in the

country, you'll find that prices will come down by about 50%. Once the shopkeeper agrees to your offer, you are expected to pay. Going on to offer a lower sum is not polite. Even in shopping centres in Dubai you can ask for a discount or for their 'best price'. Saying you are not a tourist sometimes brings better prices! Most hotels will offer a discount if you ask for it, but the prices of meals and taxis are always fixed.

Taxes & Refunds

Most hotel and restaurant bills will have 10% tacked on for service and another 10% for municipality tax. If a price is quoted 'net', this means that it includes tax and service.

POST & COMMUNICATIONS
Post Offices

The **main post office** *(Map 6, #34; Za'abeel Rd; open 8am-11.30pm Sat-Wed, 8am-10pm Thur, 8am-noon Fri)* is on the Bur Dubai side of the Creek in Karama. It has a philatelic bureau.

The **Deira post office** *(Map 4, #82; Al-Sabkha Rd; open 8am-midnight Sat-Wed, 8am-1pm & 4pm-8pm Thur)* is near the intersection with Baniyas Rd. Other post offices around the city include **Al-Musalla post office** *(Map 4, #53; open 8am-1pm & 4pm-7pm Sat-Thur)* at Al-Fahidi Roundabout in Bur Dubai, **Satwa post office** *(Map 7, #18; Al-Satwa Rd; open 8am-1pm & 4pm-7pm Sat-Thur)* and **Al-Rigga post office** *(Map 5, #47; open 8am-1pm & 4pm-7pm Sat-Thur)* near the Clock Tower Roundabout. There are post boxes at most of the major shopping centres.

There are also a number of fax and postal agencies dotted along the small streets around Deira souq and Dubai Souq.

Postal Rates

Letters up to 20g cost Dh3 to Europe and most African countries; Dh3.50 to USA, Australia and the Far East; Dh2.50 to the subcontinent; Dh1.50 to Arab countries; and Dh1 within the Gulf. Double these rates for letters weighing 20g to 50g. For letters weighing 50g to 100g, rates to these destinations are Dh13/11/9/6/4.

Postcard rates are Dh2 to Europe, the USA, Australia and Asia; Dh1 to Arab countries; and 75 fils within the Gulf.

Parcels weighing between 500g and 1kg cost Dh68 to the USA, Australia and the Far East; Dh45 to Europe and Africa; Dh36 to the subcontinent; Dh34 to other Arab countries; and Dh23 within the Gulf. For parcels weighing between 1kg and 2kg, the rates to the these destinations are Dh130/85/68/64/45.

Rates for surface mail are roughly half those for airmail.

Sending Mail

Mail generally takes about a week to 10 days to Europe or the USA and eight to 15 days to Australia. There does not seem to be any way of tracing packages that have gone missing, however.

Mumtaz Speed Post is available at post offices, but it is very expensive (Dh100 to send a letter to Australia). If you need to send something in a hurry it will cost you half as much to use a courier company, and they will come and collect the package from you. Recommended courier agencies include **Kanoo Rapid Transport** *(☎ 347 4845; PO Box 290, Dubai)* or **FedEx** *(☎ 800 4050; PO Box 9239, Dubai)*.

Cargo Shipping

There are probably more shipping and cargo agencies in Dubai than anywhere else in the world. You won't have any trouble finding them. All cargo is handled through the Dubai Cargo Village (Map 5, #15) next to the airport. Most travel agencies can arrange cargo shipping to any part of the world. Alternatively, you can contact a cargo company directly. They are all quite reliable – we haven't heard any horror stories of damaged or lost goods – but prices vary quite considerably so ring around for quotes.

To give you a rough idea of air freight charges, the average cost per kilogram to Australia is Dh10 for under 45kg, Dh8 for more than 45kg. To the UK it costs around Dh5 per kilo for 50kg to 100kg or Dh7 for under 50kg. You could pay double these rates for door-to-door service. There is also a handling charge and a fee for packing up your

items. This could be anywhere from Dh50 to Dh350, depending on the company. Sea freight is about half the cost of air freight.

There are dozens of cargo companies, which will collect goods from wherever you're staying. Look under Shipping in the UAE Business Directory or Yellow Pages, both of which should be available in your hotel. Some reputable cargo and courier companies include:

Allied Pickfords (☎ 338 3600, fax 338 3700)
DHL (☎ 299 5333, fax 299 5364)
Kanoo Group (☎ 393 4440, fax 393 5019)
TNT Express (☎ 285 3939, fax 286 1109)

Receiving Mail

Poste restante facilities are not available in Dubai. As the local postal service doesn't at present deliver to residential properties, most residents get their mail posted via the post office box of their place of work. However, there are plans to introduce a mail delivery service in the near future. The AmEx office will hold mail for AmEx clients (see Exchanging Money earlier in this chapter for the AmEx office address). If you are staying at a five-star hotel, the reception desk will usually hold letters and small packages for two or three days prior to your arrival. It's a good idea to mark these 'Guest in Hotel' and, to be sure, 'Hold for Arrival'.

Telephone

The UAE has an efficient telecommunications system. Calls within Dubai Emirate, not including Hatta, are free. The state telecommunications monopoly is **Etisalat** *(Map 5, #59; cnr Baniyas & Omar ibn al-Khattab Rds; open 24 hrs)*, recognisable by the giant, sparkling golf ball on top of its headquarters. There is another office in Al-Khaleej Shopping Centre *(Map 4, #40; Al-Mankhool Rd)*.

If you need to make a call from the airport, there are telephones at the far end of the baggage-claim area. Some of the lounges at the gates in the departures area also have phones from which you can make free local calls. Coin phones have almost completely been taken over by cardphones.

Phonecards are available in denominations of Dh30 from grocery stores, supermarkets, petrol stations and street vendors.

To phone another country from the UAE, dial ☎ 00, followed by the country code. If you want to call the UAE, the country code is ☎ 971. The area code for Dubai is ☎ 04, though if you are calling from outside the UAE you drop the zero.

There are Home Country Direct services to 43 countries. Dialling these codes connects you directly to an operator in the country being called. A list of access codes to these countries is in the Etisalat Services section of the phone book.

Mobile Phone Mobile numbers begin with 050 in the UAE. Often people will give their seven-digit mobile number without mentioning this prefix.

If you want to use your mobile phone in Dubai, you can buy a prepaid SIM card from Etisalat. It costs Dh300 and is valid for 60 days or until the credit runs out, whichever comes first. Just pay more money if you want to increase the credit available. You can hire mobiles from car-rental companies at the airport arrivals area.

Mobile Madness

This little accessory, which fits so nicely inside the pocket of a *dishdasha* (the shirt dress Emirati men wear), has to be the gadget of the century in Dubai. There are an estimated one million mobiles in the UAE. You can't go anywhere without hearing annoying electronic renditions of the William Tell Overture or Beethoven's Ninth. Emiratis just love to talk on the phone. They love it so much in fact that most of them have more than one mobile, sometimes as many as four. The dexterity with which these guys can juggle three simultaneous conversations on three different phones is astounding.

The police have banned people using handheld mobiles while driving, which has led to an explosion in the number of people using handless sets at 120km/h.

Useful Phone Numbers Some useful telephone numbers include the following:

Directory information (Arabic)	☎ 181
Directory information (English)	☎ 180
Operator	☎ 100
Talking clock	☎ 140

Call Charges The following are some direct-dial rates per minute from the UAE:

to	peak (Dh)	off-peak (Dh)
Australia	4.19	2.54
Canada	4.19	2.54
France	4.19	3.21
Germany	4.19	3.60
India	4.29	3.67
Japan	4.19	3.60
Netherlands	5.45	4.50
UK	4.19	3.21
USA	4.19	3.00

There is a complete list of rates in the green pages section at the back of the Dubai phone book. The off-peak rates apply from 9pm to 7am daily and all day on Friday and national holidays.

Fax, Telex & Telegraph

Most Etisalat offices are also equipped to send and receive fax, telex and telegraph messages. They may ask for your local address and contact number before they'll send a fax, and though the service is fairly good, it is expensive at Dh10 per page to most international destinations. Most typing and photocopying shops also have fax machines you can use. You'll find the highest concentration of these just north of the Clock Tower Roundabout on Abu Baker al-Siddiq Rd.

Email & Internet Access

Etisalat is the sole provider of Internet access in Dubai. Private Internet access is quite cheap at Dh20 per month for rental and Dh2 per hour for use. As you would expect, the Internet is heavily censored in the UAE, and access to gaming sites or anything pornographic is blocked. Many hotels and hotel residences offer Internet access to their guests, though sometimes this is only available to executive guests who are paying a premium for their rooms. Etisalat has a 'Dial 'n' Surf' service at ☎ 500 5333; all you need is a modem and a phone line. No account number or password is needed. It is charged at 15 fils per minute directly to the telephone you are connected to. If you're staying at a hotel you should check whether the hotel will charge you an additional fee for using their phone line.

There are a few specialist Internet cafés around the city, and the major shopping centres have a few terminals for hire as well. These include **Al-Jalssa Internet Café** (Map 4, #43; ☎ 351 4617; Al-Ain Centre, Al-Mankhool Rd; open 9am-1am daily) and **Inet** (Map 5, #11; ☎ 344 2602; Hamarain Centre, Abu Baker al-Siddiq Rd, Rigga), both of which charge Dh10 an hour.

The **Internet Cafe** (Map 7, #4; ☎ 345 3441; Al-Dhiyafah Rd, Jumeira; open 10am-3am Sat-Thur, 2pm-3am Fri) charges Dh15 per hour, and has snacks and coffee as well. The fanciest must be **Formula One** (Map 7, #26; ☎ 345 1232; Palm Strip Shopping Centre, Jumeira Rd; open 10am-10pm), decked out in racing car decor. Access costs Dh15 per hour.

DIGITAL RESOURCES

There are several websites on Dubai, possibly reflecting the government's commitment to e-governance (you can check how many parking tickets you have online at W www.dxbtraffic.gov.ae). The official government tourism website is W www.dubaitourism.com. Another excellent official website is W www.uaeinteract.com, run by the UAE's Ministry of Information and Culture. For local events, check out W www.dubaicityguide.com and W www.timeoutdubai.com. Local newspaper websites worth checking out include W www.khaleejtimes.com and W www.gulf-news.com.

Another handy website is W www.godubai.com, a large site with lists of travel agencies, airlines, libraries and links to other sites. It also has information on the Emirates Environmental Group, as well as promotions and giveaways. For shopping online, try W www.uaemall.com.

Etisalat's *Yellow Pages* can be found at W www.etisalatyp.com while the *White Pages* are at W cc.emirates.net.ae:82.

The map website W www.dubailocator .com has a highly detailed digital map of the city, which includes every city landmark and hundreds of businesses. It's very handy if you need to find a particular apartment building or company office. It does take a while to download and navigate though.

One of Dubai's more interesting sites is W www.sheikhmohammed.co.ae, the personal website of the crown prince of Dubai, Sheikh Mohammed bin Rashid al-Maktoum. It features critiques of his poetry, links to his Internet education portal, a photo gallery of Dubai, and reports on local sporting events, especially horse racing. The website aptly illustrates the diverse interests of this Arabian Renaissance man.

For information on business websites, see the Doing Business section at the end of this chapter.

BOOKS

Books in Dubai aren't cheap. The reason given for the high prices are that consumers in Dubai expect the latest material to be on the shelves as soon as possible, which means that books must be air-freighted in. However, this doesn't explain why books have the same exorbitant price tag a year later. We suggest you bring your own reading material.

Most books are published in different editions by different publishers in different countries. Your local bookshop or library is best placed to advise you on the availability of the following recommendations.

Lonely Planet

Lonely Planet's *Oman & the UAE* covers the whole of the UAE in detail; *Middle East* is a comprehensive guide to the region as a whole and includes a chapter on the UAE, as well as the other countries of the Gulf.

Guidebooks

Dubai Explorer, from Explorer Publishing, is a book of listings, aimed mainly at expats, with information on just about everything there is to see and do in this city, from paragliding to Mexican restaurants, as well as all kinds of clubs and societies.

UAE Off-Road Explorer, also by Explorer Publishing (Dh95), is the best guide available if you're planning a 4WD trip, with 20 detailed routes from the Musandam Peninsula in the north to Al-Ain in the south. It covers all the practicalities of 4WD travel, from lessening your impact on the environment to driving on soft sand.

Off Road in the Emirates I and *II* by Dariush Zandi is also worth a look, although directions given to sites can be vague and confusing. They are published by the UAE-based Motivate Publishing and are widely available for Dh55.

UAE: A Meed Practical Guide is the most comprehensive business guide to the country. It gives a good background to the finance and trade of the country.

Don't They Know it's Friday by Jeremy Williams is a guide to social and business etiquette written by an expat who has lived and worked all over the Gulf and now runs courses for Westerners on doing business with Arabs. It's very interesting and straightforward and should be compulsory reading for those intending to live and work in the Gulf.

Serve Them Right by Kate Dickens is a practical guide to working with and serving Dubai's multicultural population.

Eating Out in the Emirates is a spiral-bound publication that features a section on dining out in Dubai, although it seems to describe every place as being fabulous no matter what.

History & Society

Father of Dubai: Sheikh Rashid bin Saeed al-Maktoum by Graeme Wilson is a tribute to the acknowledged founder of modern Dubai.

The Merchants by Michael Field gives a brief sketch of the rise of Dubai as a trading centre, although you may find it difficult to track down.

Arabia Through the Looking Glass by Jonathan Raban has a lengthy section on Dubai and is well worth reading.

Dubai Tales by Muhammed al-Murr, one of the UAE's best known writers, is a collection of short stories that provide an intimate view of the lives and values of the people of Dubai.

Mother Without a Mask: A Westerner's Story of her Arab Family by Patricia Horton is the account of a British woman's experiences with a wealthy Emirati family. It offers fine insights into the often misunderstood realm of Arab women, and also captures the amazing transition that the Emiratis have made from desert camps to urban villas in one generation. Highly recommended.

Arabian Destiny by Edward Henderson (Motivate Publishing, Dh55) is a memoir by a British colonial official. He's the classic stiff-upper-lip type who gets through six years of fighting in WWII in one paragraph ('afterwards it was back to Libya, followed by the Salerno landings, and then to Britain in time for D-Day', he says). But he's also a wry, perceptive observer of the society he lived in. As he puts it, Dubai hasn't simply changed since the 1950s, it has become a different place altogether.

The United Arab Emirates AD 600 to the Present by Aqil Kazim is a highly detailed and rather dense read. Its secondary heading, 'A sociodiscursive transformation in the Arabian Gulf', gives you an idea of the academic jargon contained within. Nevertheless it covers the economics, history and society of the period in question in precise detail.

General

Dubai Life & Times: Through the Lens of Noor Ali Rashid is a pictorial history of Dubai over the last four decades by a man who was the royal photographer during most of this time. The photographs are absolutely stunning and very candid.

Dubai – A Pictorial Tour is a collection of pictures by various photographers depicting the modern aspects of Dubai as well as the traditional.

Dubai – An Arabian Album by Ronald Codrai is a collection of mid-20th century photos of Dubai.

1001 Arabian Nights at the Burj al-Arab is a glossy 160-page coffee-table book with more than 200 photos of the world's most jaw-dropping hotel. The photography is superb.

The Complete UAE Cookbook by Celia Ann Brock-Al-Ansari covers the local Emirati cuisine comprehensively, everything from cinnamon tea to *harees* (a meat and wheat puree).

NEWSPAPERS & MAGAZINES

Gulf News, *Khaleej Times* and *Gulf Today*, all published in Dubai, are the three English-language newspapers in Dubai. They cost Dh2 and carry pretty much the same international news, though *Gulf News* is probably the best of the bunch. Local news consists largely of 'business' stories, which are little more than advertisements masquerading as news. The local papers tend to have fairly comprehensive coverage of the Indian, Pakistani and Filipino political and entertainment scenes. *Gulf Business* (Dh15) is a glossy business magazine published locally, as is the English-language fashion and lifestyle magazine *Emirates Woman* (Dh15).

International newspapers and news magazines such as the *International Herald Tribune* (Dh15) and the *Economist* (Dh28) are fairly easy to find, though not cheap and sometimes several days or a week out of date. Many newsagencies and bookshops sell Indian newspapers such as *Malayalam Manorama* and the *Times of India* (Dh2 to Dh3).

The Arabic dailies are *Al-Bayan* (published in Dubai), *Al-Khaleej* and *Al-Ittihad* (both published in Abu Dhabi). Foreign newspapers are available in larger bookshops and hotels as well as Spinney's and Choitram's supermarkets.

Time Out Dubai is a monthly magazine with excellent listings of current events and some delightfully barbed restaurant reviews. It costs Dh10. *What's On* is another listings monthly with more of an emphasis on advertorials and photos of expats getting blitzed at functions. The magazine costs Dh12, though you will often find it free in five-star hotels. *Connector* is a monthly publication aimed at Western expats with plenty

What You Won't Read

Your first impression on reading the headlines each day will most likely be that a sheikh has said something wise or had a successful meeting. Most days you'll read a call for Arab unity, and notice Indian politics has reached yet another crisis point. But there's plenty you won't read about. Local newspapers and magazines, both in Arabic and English, have to follow a careful policy of self-censorship. For expatriate journalists, the alternative can be a sudden one-way ticket home.

The unspoken rules are that it is forbidden to say anything against the government or anyone in authority, from the Sheikh down to the lowliest policeman. This includes the governments of allies. Basically, the journalist is as guilty as the person who criticises the government whom they're reporting. There can be no reporting of a crime without the police permitting it, no coverage of a court case without a briefing from the court, and certainly no reporting of a civil commotion, disturbance or protest. If there is a major local or regional disturbance, journalists have to wait for the government to give the go-ahead to report it. Sometimes this comes days after the event, such as the Iraqi invasion of Kuwait in 1990, and sometimes it never comes at all. The news 'angle' is usually the reaction of the senior-most official responsible, for example, 'Police chief warns polluters' rather than 'Polluters threaten wildlife'.

Recently these rules have been loosening a bit. Qatar's Al-Jazeera satellite TV station has revolutionised Arab TV with its hard-hitting news reports. It can't, however, criticise the Qatari ruling family. Similarly, media companies such as Reuters and CNN based at Dubai Media City are free to report international events as they like. The Internet is a growing hole in the news blockade, making it possible for Emiratis to read on the computer screen about local events that the local newspapers and TV channels can't report. Nevertheless, expatriate journalists on local newspapers have to tread carefully.

of advertisements but useful listings pages in the green section at the back of the book.

RADIO & TV

The Dubai English-language radio station, Dubai FM, is at 92 FM, while Ajman's Channel 4 FM (also English-language) is on 104.8 FM. Both have DJs playing mainstream chart music alongside occasional speciality music programmes featuring classical or country and western. Emirates FM's music station, EFM1 is at 99.3 FM and carries much of the same music and style as the others, while EFM2 at 98.7 FM tends towards a mix of news and talk shows. The music played on these stations can be a bit stale – endless classic rock – but on Thursday and Friday night you can hear cutting-edge dance music.

QBS from Qatar at 97.5 FM and 102.6 FM features radio plays in English, jazz specials and world-music shows. QBS also has French-language broadcasts between 4pm and 7pm at 100.8 FM. Several stations play Hindi, Arabic and Indian regional music, and there's one channel which has nothing but recitations of the Quran – very soothing when you're stuck in traffic.

Channel 33 shows an English-language movie and one or two American sitcoms most days of the week as well as news in English. It can be picked up on 33 UHF. Dubai TV, the Arabic channel, features religious and educational programmes as well as the occasional variety show or drama serial from Egypt or Lebanon. It can be picked up on 2 and 10 VHF or 30, 38 or 41 UHF. The Dubai Business Channel covers business around the world with a particular focus on business in Asia and the Middle East. It broadcasts continuously from 6pm until 2pm the next day.

Most hotels, even the smaller ones, have satellite TV. This usually consists of the standard package of four channels from Hong Kong-based Star TV: a music video channel, a sports channel, a movie channel and the BBC World Service. There may also be one or two Indian or Pakistani services (Zee TV/PTV) and sometimes one or more of the Arabic satellite services (MBC, Dubai Satellite Channel, Nilesat, ART).

VIDEO SYSTEMS

Video tapes bought in Dubai are for use with the PAL system, which is prevalent in most of Western Europe and Australia. Note that they are incompatible with the North American NTSC system and France's Secam system. They can be played on multisystem VCRs, which are available from electronics shops in Dubai.

PHOTOGRAPHY & VIDEO

Dubai's intense seasonal heat and humidity can cause havoc with cameras. We've had reports from travellers that their pricey new digital cameras broke down because condensation seeped in. Many owner manuals for cameras warn you not to use it in temperatures above 40°C and that it should be kept in a sealed plastic bag in humid conditions. At times, Dubai amply fills both these criteria. You might consider bringing a cheap disposable camera if you're planning to snap away in Dubai between April and October.

Film & Processing

Getting colour prints developed is never a problem – 20-minute services are advertised by photo developers on nearly every street in the city. These places will also take four passport photos for Dh12. A 24-exposure print film costs Dh12; a 36-exposure print film costs Dh15. Developing charges are Dh5, plus Dh1 for each photo, and you'll usually get a replacement film and a photo album thrown in. The best place to get slides and B&W film developed is **Prolab** (Map 5, #6; ☎ 266 9766; Abu Baker al-Siddiq Rd). It costs Dh33 for a 36-exposure slide film and Dh36 for developing and mounting. Prolab offers same-day service and is one of the few places where you can buy slide film, though some shops in larger hotels may also sell it.

When taking photographs during the day in Dubai you should use a UV filter on your lens, since the glare is very strong (you could also try reducing your aperture by around 1 f-stop).

Restrictions

Do not photograph anything even vaguely military. This includes airports, palaces, the

Diwan building, police stations (or police officers), the Dubai Courts, consulates and government ministries. It's discourteous to photograph people without their permission; and never photograph women.

TIME

Dubai is four hours ahead of GMT. The time does not change during the summer. Not taking daylight saving into account, when it's noon in Dubai, the time elsewhere is:

city	time
Auckland	8pm
London	8am
Los Angeles	midnight
New York	3am
Paris, Rome	9am
Perth, Hong Kong	4pm
Sydney	6pm

ELECTRICITY

The electric voltage is 220V AC. British-style three-pin wall sockets are used, although most appliances are sold with two-pin plugs. Adaptors are available in small grocery stores and supermarkets and cost Dh5. The two-pin plugs will work, but it's a tricky technique.

WEIGHTS & MEASURES

The UAE uses the metric system (see the conversion chart at the back of this book if you are not familiar with it).

LAUNDRY

There are no self-serve laundrettes in Dubai, but small laundries can be found in many spots around central Deira and in Bur Dubai. On average you will be charged Dh2 for T-shirts, Dh5 for trousers, Dh1 for underwear, Dh10 for dresses and Dh7 for blouses and skirts. You can also have clothes ironed for Dh1 to Dh2 per item. Turnaround time at these places is usually 24 hours.

Dry-cleaning services are also available around the city and from most mid-range and top-end hotels. In Deira try **Tide Dry Cleaners & Laundry** (Map 4, #73; ☎ 227 7796; north side of Baniyas Square). In Bur

Dubai try **Red Rose Laundry** (Map 4, #31; ☎ 337 2933; Al-Esbij St), near the corner with Khalid bin al-Waleed St. In Satwa you could try **Adnan Ali Laundry** (Map 7, #7; ☎ 398 5055; 6B St), just off Al-Dhiyafah Rd. Spinney's supermarkets also offer dry-cleaning services.

TOILETS

The best advice is to go when you can. The very few public toilets on the streets are usually only for men. Public toilets in shopping centres, museums, restaurants and hotels are Western style and are generally well maintained. Outside Dubai you might have to contend with 'hole in the ground' loos at the back of restaurants or petrol stations.

LEFT LUGGAGE

Dubai airport has a **left luggage office** (☎ 224 5555) in the arrivals hall, which charges Dh20 per item per day (24 hours). If you are staying at a mid-range or top-end hotel you will be able to leave your luggage at reception for up to a day.

HEALTH

Dubai has a good standard of hygiene, advanced healthcare and efficient hospitals. Although the standard of healthcare is quite high throughout the UAE, it's not cheap. Western medicines are widely available at pharmacies. Emergency medical care is free at government hospitals. Travel insurance is recommended to cover you for nonurgent or urgent care. Should you need to see a doctor, consult either the hotel doctor (if you are in a big hotel) or check with your embassy or consulate for a list of recommended doctors and clinics. Expats are covered by a health card entitling them to free care at government hospitals and clinics.

Preparation

There are no vaccination requirements for entry to Dubai unless you are arriving from a yellow-fever infected part of the world such as most of Africa and South America. In this case you will need a vaccination certificate for yellow fever. As a general rule, and especially before you travel anywhere, it's a good idea to make sure you are up-to-date with 'routine' vaccinations such as tetanus, diphtheria and polio (boosters are required every 10 years). Other vaccinations (such as hepatitis A or B) may be recommended for a longer-term stay – discuss your requirements with your doctor at least six weeks before you intend to travel.

If you require a particular medication take an adequate supply with you, as it may not be available locally. Take part of the packaging showing the generic name rather than the brand, which will make replacements easier to find. It's a good idea to have a legible prescription or letter from your doctor to show that you legally use the medication to avoid any problems.

Jet Lag

When we travel long distances rapidly, our bodies take time to adjust to the 'new time' of our destination, and we may experience fatigue, disorientation, insomnia, anxiety, impaired concentration and loss of appetite. These effects will usually be gone within three days of arrival, but to minimise the impact of jet lag:

- Rest for a couple of days prior to departure.
- Try to select flight schedules that minimise sleep deprivation; arriving late in the day means you can go to sleep soon after you arrive. For very long flights, try to organise a stopover.
- Avoid excessive eating, as well as alcohol (which causes dehydration) during the flight. Instead, drink plenty of noncarbonated, non-alcoholic drinks such as fruit juice or water.
- Make yourself comfortable by wearing loose-fitting clothes and perhaps bringing an eye mask and ear plugs to help you sleep.
- Try to sleep at the appropriate time for the time zone you are travelling to.

Food & Water

The tap water in Dubai is safe to drink but, as it comes from desalination plants, it doesn't taste great. Many residents stick to bottled water, which is readily available from shops and from vending machines all over the city.

In general, the standard of hygiene in restaurants, even the smaller ones, is very high. Health department inspectors take their jobs seriously and even small roadside grilled-meat joints are scrupulously checked. If you are eating at some of the smaller Indo-Pakistani restaurants, you may want to avoid raw salads.

Heat-Related Problems

The heat can really take it out of you, so take time to acclimatise to high temperatures, drink sufficient liquids and do not do anything too physically demanding, at least until you have acclimatised. You can get sunburnt surprisingly quickly in Dubai, even if it's cloudy. If you are at the beach, you are more susceptible to sunburn due to the reflection from the water and sand. Use sunscreen, a hat and a barrier cream for your nose and lips. Calamine lotion is good for mild sunburn. The glare in Dubai is very strong. Protect your eyes with good-quality sunglasses.

Prickly heat is an itchy rash caused by excessive perspiration trapped under the skin. It usually strikes people who have just arrived in a hot climate. Keeping cool, bathing often, drying the skin and using a mild talcum or prickly heat powder or resorting to air-con may help.

Warm, moist conditions also encourage fungal skin infections. To help prevent these, wear loose clothing, wash frequently, and dry yourself carefully. If you do get an infection, an antifungal cream or powder may help, and try to expose the infected area to sunlight as much as possible.

Dehydration and salt deficiency, caused by diarrhoea, profuse sweating or by not drinking enough, can cause heat exhaustion.

Diarrhoea

Simple things like a change of water, food or climate can all cause a mild bout of diarrhoea, but a few rushed toilet trips with no other symptoms is not indicative of a major problem. With any type of diarrhoea, dehydration is the main danger, particularly in children or the elderly. Fluid replacement (at least equal to the volume being lost) is the most important thing to ensure. Weak black tea, with a little sugar, soda water or soft drinks allowed to go flat and diluted 50% with clean water are all good. With severe diarrhoea, a rehydrating solution is preferable to replace minerals and salts lost. Commercially available oral rehydration salts (ORS) are very useful; add them to boiled or bottled water.

Hepatitis
Hepatitis A is a viral infection of the liver that is common worldwide. It's transmitted by contaminated food and drinking water. You should seek medical advice, but there is not much you can do apart from rest, drink lots of fluids, eat lightly and avoid fatty foods. Hepatitis E is transmitted in the same way as hepatitis A and can be particularly serious in pregnant women.

Hepatitis B is spread through contact with infected blood, blood products or body fluids (for example, through sexual contact, unsterilised needles, or contact with blood via broken skin). Other risk situations include being shaved, tattooed or body pierced with contaminated equipment. The symptoms of hepatitis B may be more severe than type A and the disease can lead to long-term problems such as chronic liver damage, liver cancer or a long-term carrier state. Hepatitis C and D are spread in the same way as hepatitis B and can also lead to long-term complications.

There are vaccines against hepatitis A and B, but there are currently no vaccines against the other types of hepatitis. Following basic hygiene rules about food and water and avoiding risk situations for hepatitis B, C and D are important preventative measures.

HIV & AIDS
Infection with the human immunodeficiency virus (HIV) may lead to acquired immune deficiency syndrome (AIDS), which is a fatal disease. Any exposure to blood, blood products or body fluids may put the individual at risk. The disease is transmitted through sexual contact or dirty needles – vaccinations, acupuncture, tattooing and body piercing can be potentially as dangerous as intravenous drug use. The UAE has tried to keep HIV out of the country by requiring all expatriate workers to be screened for the virus. The Dubai police were reported as saying that about 500 expatriates are deported annually for testing positive. However most prostitutes, often from places with established HIV epidemics such as India, the former Soviet countries and southern and eastern Africa, enter Dubai on short-term visas under which they don't require testing. No official statistics on HIV infection rates among expatriates or nationals in Dubai are available.

Women's Health
Dubai's pharmacies sell a full range of contraceptive pills, which sometimes need to be bought with a prescription, depending on the type.

Antibiotic use, synthetic underwear, sweating and contraceptive pills can lead to fungal vaginal infections, especially when travelling in hot climates. Fungal infections are characterised by a rash, itch and discharge. Nystatin, miconazole or clotrimazole pessaries or vaginal cream are the usual treatment. Maintaining good personal hygiene and wearing loose-fitting clothes and cotton underwear may help prevent these infections.

Sexually transmitted infections are another cause of vaginal problems. Seek medical attention, and remember that male sexual partners must also be treated.

Medical Services
The following government hospitals have emergency departments:

Al-Maktoum Hospital (Map 5, #1; ☎ 222 1211) Al-Maktoum Hospital Rd, near the corner of Omar ibn al-Khattab Rd, Rigga
Al-Wasl Hospital (Map 3, #40; ☎ 324 1111) Oud Metha Rd, south of Al-Qataiyat Rd, Za'abeel
New Dubai Hospital (Map 3, #3; ☎ 222 9171) Abu Baker al-Siddiq Rd, near the corner of Al-Khaleej Rd, Hor al-Anz
Rashid Hospital (Map 3, #25; ☎ 337 4000) off Oud Metha Rd, near Al-Maktoum Bridge, Bur Dubai

If you need nonurgent care, ask your consulate for the latest list of recommended doctors and dentists. Some are listed here in case you need to find one and your consulate is closed:

Al-Zahra Private Medical Centre (Map 3, #52; ☎ 331 5000) Zaabeel Tower, Sheikh Zayed Rd
Dubai London Clinic (Map 3, #65; ☎ 344 6663) Al-Wasl Rd, Jumeira. The clinic also has an emergency section.
General Medical Centre (Map 7, #30; ☎ 349 5959) 1st floor, Magrudy's Shopping Centre, Jumeira Rd. The clinic also has an emergency section.
Manchester Clinic (Map 3, #44; ☎ 344 0300) Jumeira Rd, just north of McDonald's

There are pharmacies on just about every street in Dubai. See the *Gulf News* for a list of pharmacies that are open 24 hours on that day. If you can't get to a newspaper and you need to get to a pharmacy urgently, call ☎ 223 2232, a hotline that will tell you where the nearest open pharmacy is.

WOMEN TRAVELLERS
Attitudes Towards Women
In general, Dubai is one of the best places in the Middle East for women travellers.

Checking into hotels is not usually a problem, though unaccompanied women might want to think twice about taking a room in some of the budget hotels in Deira and Bur Dubai. They are renowned for accommodating prostitutes from the CIS (Commonwealth of Independent States) and Africa and you run the risk of being mistaken for one (this happened to the author of the 1st edition a couple of times).

Although things might be better in Dubai than in other parts of the Gulf, it does not mean that some of the problems that accompany travel in the Middle East will not arise here as well, such as unwanted male attention and long, lewd stares. You may be beeped at by men in passing cars, though often these are taxi drivers touting for business. Try not to be intimidated; it helps to retain a sense of humour.

Safety Precautions
You'll find that Dubai, as opposed to other places in the region, is a very liberal place and people here are used to Western women and their ways. It's once you're out of Dubai that you might encounter a different attitude. Apply common sense – don't wear tight and revealing clothes that are just going to make

Women in Dubai

The young, modern Emirati woman, confidently strolling through a Dubai shopping centre while chatting on her mobile phone, is an enormous contrast to the older Emirati woman, covered from head to toe, selling handicrafts in a country souq.

The modernisation of Dubai has dragged many women with it. Attitudes towards the traditional role of women are gradually shifting, and women now have a strong presence in public life.

Although there are no published statistics for Dubai alone, the number of Emirati women in the workforce, in both private and government sectors, has increased enormously over the past two decades. In the civil service, women now account for over 40% of employees. Apart from the traditionally women-dominated professions (such as teaching and nursing), Emirati women can be found in the media, military, travel and tourism industry, and police force.

It may surprise you to hear that female students outnumber male students in universities by three to one. This means that more women than men are demanding and obtaining a variety of jobs at graduate level.

This doesn't mean that the traditional role of women in UAE society has been abandoned. Handicrafts, such as weaving, are still practised and encouraged. The role of women as carers, mothers and nurturers is still very much in place, and the family is still considered the most important unit in UAE society. The task at hand for Emirati women is to strike a comfortable balance between these two roles.

your life difficult. Sit in the back seat of taxis and avoid making chitchat. You'll find that you'll often be asked to take the front seat in buses or be asked to sit next to other women. This is so you can avoid the embarrassment of men's stares.

In banks, Etisalat offices, post offices and libraries there are usually separate sections or windows for women – great when there's a queue. In small Arab and Indo-Pakistani restaurants you will often be ushered into the 'family room'. You don't have to sit here but the room is there to save you from being stared at by men.

Organisations

The green pages at the back of *Connector* magazine lists a variety of cultural and social groups, from gardening clubs to support groups for single mothers. Listed here are some of the larger organisations which women travellers may find useful.

International Business Women's Group (☎ 345 2282; e ibwg_dxb@emirates.net.ae) With over 200 members, this is a networking support group for women in the UAE who are in senior management or who own their own companies. It meets on the second Monday of each month and is open to all nationalities.

Dubai & Sharjah Women's Guild (☎ 394 5331) This is a social group of predominantly Western women who meet twice a month to hear a guest speaker or to go on an excursion. It's also a fundraising organisation that donates to various local and overseas charities.

American Women's Association (☎ 050-768 8657) This is a 300-member strong social and philanthropic club, which meets once a month. Sporting activities and outings are also arranged. You can only become a full member if you or your spouse has a US passport or Green Card; a number of associate memberships are also available.

German Women's Club (☎ 050-444 5709; e dfk_dubai@yahoo.de) This is a club for German-speaking women in Dubai. Similar to the American Women's Association, it puts on social events and provides support to members.

GAY & LESBIAN TRAVELLERS

Officially, homosexuality is illegal in the UAE and can incur a jail term. However, we have had a number of letters from gay travellers who have had no trouble travelling in the UAE and have met other gays quite easily. Men walking hand in hand is quite common, and doesn't indicate their sexual orientation. Women walking hand in hand is not as commonly seen.

Dubai has made a huge effort to promote itself as a tolerant, safe tourist destination, and the authorities were keen to indicate to us that gay and lesbian travellers won't face any discrimination or legal trouble, short of staging a gay-pride march down Sheikh Zayed Rd. In the Arab way, there's only a problem when it's unavoidably public. For example, one nightclub which had a strong gay following crossed the line when it posted flyers around the city calling on local gays and drag queens to come out. Only then were the authorities compelled to shut the place.

The official line from the religious authorities is that homosexuality is a Western disease that dates from the 1960s, and which doesn't exist in Arab culture. Unofficially, it's not so uncommon for young Arabs to experiment, perhaps because relations with the opposite sex are so much more restricted.

Jules Bar *(Map 3, #10)* near Le Meridien Dubai has a reputation as a place for gay people to mingle, especially on Thursday night.

DISABLED TRAVELLERS

The DTCM has a highly detailed list of facilities for disabled people at dozens of hotels, which they will fax or email to you on request. All the major shopping centres have wheelchair access, but ramps in car parks and into most buildings in the city are few and far between. There are a number of car parks for disabled drivers.

Dubai Transport *(☎ 208 0808)* has taxis that can take wheelchairs. The airport has facilities for the disabled including low check-in counters but things get more difficult once you are out of the airport. Dubai Museum has ramps; however, other tourist attractions are difficult for disabled visitors to get around on their own. Dubai airport has modern facilities for people with disabilities, including lounges and carts for getting around the concourse.

SENIOR TRAVELLERS

For a country that traditionally respects its elders, it is surprising to learn that no discounts are available to senior travellers for things such as admission fees and public transport. One good thing is that all hotels have elevators, even the cheapest ones, so you won't have to contend with endless flights of stairs.

DUBAI FOR CHILDREN

As in most Gulf cities, families are well looked after in Dubai and there are plenty of activities for children. All the parks mentioned in this book have kids' playgrounds and there are plenty of grassy stretches where they can expend energy (see Parks in the Things to See & Do chapter). All the shopping centres have nurseries or play areas for little kids though most of the time you won't be able to leave them unattended. *Kids Explorer* (Dh25) lists dozens of fun things for kids to do around the UAE.

Magic Planet *(Map 3, #21; Deira City Centre, Baniyas Rd; bus Nos 3, 4, 6, 11, 15, 23 & 33; open 10am-midnight Sat-Thur, 2pm-midnight Fri)* has various rides, amusements and play areas aimed primarily at kids under 12. It also has a minigolf course and numerous video games that usually attract much larger kids. Individual rides cost from Dh2.50 or you can pay Dh40 for unlimited rides with six video game tokens thrown in.

Encounter Zone *(Map 3, #34; Wafi City; bus Nos 14, 16 & 44; open 10am-11pm Sat-Tues, 10am-midnight Wed-Thurs)* is a techno-adventure playground for kids of all ages. It is divided into Galactica, which has amusements and rides for teenagers and adults, and Lunarland, which is a play area for kids under 10. Individual rides cost Dh5 or you can pay Dh40 (Dh50 on Thursday) to go on everything. Younger children can be left under the supervision of employees at Lunarland for Dh40 for half a day.

By far the most appealing place for older kids is the **Wild Wadi Waterpark** *(Map 2, #19)* 14km south of Jumeira. The rides are some of the most exciting in the world (see Activities in the Things to See & Do chapter for more information).

If you are planning to take a trip outside Dubai, there are plenty of places to take the kids. **Dreamland Aquapark** *(adult/child Dh30/20; open 10am-7pm daily)* in Umm al-Qaiwain claims to be the largest water park in the Gulf. It has all kinds of wet rides plus a go-kart track, a video-game parlour and a number of swimming pools, kiosks and restaurants. Admission gives you unlimited use of the rides. If you're catching public transport, you'll need to take a minibus towards Ras al-Khaimah (Dh20) as the water park is 10km out of Umm al-Qaiwain on the road to Ras al-Khaimah. Alternatively, an engaged taxi will cost you Dh50.

One place guaranteed to keep children and adults fascinated for a couple of hours is the **Sharjah Desert Park** (see the Excursions chapter for details).

The best time of year for kids is during special events such as the Dubai Shopping Festival and Dubai Summer Surprises. Every day there are activities for children at one shopping centre or another. You have to wonder at the intelligence behind events such as burger-eating competitions, though.

USEFUL ORGANISATIONS

The following is a list of organisations that might be of interest to those living and working in Dubai (see Ecology & Environment in the Facts about Dubai chapter for a list of ecologically minded community groups).

Australian & New Zealand Association (☎ 511 579) PO Box 28691, Dubai. A society for Australian and New Zealand expats in Dubai, this group organises activities, events and social gatherings, and produces a newsletter.

British Community Assistance Fund (☎ 337 1413) PO Box 51299, Dubai. This voluntary organisation helps British citizens in Dubai and the northern Emirates who find themselves in distress. It offers legal, financial and medical assistance and can help with repatriation.

Dubai Caledonian Society (☎ 394 7506; ⓦ www .scotsindubai.com) This group has more than 200 members, and organises social events such as Burns' Night, the St Andrew's Day Ball as well as ceilidhs, golf outings and race nights. It also raises money for charity.

Dubai Irish Society (☎ 399 2280) PO Box 37208, Dubai. Primarily a social group for Irish expats, in addition to a couple of social events each month, the society also organises sporting events and, of course, the ever-popular St Patrick's Day Ball. The society can also give support or advice for Irish people who find themselves in trouble or distress.

Dubai Welsh Society (☎ 394 7825, 394 0762; W www.dubaiwelshsociety.com) As you may have guessed, this is a society for Welsh people. It organises a St David's Day Ball, regular golf meets and other social events.

LIBRARIES

If you forget to bring books with you, or have a special interest, there are some libraries that may be of use.

Archie's Library (*Map 6, #26;* ☎ *396 7924; Sheikh Khalifa bin Zayed Rd, Karama; open 10am-2pm & 5pm-10pm Sat-Thur, 5pm-10pm Fri*) is in the Pyramid Building, near the Ministry of Health. It has a huge collection of books in English – mostly pulp novels – as well as children's books and magazines. You can read books on site for a small charge, but you have to be a member to take books home. This costs Dh75 per year plus a Dh100 deposit.

The **British Council** (*Map 3, #24;* ☎ *337 0109; open 9am-8pm Sat-Thur*), just south of Al-Maktoum Bridge, has a reference library for students of its courses so the collection's emphasis is on business studies and English literature. It also has educational videos and reference CD-ROMs. You must become a member to take books home. This will cost you Dh350 per year. Internet access is also available.

Dubai Lending Library (*Map 3, #43;* ☎ *344 6480; Dubai International Arts Centre, Jumeira; open 10am-noon & 4pm-6pm Sat-Thur*) has 14,000 books in a variety of genres, including adult fiction, children's books, biographies and reference. You must be a member to take books out, which costs Dh80 per year if you want to take out five books at a time or Dh50 if you want to take out two. Each book has a minimal hiring fee, from Dh1 for romance novels to Dh4 for in-demand books.

Juma al-Majid Cultural & Heritage Centre (*Map 5, #9;* ☎ *262 4999; cnr 44B & 21C Sts, Hor al-Anz; library open 8am-7.30pm Sat-Thur*), just off Salahuddin Rd in the Hor al-Anz district, is a nonprofit reference library and research institute. It has a large collection of books, periodicals and journals in English on the history, politics and culture of the UAE and other Gulf countries. Much of the collection is on Arab and Islamic themes. It also has titles in French, German, Russian and other languages. You cannot take books home, but you are welcome to use the reading room.

The **public library** (*Map 4, #12;* ☎ *226 2788; Baniyas Rd, Deira; open 7.30am-9.30pm Sat-Wed, 7.30am-2.30pm Thur*) is at the western end of Baniyas Rd, in Al-Ras district in Deira. Everyone is welcome to browse the collection and use the reading rooms. The English collection covers mainly the social sciences. Although there are some works on the Gulf, the main focus of the collection is international. You can only take books home if you are a member, which means you must have a residence visa and pay a Dh200 deposit for one year.

CULTURAL CENTRES

Dubai has become such a multi-ethnic melting pot that cultural centres have sprung up all over town.

Alliance Française (Map 3, #30; ☎ 335 8712) Oud Metha Rd, Za'abeel. Promotes French culture and teaches French. Events such as concerts, lectures and ballets are occasionally organised.

British Council (Map 3, #24; ☎ 337 0109) Just south of Al-Maktoum Bridge, near the Dubai Courts building, this centre conducts English and Arabic classes as well as courses in computer studies and business. There is also a reference library with videos and CD-ROMS providing information on studying in Britain.

Sheikh Mohammed Centre for Cultural Understanding (Map 3, #45; ☎ 344 7755; e smccu@ emirates.net.ae) Beach Centre, Jumeira Rd. This centre was set up to help break down cultural barriers between Emiratis and foreigners. It seeks to teach visitors more about Arab and Islamic culture and arranges cultural tours and outings. There is a one-hour tour (in English) of Jumeira Mosque every Sunday and Thursday at 10am. During Ramadan the centre arranges for non-Muslim families to share *iftar* (post-sunset fast-breaking meals) with Emirati families. These are very popular, and bookings are essential. The SMCCU plans to move to new premises in the Bastakia district of Bur Dubai, possibly by 2003.

DANGERS & ANNOYANCES

On the whole, Dubai is a very safe city, but you should exercise the same sort of caution with your personal safety as you would anywhere.

There is one real danger in Dubai, and that is bad driving. We have received a number of letters from travellers reiterating this sentiment. Be wary of drivers, whether you're behind the wheel or on foot. Don't expect them to drive carefully, sensibly or courteously. Blocking the lane for someone who wants to speed along the inside lane can provoke a serious attack of road rage.

Finally, we don't recommend that you swim, water-ski or jet-ski in the Creek. The tides in the Gulf are not strong enough to flush the Creek out on a regular basis so it is not a clean waterway, despite what the tourist authorities might tell you.

EMERGENCIES

In an emergency, you can try calling one of the following numbers:

Ambulance	☎ 998 or 999
Electrical faults	☎ 991
Fire department	☎ 997
Police	☎ 999

LEGAL MATTERS

Dubai maintains the death penalty for drug importation, though no executions have been made. A very long jail term is the current penalty. Jail sentences for being involved in drugs just by association are also likely. That means that even if you are in the same room where there are drugs, but are not partaking, you could be in as much trouble as those who are. The UAE has a small but growing drug problem, and the authorities are cracking down hard on it. The secret police are pervasive, and they include officers of many nationalities. Theft and writing bad cheques are also taken pretty seriously and usually involve jail and deportation.

If you are arrested you have the right to a phone call, which you should make as soon as possible (ie, before you are detained in a police cell or prison pending investigation, where making contact with anyone could be difficult). Call your embassy or consulate first. If there is an accident, it's a case of being guilty until proven innocent. This means that if you are in a road traffic accident, you may be held under police guard until an investigation reveals whose fault the accident was.

One common myth is that it is illegal for non-Arabs to wear traditional Arab clothing. In 2001 this was tested in a bizarre case in which a British man was arrested in the Gold Souq for dressing in women's clothing. After a considerable amount of legal discussion the judges decided that cross-dressing in Arab garb was not a crime.

Note that drinking alcohol in a public place that is not a licensed venue is illegal. The penalties vary from a warning to a fine. If the police should come across you when you're camping, put away any alcohol.

BUSINESS HOURS

The weekend here is Thursday and Friday. Government offices start work at 7.30am and finish at 1pm or 1.30pm Saturday to Wednesday. Businesses are open from 8am or 9am to 1pm or 1.30pm and reopen from 4pm to 7pm or 8pm Saturday to Wednesday. Some businesses, especially those run by Western staff, are open from 8am to 5pm, and their weekend may be Friday and Saturday instead of Thursday and Friday.

Shops open from 8am to 1pm and from 4.30pm or 5pm to 8pm or 9pm daily except Friday morning. Most shopping centres are open from 10am to 10pm or midnight Saturday to Thursday and around 2pm to 10pm on Friday. Souqs start up early, usually from around 7am until noon, and from 5pm to 7pm or 8pm daily except Friday morning. Opening hours are generally pretty flexible, except during Ramadan.

During Ramadan shops are open from 9am or 10am until 1.30 pm, and then from 7pm until 1am. On Friday during Ramadan, shops close at 10pm.

PUBLIC HOLIDAYS

See the 'Table of Islamic Holidays' for the approximate dates of the religious holidays observed in Dubai. Lailat al-Mi'raj is the celebration of the Ascension of Prophet Mohammed. Eid al-Fitr is a three-day celebration that occurs after Ramadan, and Eid al-Adha is a four-day celebration that occurs after the main pilgrimage to Mecca, or *haj*.

Secular holidays are New Year's Day (1 January) and National Day (2 December). The death of a minister, a member of the royal family or the head of state of another Arab country is usually marked by a three-day holiday. These holidays are announced in the newspaper on the day they occur. If a public holiday falls on a weekend (ie, Thursday or Friday), the holiday is usually taken at the beginning of the next working week.

The Islamic calendar starts at the year AD 622, when Prophet Mohammed fled Mecca for the city of Medina. It is called the Hejira calendar (*hejira* means 'flight'). As it is a lunar calendar, it's 11 days shorter than the Gregorian (Western) calendar, which means that Islamic holidays fall 11 days earlier each year. This is not a fixed rule, however, as the exact dates of Islamic holidays depend upon the sighting of the moon at a particular stage in its cycle. This can be as informal as a group of elderly imams being taken on a night-time drive into the desert to confer on whether or not the new moon is visible. This is why Islamic holidays are not announced until a day or two before they occur, and why they differ from country to country.

Ramadan

This is the month during which Muslims fast from dawn until dusk. Government offices ease back to about six hours work a day. Bars and pubs are closed until 7pm each night, live music is prohibited and dance clubs are closed throughout the month. Camel racing ceases too. Some restaurants do not serve alcohol. People with a liquor licence (see Drinks in the Places to Eat chapter for more details) can still buy alcohol for consumption at home. Everyone, regardless of their religion, is required to observe the fast in public. That not only means no eating and drinking but no smoking in public as well.

Some hotels still serve breakfast and lunch to guests, but most of the time eating during the day means room service or self-catering. Non-Muslims offered coffee or tea when meeting a Muslim during the day in Ramadan should initially refuse politely. If your host insists, and repeats the offer several times, you should accept so long as it does not look as though you are going to anger anyone else in the room who may be fasting.

SPECIAL EVENTS

Dubai hosts two main tourist-oriented events during the year. One is the Dubai Shopping Festival (DSF), which is fiercely promoted to the extent of having the festival logo painted on the Emirates fleet of 747s. It runs for the whole month of March and shopping centres bust themselves to bring in the spenders. In 2001 the festival brought in 2.5 million visitors. Every time you make a purchase you get raffle tickets that can win you cash, cars and shopping vouchers. Shopping centres hold entertainment for kids and displays of traditional culture.

Dubai Summer Surprises is designed, along with cheap hotel rates, to attract tourism and dollars to Dubai during the

Table of Islamic Holidays

Hejira Year	New Year	Prophet's Birthday	Lailat al-Mi'raj	Ramadan Begins	Eid al-Fitr	Eid al-Adha
1423	15.03.02	23.05.02	02.10.02	05.11.02	05.12.02	12.02.04
1424	04.03.03	12.05.03	21.09.03	25.10.03	24.11.03	01.02.04
1425	22.02.04	01.05.04	10.09.04	14.10.04	13.11.04	21.01.05
1426	10.02.05	19.04.05	31.08.05	03.10.05	02.11.05	10.01.06

tourist slump. The 'surprises' include food and cooking exhibitions, technology displays, events for children, ice sculpting and traditional culture displays such as henna painting and art shows. Most events are held at the shopping centres and big hotels. Some shops, though not all, offer big discounts on their merchandise and every Dh100 you spend entitles you to a raffle ticket. There are daily draws of Dh10,000 worth of shopping vouchers, weekly draws of a car and the end of festival draw of Dh1 million.

DOING BUSINESS

Business comes first in Dubai. If you need proof of this then consider the fact that, in 1998, Dubai's prisoners were given access to phones, faxes, conference rooms and secretaries to enable them to keep their business going while they served their sentence!

Foreign investors have been pouring into Dubai over the last two decades, making it the major business hub of the GCC. The reason for this is predominantly Dubai's relaxed business policies: no tax on profits or income (direct taxation goes against the traditions of the UAE and it is highly unlikely that it will be introduced in the future), no foreign exchange controls and 100% repatriation of capital and profits. There are no import duties on food, building materials, unworked silver and gold, agricultural products, medical products and anything destined for the Jebel Ali Free Zone. Other products attract a 4% duty. Dubai is well positioned between the major markets of Europe and Asia and has excellent airport, port, storage and shipping facilities. The major areas of investment are mining, construction, banking and finance, trade and manufacturing.

Trade laws are such that only UAE or other GCC nationals can own the lion's share of commercial companies. The most a foreign investor can hold is 49%. Foreign companies and individuals are not permitted to own real estate in Dubai. All property must be rented or leased.

To set up a bank account in Dubai you need to have a residence visa and a sponsorship letter from your employer, plus your passport and a photocopy of it.

Jebel Ali Free Zone

The Jebel Ali Free Zone was set up in 1985 to provide incentives to foreign investors. The legal status here is quite different to the rest of Dubai as companies enjoy the benefits of being 'offshore'. It is most suited to companies intending to use Dubai as a manufacturing or distribution base where most of their turnover is outside the UAE. The added incentives of the free zone include 100% foreign ownership; exemption from export and import duties; a guarantee of no corporate taxes for 15 years, which is then renewable for another 15 years; and abundant energy and administrative support from the Jebel Ali Free Zone Authority.

Useful Organisations & Government Departments

Listed here are some organisations you may find helpful if you are doing business in Dubai.

American Business Council (☎ 331 4735, fax 431 4227; W www.abcdubai.com) PO Box 9281, Dubai
British Business Group (☎ 397 0303, fax 3970939; W www.britbiz-uae.com) PO Box 9333, Dubai
Department of Economic Development (☎ 222 9922, fax 22 5577; W www.dubaided .gov.ae) PO Box 13223, Dubai
Dubai Airport Free Zone Authority (☎ 202 7000, fax 299 5500; W www.dafza.gov.ae) PO Box 2525, Dubai
Dubai Chamber of Commerce & Industry (☎ 228 0000, fax 221 1646; W www.dcci .gov.ae) PO Box 1457, Dubai
Jebel Ali Free Zone Authority (☎ 881 5000, fax 881 6093; W www.jafza.co.ae) PO Box 17000, Jebel Ali

Publications

If you intend to set up a business and live in Dubai it's worth reading *UAE – A MEED Practical & Business Guide*. Although it hasn't been updated since 1999, it spells out the requirements for obtaining trade licences, discusses trade laws, has thorough profiles of the major industries and provides listings of trade organisations and useful government departments. It is available from major bookshops and costs Dh65. The Dubai Chamber of Commerce & Industry on Baniyas Rd sells a number of publications at a cheaper price than the bookshops. *Dubai Business Handbook* has information on setting up a business in Dubai, trade laws and useful organisations; it costs Dh80 and is updated every year. The *Dubai Industrial Directory* has alphabetical listings of companies by industry and information on setting up a business. It costs Dh35. The *Dubai Commercial Directory* is the same sort of thing, but concentrates on listings of commercial companies; it costs Dh60.

Business Facilities & Services

Dubai's hotels are very much geared towards business travellers and almost all of the mid-range and top-end hotels mentioned in this book have business centres where guests can use computers, faxes and the Internet, and hire secretarial services. All the Western consulates and embassies in Dubai have commercial attaches whose business is to help you.

The **Dubai World Trade Centre** *(Map 7, #19; ☎ 322 1000, fax 306 4033;* **W** *www .dwtc.com)* is the largest venue and its exhibition hall can take up to 4500 people. The **Dubai Chamber of Commerce & Industry** *(Map 5, #53; ☎ 228 0000, fax 221 1646)*, on Baniyas Rd near the Sheraton Dubai, **Dubai Creek Golf & Yacht Club** *(Map 3, #19; ☎ 295 6000, fax 295 6083)* and the **Nad al-Sheba Club** *(Map 2, #32; ☎ 336 3666, fax 336 3717)* also offer substantial facilities for receptions and conferences. Many of the five-star hotels listed in this book have conference and exhibition facilities.

For all the information you could possibly need on business laws, trade licences, business organisations and statistics, go to **W** www.dubaicity.com.

The Dubai Chamber of Commerce and Industry (**W** www.dcci.gov.ae) also has a comprehensive website.

Business Etiquette

The biggest business blunder you can make is to offend prospective clients, employers and colleagues. Here are some issues to bear in mind when you are doing business with Emiratis (see also Society & Conduct in the Facts about Dubai chapter for more information).

- Many Gulf Arabs prefer to begin meetings with small talk. In such situations you may cause offence if you try to move directly to business. This tradition for chitchat becomes more pronounced in rural areas and when dealing with older people.
- Remember that 'timing' and not 'time' is important. If someone fails to appear for a meeting, try not to take offence. This simply means that something more important has come up.
- According to Jeremy Williams, who has written a book on the subject of business etiquette (see Books earlier in this chapter), 95% of time spent on business activity in the Gulf will be taken up with waiting, the other 5% will involve intense work to meet extremely demanding deadlines.
- Never cause someone to lose face in a public situation. If someone has made a mistake it's best to take them aside, explain the situation and take the blame yourself as much as possible.
- Meeting agendas are considered too static for most people, who will prefer to discuss things as the mood takes them rather than stick to a rigid list of topics.
- Gulf Arabs do not make harsh divisions between business and pleasure. Meetings may occur over dinner or coffee or after hours, so be prepared to talk business at any time of the day.
- Family comes first in Arab culture. If a Gulf Arab fails to arrive at a meeting because he had to meet his father at the airport at short notice, don't take offence.
- Don't telephone an Arab colleague for a business chat during siesta time, between about 2pm and 5pm. And remember, Friday is a day of prayer and rest.

WORK

You can pre-arrange work in the UAE, but if you enter the country on a visit visa and then find work, you will have to leave the country for one day and re-enter under your employer's sponsorship.

If you have arranged work in Dubai you will enter the country on a visit visa sponsored by your employer while your residence visa is processed. This process involves a blood test for HIV/AIDS and lots of paperwork. Those on a residence visa who are sponsored by a spouse who is in turn sponsored by an employer, are not officially permitted to work. This rule is often broken, and it is possible to find work in the public or private sector. If you are in this situation, remember that your spouse, and not the company you work for, is your sponsor. One effect of this is that you may only be able to apply for a tourist visa to another Gulf Arab country with a consent letter from your spouse. In some cases you will need to be accompanied by your spouse who has company sponsorship. Similarly, if you want to apply for a driving licence you will also need a consent letter from your spouse.

If you obtain your residence visa through an employer and then quit because you've found something better, you may find yourself under a six-month ban from working in the UAE. This rule is designed to stop people from job hopping.

If you are employed in Dubai and have any work-related problems you can call the **Ministry of Labour Helpline** (☎ 269 1666) for advice.

Finding Work
Sending off a CV to a few companies or recruitment agencies in Dubai from home is unlikely to bring much success; like elsewhere, there's nothing like knocking on doors yourself for discovering employment opportunities. Plenty of people turn up in Dubai on a visit visa, decide they like the look of the place and then scout around for a job. The *Khaleej Times* and the *Gulf News* publish employment supplements several times a week. When you find a job, you will be offered an employment contract in Arabic and English. Get the one in Arabic translated before you sign it. Besides the recruitment agencies listed below, there's a comprehensive list on the Web at W www .godubai.com/citylife/empagencies.asp

Business Aid Centre (☎ 337 5747, fax 337 6467; W www.bacdubai.com) PO Box 8743, Dubai

Clarendon Parker (☎ 331 1702, fax 331 5668; W www.clarendonparker.com) PO Box 26359, Dubai

Job Hunt Recruitment Services (☎ 355 4469, fax 359 4919; W www.jobhuntdubai.com) PO Box 62589, Dubai

SOS Recruitment Consultants (☎ 396 5600, fax 396 5900; W www.sos.co.ae) PO Box 6948, Dubai

Getting There & Away

AIR

You can fly direct to Dubai from most of Europe and Asia. Flights from North America involve changing flights in Europe or Asia. Dubai's reputation as the travel hub of the Gulf, and increasingly as the major stopover between Europe and Asia, was built on a combination of easy landing rights for aircraft in transit and a large, cheap duty-free centre at the airport.

For general airport information in Dubai call ☎ 224 5555; for flight inquiries dial ☎ 206 6666.

The national carrier is Emirates Airlines, which flies to about 50 destinations in the Middle East, Europe, Australia, Africa and the subcontinent. The secondary carrier is the regional airline, Gulf Air. It flies to many of the same destinations as Emirates, although all flights go via Bahrain. Emirates has a perfect safety record, whereas Gulf Air doesn't.

Warning

The information in this chapter is particularly vulnerable to change as prices for international travel are volatile; routes are introduced and cancelled; schedules change; special deals come and go; and rules and visa requirements are amended. Airlines and governments seem to take a perverse pleasure in making price structures and regulations as complicated as possible. You should check directly with the airline or a travel agent to make sure you understand how a fare (and ticket you may buy) works. In addition, the travel industry is highly competitive and there are many lurks and perks.

The upshot of this is that you should get opinions, quotes and advice from as many airlines and travel agents as possible before you part with your hard-earned cash. The details given in this chapter should be regarded as pointers and are not a substitute for your own careful, up-to-date research.

Remember when buying air tickets that direct flight routes are generally more expensive than nondirect routes. This means that flying Emirates or British Airways between London and Dubai, for instance, is going to be more expensive than flying Gulf Air via Bahrain or Qatar Airways via Doha. Sometimes, however, connecting flights can be more trouble than they're worth and you should check how long you'll be stuck at an airport before you buy that cheaper ticket. For all the talk of free markets, air fares out of the UAE are just as strictly regulated as anywhere else. There are no bucket shops.

High season for air travel varies from airline to airline. Generally, it is from late May or early June to the end of August, and from the beginning of December to the end of January. Low season is generally any other time. Regardless, special fares are offered throughout the year by different airlines and travel agents, so it pays to shop around.

Departure Tax

Dubai international airport has no separate airport departure tax; it's included in the price of your ticket.

The UK

As yet there are no charter flights from the UK to Dubai. A direct flight from London takes about seven hours. From London return you will pay around UK£260 on Air France via Paris and Qatar Airways via Doha. The cheapest nonstop return flight is with Biman for UK£340 – if you call flying with the Bangladeshi national airline a bargain. If you're lucky enough to strike a British Airways special offer you'll pay around UK£360. A direct flight between London and Dubai with Emirates costs UK£360 return, and you might find a British Airways special offer for a similar price. Flights from Birmingham and Manchester are almost identical in price to the London fare.

Air Travel Glossary

Alliances Many of the world's leading airlines are now intimately involved with each other, sharing everything from reservations systems and check-in to aircraft and frequent-flyer schemes. Opponents say that alliances restrict competition. Whatever the arguments, there is no doubt that big alliances are the way of the future.

Courier Fares Businesses often need to send urgent documents or freight securely and quickly. Courier companies hire people to accompany the package through customs and, in return, offer a discount ticket which is sometimes a bargain. However, you may have to surrender all your baggage allowance and take only carry-on luggage.

Fares Airlines traditionally offer 1st class (coded F), business class (coded J) and economy class (coded Y) tickets. These days there are so many promotional and discounted fares available that few passengers pay full fare.

Lost Tickets If you lose your airline ticket, an airline will usually treat it like a travellers cheque and, after inquiries, issue you with another one. Legally, however, an airline is entitled to treat it like cash and if you lose it then it's gone forever. Take very good care of your tickets.

Onward Tickets An entry requirement for many countries is that you have a ticket out of the country. If you're unsure of your next move, the easiest solution is to buy the cheapest onward ticket to a neighbouring country or a ticket from a reliable airline which can later be refunded if you do not use it.

Open-Jaw Tickets These are return tickets where you fly out to one place but return from another. If available, this can save you backtracking to your arrival point.

Overbooking Since every flight has some passengers who fail to show up, airlines often book more passengers than they have seats. Usually excess passengers make up for the no-shows, but occasionally somebody gets 'bumped' onto the next available flight. Guess who it is most likely to be? The passengers who check in late. If you do get 'bumped', you are normally offered some form of compensation.

Reconfirmation Some airlines require you to reconfirm your flight at least 72 hours prior to departure. Check your travel documents to see if this is the case.

Restrictions Discounted tickets often have various restrictions on them – such as needing to be paid for in advance and incurring a penalty to be altered or cancelled. Others are restrictions on the minimum and maximum period you must be away.

Round-the-World Tickets RTW tickets give you a limited period (usually a year) in which to circumnavigate the globe. You can go anywhere the carrying airlines go, as long as you don't backtrack. The number of stopovers or total number of separate flights is decided before you set off and they usually cost a bit more than a basic return flight.

Ticketless Travel Airlines are gradually waking up to the realisation that paper tickets are unnecessary encumbrances. On simple one-way or return trips, reservations details can be held on computer and the passenger merely shows ID to claim their seat.

Transferred Tickets Airline tickets cannot be transferred from one person to another. Travellers sometimes try to sell the return half of their ticket, but officials can ask you to prove that you are the person named on the ticket. On an international flight, tickets are compared with passports.

From Dubai, the cheapest flight to London is with Biman, for Dh1010 one way and Dh1840 return. During the summer and Christmas seasons, when many expats return home, European airlines lock horns and return fares to London can be as low as Dh2000 return.

Discount air travel is big business in London. Advertisements for many travel agencies appear in the travel pages of the weekend broadsheet newspapers, in *Time Out*, the *Evening Standard* and in the free magazine *TNT*.

STA Travel (☎ 0870 160 0599; Ⓦ *www .statravel.co.uk*) is a popular travel agency in the UK and has branches across the country. STA sells tickets to all travellers, but caters especially to young people and students.

Continental Europe

From Paris to Dubai, return fares start at €548 with British Airways and €580 with Emirates (direct). From Geneva, return fares start at about SF840 with Lufthansa or SF900 with Kuwait Airways.

From Amsterdam, the cheapest direct return fare is €520 with KLM. There are many cheaper options involving a change of flight, such as €476 with Turkish Airlines via Istanbul, or €480 with Czech Airlines via Prague.

There are also many options from Germany. The cheapest direct return flights are with Lufthansa for €600. Nondirect return flights include €516 with Cyprus Airways, €560 with Gulf Air and €580 with Austrian Airlines.

There are daily services from Dubai to most major European hubs. To Paris the cheapest fare is with Kuwait Airways (via Kuwait) for Dh1345 one way. To Frankfurt the cheapest fare is with Olympic Airways via Athens for Dh1700. Return fares to Paris, Frankfurt and Amsterdam range from Dh2500 to Dh3500. A return ticket to Athens costs Dh1850 with Olympic Airways; a one-way fare is Dh1450. A one-way fare with Emirates to Athens costs Dh1550. To Rome, Olympic Airways offers a one-way fare via Athens for Dh1700.

STA Travel (Ⓦ *www.statravel.com*) has offices throughout the region. Check its website for office locations and contact details.

Nouvelles Frontières (Ⓦ *www.nouvelles-frontieres.com*) also has branches throughout the world.

France has a network of student travel agencies that can supply discount tickets to travellers of all ages. **OTU Voyages** (☎ 0820 817 817; Ⓦ *www.otu.fr*) and **Voyageurs du Monde** (☎ 01 42 86 16 40; Ⓦ *www.vdm.com*) have branches throughout the country and offer some of the best services and deals.

A recommended agency in Germany is **STA Travel** (☎ 01805 456 422; Ⓦ *www.sta travel.de*), which has branches in major cities across the country.

In Italy, **CTS Viaggi** (☎ 840 501 150; Ⓦ *www.cts.it*) is a student and youth specialist with branches in major cities.

In Spain, a recommended agency is **Barcelo Viajes** (☎ 902 116 226; Ⓦ *www .barcelo-viajes.es*), which has branches in major cities.

The USA & Canada

There were no direct flights between North America and Dubai at the time of writing, although Emirates plans to start nonstop flights to New York in 2003. From New York to Dubai, you'll pay around US$1700 return on Air France (via Paris), Malaysia Airlines (via Istanbul) or Austrian Airlines (via Vienna).

From Chicago, British Airways flies via London for US$1912. From the West Coast, Singapore Airlines flies via Singapore for US$1915 return or there's the option of going via London for US$1923 with British Airways.

From Dubai, all flights go via Europe and return fares cost between Dh4500 and Dh5000. The cheapest one-way tickets to New York at the time of writing were with Emirates and Continental Airlines for Dh3270, and with Swiss for Dh3350. To Los Angeles, San Francisco or Vancouver the lowest return fares are with Singapore Airlines (via Singapore) for Dh4100.

The best deal from Vancouver to Dubai is with Singapore Airlines for C$1700 return.

From eastern Canada, flights to Dubai go via Europe and cost around C$1900 to C$2100 on British Airways. One-way tickets on all these flights are generally about US$500 cheaper.

STA Travel (☎ 800-781 4040; **W** www.sta travel.com) has offices in Boston, Chicago, Miami, New York, Philadelphia, San Francisco and other major cities. Call the toll-free 800 number for office locations or visit its website.

Travel Cuts (☎ 800-667 2887; **W** www .travelcuts.com) is Canada's national student travel agency and has offices in all major cities.

Australia & New Zealand

Emirates flies from Melbourne and Sydney to Dubai via Singapore for A$1770 return. Other carriers include Malaysia Airlines via Kuala Lumpur for A$1780, and Qantas with British Airways for A$1870. Return fares from Perth start at A$1520 with Royal Brunei Airlines. Emirates is planning to start direct flights from Dubai to Perth in 2003.

Fares from Auckland are NZ$2200 with Malaysia Airlines via Kuala Lumpur or NZ$2300 with Cathay Pacific via Hong Kong.

A return air fare from Dubai to Melbourne (via Singapore) costs Dh3800 to Dh4200 on Emirates, depending on the season. Singapore Airlines and Malaysia Airlines are usually a cheaper alternative to Australia or New Zealand. Prices vary, depending on the season, between Dh3600 and Dh4100.

Two well-known agents for cheap fares are **STA Travel** (☎ 1300 360 960 Australia-wide; **W** www.statravel.com.au) and **Flight Centre** (☎ 131 600 Australiawide; **W** www .flightcentre.com.au). STA Travel has offices in major cities and on many university campuses; call its Australiawide number for the location of your nearest branch. Flight Centre has dozens of offices throughout Australia.

Flights to Anywhere & Nowhere

Besides well-known major international airlines such as British Airways, Lufthansa and Singapore Airlines, Dubai airport is also a base for a colourful array of regional airlines. Need that direct flight to Hargeisa, capital of the unrecognised state of Somaliland? Try Daallo Airlines or Damal Airlines, with flights three times a week. Looking for a weekend getaway to Khartoum? Jump aboard Sudan Airways. Business in Krasnoyarsk, Siberia? Try Kras Air Krasnoyarskavia, which is just one of a flock of 'babyflot' airlines descended from the old Aeroflot which fly to Dubai. Most of these smaller airlines leave from Terminal 2.

A mix of inter-emirate rivalry and free-spending petrodollar economics has left the UAE particularly well catered for in international airports. There are six across an area not much bigger than Switzerland, and Ajman plans to build one more. The competition for business is fierce; Dubai has most of the passenger market, while Sharjah is a competitor in the cargo business. Sharjah has such a weird and wonderful collection of aircraft from the former Soviet Union that a British 'plane spotters' travel agency runs tours for devotees.

One remaining niche market is the visa run. Every month hundreds of people working in the UAE without residency papers must leave the country before their visa expires, but have to get back before they lose their job. So they invented the visa run flight, which flies off to somewhere in the neighbourhood, such as Bahrain, Oman or Iran's Kish Island, sits on the tarmac, then flies back. One airport has perfected the visa run further. The plane takes off, flies a loop and lands. The passengers get off and get a new stamp in their passport. Sometimes, we're told by reliable sources, the company organising these flights even economises on flying. The passengers get on the plane, wait for a respectful time, then disembark and go back through immigration. These must be the safest flights in the world.

Asia & the Subcontinent

There are daily flights from Dubai to major Asian travel hubs. A return flight to Bangkok on Qatar Airways costs Dh1710, with other carriers such as Emirates and Thai Airways International, fares are around Dh2200. Cathay Pacific has a one-way fare to Bangkok for Dh1500.

The best return fare to Singapore is with Royal Brunei Airlines for Dh2150, which also has a one-way fare of Dh1569. To Hong Kong it costs Dh2550 return on Cathay Pacific Airways. A return flight to Kuala Lumpur on Qatar Airways costs Dh2130.

Dubai probably has the best air links to Pakistan and India of any city in the world, with direct links to more than 10 cities. The cheapest return ticket to Karachi is Dh590 with Aeroasia, a Pakistani airline. Lahore is more expensive at Dh980/525 for return/one-way tickets on Aeroasia.

Fares to/from India don't vary much between airlines. An average fare to Mumbai and New Delhi is Dh1400 return, a one-way fare is Dh960. Flights to southern India are slightly more expensive, but plentiful. Flights to Kerala (Kochi or Thiruvananthapuram) cost around Dh1900 return or Dh1200 one way.

The Middle East & Africa

There are no flights within the UAE except for expensive business flights between Dubai and Abu Dhabi, the capital. The 20-minute flight costs Dh550 return with Emarat Link Aviation, which runs nine-seater Cessna Caravan seaplanes. Flights depart 12 times daily from next to the Dubai Creek Golf and Yacht Club (Map 3, #20) on Dubai Creek and land (if that's the right word) in Abu Dhabi near the Hiltonia on the Abu Dhabi Corniche.

There are daily services to most Middle East capitals. The best direct fares available at the time of writing were:

destination	one way (Dh)	return (Dh)
Amman	995	1550
Bahrain	300	450
Beirut	895	1140
Cairo	820	1370
Damascus	795	1630
Doha	890	710
Jeddah	1565	1970
Kuwait	745	1170
Muscat	705	670
Riyadh	950	1260
San'a	1245	1870
Tehran	570	410

One-way flights to regional Iranian cities are generally cheaper than the Dh570 listed earlier for Tehran. Flights to Shiraz cost Dh340/610 one way/return on Iran Asseman, while flights to Bandar-e Abbas on Iran Air cost Dh310/710 one way/return.

Visa-change flights (if you come in on a tourist visa, find a job, then need to leave and return to start work on a residence visa) are widely advertised. The cheapest fares we saw were Dh260 on Gulf Air to Bahrain and back, and Dh250 return on Oman Air to Muscat. Visa-change flights are usually up around Dh300.

From Dubai to Africa, flights to Johannesburg cost Dh1630 one way and Dh2310 return with Kenya Airways. This airline also flies direct to Nairobi for Dh1145.

Airline Offices

The following is a selection of carriers that fly to and from Dubai. Many of them also have desks at the DNATA (Dubai National Air Travel Agency) Airline Centre (Map 5, #19) on Al-Maktoum Rd in Deira.

Air France (Map 5, #18; ☎ 294 5991, fax 294 0049) Al-Shoala Complex, cnr Al-Maktoum Rd & 9 St, Deira

Air India (Map 5, #38; ☎ 227 6787, fax 227 1293) Al-Maktoum Rd, Deira

Alitalia (Map 5, #50; ☎ 224 2257, fax 223 6148) 16th floor, Green Tower, Baniyas Rd, Deira

British Airways (Map 3, #54; ☎ 307 5555, fax 307 5790) 10th floor, Kendah House, Sheikh Zayed Rd

Cathay Pacific Airways (Map 3, #19; ☎ 295 0400, fax 295 0708) Al-Shoala Complex, cnr Al-Maktoum Rd & 9 St, Deira

Czech Airlines (Map 5, #42; ☎ 295 9502, fax 295 7555) Al-Maktoum Rd, Deira

EgyptAir (Map 5, #39; ☎ 224 7055, fax 227 3300) Al-Maktoum Rd, Deira

Emarat Link Aviation (Map 3, #22; ☎ 295 9779, fax 295 9778) 3rd floor, Al-Yamamah Towers, cnr Baniyas Rd & 9 St, Deira
Emirates (☎ 214 4444, fax 204 4040) • (Map 5, #19) DNATA Airline Centre, Al-Maktoum Rd, Deira • (Map 2, #30) Sheikh Zayed Rd, near Interchange No 2
Ethiopian Airlines (Map 4, #69; ☎ 228 4338, fax 227 3306) 2nd floor, Pearl Bldg, 18 St, Deira
Gulf Air (Map 5, #3; ☎ 713 111, fax 736 465) Salahuddin Rd, Deira
Iran Air (Map 5, #49; ☎ 224 0200, fax 223 7487) Al-Salemiyah Tower, Baniyas Rd, Deira
Iran Asseman (Map 4, #62; ☎ 299 6611, fax 299 5406) Al-Maktoum Rd, near the Inter-Continental Hotel, Deira
KLM (Map 4, #31; ☎ 335 5777, fax 335 4854) 9th floor, Gulf Towers, cnr Oud Metha Rd & 20 St, Oud Metha
Lufthansa Airlines (Map 3, #62; ☎ 343 2121, fax 343 1687) 2nd floor, Lufthansa Bldg, Sheikh Zayed Rd
Malaysia Airlines (Map 4, #49; ☎ 397 0250, fax 397 1286) 1st floor, National Bank of Umm al-Qaiwain Bldg, Khalid bin al-Waleed Rd, Bur Dubai
Middle East Airlines (Map 4, #71; ☎ 203 3761, fax 295 4422) 3rd floor, Dubai Tower, Baniyas Square, Deira
Oman Air (Map 6, #1; ☎ 351 8080, fax 355 4600) mezzanine floor, Al-Rais Centre, Al-Mankhool Rd, Bur Dubai
Qatar Airways (Map 5, #32; ☎ 221 4448, fax 221 5561) Doha Centre, Al-Maktoum Rd, Deira
Royal Brunei Airlines (Map 6, #3; ☎ 351 4111, fax 351 9332) 3rd floor, Rais Hassan Saadi Bldg, Al-Mankhool Rd, Bur Dubai
SriLankan Airlines (Map 5, #19; ☎ 294 9119, fax 295 5245) 3rd floor, DNATA Airline Centre, Al-Maktoum Rd
Singapore Airlines (Map 4, #69; ☎ 223 2300, fax 221 8357) 3rd floor, Pearl Bldg, 18 St, Deira
Swiss (Map 3, #22; ☎ 294 5051, fax 294 1410) 1st Floor, Al-Yamamah Towers, cnr Baniyas Rd & 9 St, Deira
Thai Airways International (Map 5, #14, ☎ 268 1702, fax 297 2098) Al-Muraqqabat Rd, Deira

BUS & MINIBUS
Departure Tax
There is a Dh20 tax to pay at UAE border posts if you leave the country by land.

Other Parts of the UAE
The only intercity route within Dubai Emirate that really matters is route No 16 to Hatta

(Dh10, 1¼ hours). It leaves from the Deira bus station (Map 4, #101), near the Gold Souq, and also stops at Bur Dubai bus station (Map 4, #23) on Al-Ghubaiba Rd, and a number of other places on the way out of town. Buses depart every hour from 6.10am to 9pm. From Hatta, buses start running at 6am and finish at 9pm.

Minibuses run from Dubai to all major cities in the other emirates. They leave every 15 or 20 minutes depending on when they fill up. They are very clean and efficient, and fares are fixed so there's no haggling over prices. Minibuses leave Deira from the minibus and taxi station (Map 5, #30) near the intersection of Omar ibn al-Khattab and Al-Rigga Rds. Minibuses for Abu Dhabi and Al-Ain leave from the Bur Dubai bus station (Map 4, #23) on Al-Ghubaiba Rd. Minibuses for Sharjah leave from both stations. Although Dubai Transport minibuses can take you out of Dubai Emirate, they can't take you back due to an inter-emirate law so minibuses always return empty on the return journey from Sharjah, Abu Dhabi etc.

Get your tickets from the ticket windows at each station. Prices per person are:

Abu Dhabi	Dh33
Ajman	Dh7
Al-Ain	Dh30
Fujairah	Dh25
Khor Fakkan	Dh30
Ras al-Khaimah	Dh20
Sharjah	Dh5
Umm al-Qaiwain	Dh10

To get to Dibba or Kalba on the east coast, you will need to get a minibus to Fujairah, then a local taxi from there.

Oman
There are two buses a day to Muscat in Oman. These depart at 7.30am and 4.30pm from the parking lot of the DNATA Airline Centre (Map 5, #19) on Al-Maktoum Rd, Deira. The trip costs Dh30/50 one way for children/adults or Dh50/90 return, and takes 5½ hours. Tickets are available at the Oman Transport office at the DNATA Airline

Centre or from the bus driver. For more information, you can call Oman Transport on ☎ 203 3923.

From Muscat they leave at 7.30am and 4.30pm from the Ruwi bus station. The fare is OR5 (Dh50) one way for adults or OR9 (Dh90) return.

If you have an Omani tourist visa in your passport, getting from Dubai to Muscat by land involves nothing more than purchasing a bus ticket. Coming the other way, however, is another story. There is no UAE border post on the road used by the bus. That means that there is no place to pick up a visa or get a stamp on your passport. If you cross the border this way – even if you already have a valid UAE visa in your passport – it is considered that you are in transit, allowing you to remain in the country for only 48 hours. After this period you will be fined Dh100 per day when you do try to leave, or when you get caught.

Jordan, Syria & Lebanon
There are a few bus companies that have services to Lebanon and Syria via Saudi Arabia and Jordan. The biggest obstacle for travellers is getting a transit visa for Saudi Arabia. The Saudi consulate currently only issues transit visas to people who have residency visas for the UAE so if you have a visit visa for Dubai, you won't be able to take the bus. If you are eligible to get a transit visa for Saudi Arabia, you'll first have to get a valid visa for your destination, ie, Lebanon, as well as transit visas for Jordan and Syria, before you approach the Saudi consulate.

The bus companies are clustered around the intersection of Al-Khaleej and Omar ibn al-Khattab Rds (Map 3, #2), not far from the Hyatt Regency Hotel. Buses leave from the adjacent car park.

With **Al-Balawi Transportation** (☎ 271 0539), however, you can get to Jordan from Dubai and back again for only Dh350/200 for adults/children. Buses leave twice a week (Monday and Thursday) from the roundabout on Al-Khaleej Rd (just north of the Hyatt Regency Hotel); the trip takes 38 hours.

Another company here is **Al-Nasr Passenger** (☎ 271 1770), which runs buses to Syria and Lebanon twice a week on Monday and Thursday. Tickets cost Dh350/225 return for adults/children for both trips and the journey to both countries takes about 48 hours.

Egypt
Al-Balawi Transportation has bus services to Egypt each Wednesday. Return tickets cost Dh850/500 for adults/children. Buses leave from the roundabout on Al-Khaleej Rd (just north of the Hyatt Regency Hotel); the trip takes three days all up so it's a serious trek. Unless money is a real concern, you'd be better off catching a plane for only a couple of hundred dirhams more.

CAR & MOTORCYCLE
There is a Dh20 tax to pay at UAE border posts if you leave the country by land.

There are no border or customs controls between the Emirates and you can freely drive into Dubai from other parts of the country with either your own UAE-registered car or motorcycle or a hire car.

Just remember that cars rented in Dubai are not covered for accidents in Omani territory. If you are driving to Hatta from Dubai you will pass through 20km or so of Omani territory. Also, if you are driving around Al-Ain and wish to pop over to the Omani town of Buraimi (which you can do without an Omani visa) you will not be covered.

If you have your own car, you can drive from Dubai to Muscat and vice versa. The trip takes nearly four hours and you do not need a *carnet de passage* or any other documentation. If you have a rental car you will not be permitted to drive it over the border unless you get Oman added to the car's insurance (for more details, see the boxed text 'Insurance Warning' at the start of the Excursions chapter).

TAXI
Long-distance taxis seem to be dying out in Dubai, but they can still take you to any other emirate on a shared or 'engaged'

basis (which means you will have to pay for all of the seats in it – generally five times the shared cost). If you do take an engaged taxi you should settle the price before you leave. Most taxi drivers will charge for your luggage if it is larger than a backpack. Taxis for Abu Dhabi, Al-Ain and Hatta leave from the Bur Dubai bus station (Map 4, #23). Taxis for all other destinations leave from the taxi and minibus station on Omar ibn al-Khattab Rd in Deira. If you're willing to pay, private taxis will take you anywhere you want to go within the emirates.

Some approximate fares to destinations within the emirates for shared and engaged taxis include the following:

destination	shared (Dh)	engaged (Dh)
Abu Dhabi	33	150
Al-Ain	30	150
Fujairah	25	150
Hatta	25	100
Ras al-Khaimah	20	100
Sharjah	6	30
Umm al-Qaiwain	12	50

BOAT

If you leave the UAE by boat, there's a Dh20 port tax.

There are ambitious plans to link Dubai and five other Gulf ports with regular ferry services in the future. For now, the only ferry services are between the UAE and Iran. The schedules can be a bit flaky, so it's worth checking in advance.

There are passenger services between Sharjah (10 minutes drive from Dubai) and the port of Bandar-e Abbas in Iran. The trip costs Dh103/163 one way/return and takes eight hours. The ferry has no sleeper berths, only economy class seats, which makes it a bit uncomfortable, especially as the boat sails overnight. The ferry leaves Sharjah's Port Khalid at 9pm every Saturday and Wednesday, arriving in Bandar-e Abbas at 5am the next day. For more details, contact **Oasis Freight Company** (☎ 06-559 6325; *Kayed Ahli Bldg, Jamal Abdul Nasser Rd, Sharjah*), the UAE agent for the Valfajre-8 ferry company. Tickets should be purchased

at least four working days in advance, and you also need an Iranian visa.

There is also a fortnightly passenger service between Dubai and Bushehr in Iran. It leaves the passenger terminal at Port Rashid every second Sunday at 6pm, and takes 24 hours to reach Bushehr. Pullman seats cost Dh165/330 one way/return, economy cabins Dh310/620, 1st-class cabins Dh420/840 and luxury cabins Dh735/1470. If you're interested, contact **Naif Marine Services** (*Map 3, #42;* ☎ 345 7878, fax 345 5570; Port Rashid) for details.

The main appeal of these ferries is the baggage limit – 200kg.

ORGANISED TOURS

Many major tour companies offer package holidays to Dubai. The programmes are either 'sea & sun' holidays or a combination of 'sea & sun' with a desert safari sightseeing trip outside Dubai. These companies tend to accommodate their clients at the beach hotels on the outskirts of Dubai or at Jebel Ali Hotel. The facilities are wonderful, but you may end up wishing that you were closer to town.

From the UK

Every high-street travel agency can line up flights and hotel packages to Dubai, and many leading tour operators organise trips to Dubai. The following is just a selection.

The **Destination Group** (☎ 020 7400 7079; **W** *www.dubai-holidays4less.com*) offers special deals at beach hotels, including five nights at the Burj al-Arab for UK£1419, five nights at the Jebel Ali Hotel & Golf Resort for UK£669, and seven nights at the Le Meridien Mina Seyahi Resort for UK£655, including return flights.

At the time of writing, the Internet-based travel company **ebookers.com** (**W** *www .ebookers.com*) was also offering some excellent deals – a return flight from London and five nights in a five-star beach hotel such as the Hilton Dubai Jumeirah for UK£659.

Kuoni (☎ 020-7374 6601; **W** *www.kuoni .co.uk*) has an extensive range of tour packages to Dubai, including five nights at the Dusit Dubai for UK£549, or five nights at the Dubai Marine Beach Resort & Spa for UK£667.

Emirates Holidays *(☎ 020-7932 9900;* W *www.emirates-holidays.com)*, the holiday package wing of Emirates Airlines, also has a base in London and offers a variety of holiday packages.

Abercrombie & Kent *(☎ 0845-0700 610;* W *www.abercrombiekent.co.uk)* also offers upmarket tours. **British Airways Holidays** *(☎ 0870-442 3820;* W *www.britishairways .com)* arranges packages to Dubai, as does **Arabian Odyssey** *(☎ 01242-224 482;* W *www .arabianodyssey.com)* and **Somak** *(☎ 020-8423 3000;* W *www.somak.com)*.

From the USA

African Travel *(☎ 1-800-421-8907;* e *ati@ africantravelinc.com)* runs five-day packages to Dubai from New York during the Shopping Festival (March) each year for around US$2600. **Global Destinations** *(☎ 757-490 3466, fax 490 3468;* e *global@visi.net)* also offers a 10-day trip to Dubai from New York for US$2725 per person.

From Australia

Contact **Abercrombie & Kent** *(☎ 03-9536 1800;* e *contact@abercrombiekent.com.au)* or **Destination Dubai** *(☎ 03-9576 0952)* for details of upmarket packages to Dubai.

Getting Around

THE AIRPORT

Dubai international airport recently completed a US$540 million expansion project. In 2001, about 13.5 million passengers passed through the expanded airport, making it the busiest in the Middle East. By 2010 this is expected to rise to 30 million passengers a year, so the airport authority is launching another building programme costing US$2.5 billion, due to be completed in 2006. The new structures will be for the exclusive use of Emirates Airlines, including a new underground third terminal and a doubling in size of the concourse. A third concourse will be built to accommodate the new A380 super jumbo aircraft.

All the major international airlines, including Emirates, use Terminal 1, the main terminal. Smaller airlines, mostly en route to East Africa or the countries of the former Soviet Union, use the much smaller Terminal 2.

TO/FROM THE AIRPORT

From the Deira bus station (Map 4, #101), bus Nos 4, 11 and 15 go to the airport every 15 to 20 minutes for Dh1.50. From the Bur Dubai bus station (Map 4, #23), bus Nos 33 and 44 go to the airport for Dh2, but No 44 takes a long and tortuous route via Karama.

Only the sand-coloured Dubai Transport taxis are allowed to pick up passengers outside the arrivals area. The minimum charge is Dh20 just to pick you up; a ride to the Deira souq area will cost about Dh30 while to Bur Dubai it costs around Dh35. A taxi ride from Deira souq area to the airport costs Dh12; from Bur Dubai it's about Dh17.

There is no bus service linking Terminals 1 and 2. A taxi takes five to 10 minutes.

BUS

Local buses operate out of the two main stations in Deira and Bur Dubai. The **Deira bus station** *(Map 4, #101)* is off Al-Khor St, near the Gold Souq. The **Bur Dubai bus station** *(Map 4, #23)*, Dubai's main bus station, is on Al-Ghubaiba Rd. In the official timetables the two stations appear as 'Gold Souq Bus Station' and 'Al-Ghubaiba Bus Station',

---

Duty-Free Frenzy

For the past 20 years, Dubai international airport has been feted for its duty-free shops. It's part of Dubai's eagerness to combine travel and commerce, promoted with endlessly upbeat heavy marketing. Dubai duty-free has picked up numerous awards from various travel magazines. This is predominantly to do with the sheer volume of items for sale, as well as for the very competitive prices compared with other airport duty-free complexes, such as Singapore.

Arriving, departing and transit passengers are all welcome to shop in the duty-free complex. Most shops are open 24 hours as flights tend to arrive or depart in the small hours of the morning.

In 2001 the airport's duty-free shops turned over almost US$250 million in sales. If people are not lured by perfumes, caviar, watches, electronics, clothes, souvenirs and rugs, the chance of winning US$1 million in cash in a lottery will bring them in. With a limited number of tickets available (5000) at Dh1000 each, the chances are high. To date US$20 million has been won.

The odds are even better in the Finest Surprise lotteries, which offer luxury cars. The shortest odds are in the raffle to win a vehicle such as a 7-series BMW, with 1000 tickets on sale for Dh500 each. The other car raffle also costs Dh500 but 1500 tickets are sold; the prize is a Bentley or a similar marque. These raffles have yielded 800 luxury cars in the last 10 years, with the cars delivered free to anywhere in the world.

You can buy tickets in these raffles online at [W] www.dubaidutyfree.com.

Dubai by Bus

Dubai	Route No
Al-Dhiyafah Rd	06, 07, 09
Al-Mankhool Rd	09
Khalid bin al-Waleed Rd, Bur Dubai	03, 05, 09, 19, 44, 61, 90, 91
Khalid bin al-Waleed Rd, Mankhool	03, 05, 21, 33, 44, 61, 90
Sheikh Khalifa bin Zayed Rd, Karama	05, 06, 21, 33, 44, 61, 90
Sheikh Zayed Rd	21, 90

Deira	Route No
Abu Baker al-Siddiq Rd	03, 06, 23
Al-Maktoum Rd	04, 05, 11, 14, 15, 16
Al-Rigga Rd	20
Baniyas Rd	04, 05, 11, 14, 15, 19, 20, 22, 25, 31
Clock Tower Roundabout	03, 04, 05, 06, 11, 15, 20, 23
Salahuddin Rd	03, 06, 13, 19, 31

Things to See	Route No
Al-Ahmadiya School & Heritage House	08, 19, 20
Bastakia Quarter	19
Dubai International Arts Centre	08
Dubai Museum	25
Heritage & Diving Villages, Sheikh Saeed al-Maktoum House	08, 19, 20, 25, 91
Majlis Gallery	19

Souqs & Shopping Centres	Route No
Al-Ghurair City	05, 06, 11, 13, 14, 15, 19, 20, 21
Al-Karama Centre	05, 06, 23, 33, 44
Beach Centre	08
Bur Juman Centre	03, 05, 21, 23, 33, 44, 61, 90
Deira City Centre	03, 04, 06, 11, 15, 23, 33
Dubai Souq	03, 05, 07, 08, 09, 12, 19, 20, 21, 25, 33, 44, 61, 90, 91

	Route No
Gold & Diamond Park	90, 91
Gold Souq	02, 04, 05, 06, 08, 11, 13, 14, 15, 16, 17, 18, 19, 20, 25, 31, 91
Lamcy Plaza	44
Markaz al-Jumeira	08
Palm Strip Shopping Centre	08
Twin Towers	04, 05, 08, 11
Wafi City	14, 16, 44

Parks	Route No
Al-Mamzar Park	22
Mushrif Park	11, 15
Safa Park	07, 12
Creekside Park	03, 05, 06, 14, 16, 23, 33, 44
Jumeira Beach Park	08

Other	Route No
Al-Maktoum Hospital	02, 06, 17, 18
Aviation Club & Irish Village	44
Consulate Area	03, 05, 06
DNATA Airline Centre	03, 04, 06, 11, 15, 23
Dubai Chamber of Commerce	04, 05, 11, 14, 15, 19, 20, 22, 25, 31
Dubai Creek Golf & Yacht Club	03, 06, 23, 33
Dubai International Airport	04, 11, 15, 33, 44
Dubai Media City	08
Dubai Police HQ	02, 03, 13, 17, 20, 31
Dubai World Trade Centre	06, 21, 23, 61, 90 98
Emirates Golf Club	90
Hatta	16
Iranian Consulate	07, 12
Jebel Ali Free Zone	90, 91, 99
Al-Mina al-Seyahi	08
Jumeira Beach Hotel, Burj al-Arab & Wild Wadi Waterpark	08

respectively. Numbers and routes are posted on the buses in English as well as Arabic. Fares are Dh1 to Dh3.50, depending on the distance travelled. You pay the driver, so keep some change handy.

You can purchase monthly bus passes, known as *taufeer*, at both bus stations. There are two versions: the Dh75 pass gets you unlimited travel for a month on one or the other side of the Creek whereas the Dh120 pass gets you unlimited travel all over the city. Neither pass can be used on the intercity buses within the Dubai emirate (ie, for trips to Jebel Ali Port and Hatta). You'll need a passport photo to buy one of these passes.

A free schedule and route map can be picked up from either bus station, or from the tourist office in Baniyas Square. The table 'Dubai by Bus' lists a selection of useful routes. Note that most buses start and finish their days a bit later on Friday. You can count on there being no Friday service from about 11.30am until about 1.30pm (except on route Nos 16, 90 and 91) while noon prayers, the most important of the week, are under way. From Saturday to Thursday, buses run from approximately 5.45am to 11.15pm, at intervals of 15 to 20 minutes.

For information on public buses you can call the 24-hour **Dubai Municipality hotline** (☎ 800 4848).

CAR

If you are planning on taking a day or overnight excursion from Dubai, hiring a car is the best and cheapest way to do it. If you decide to hire a car to get around the city, remember that traffic congestion in Dubai can be a real problem at peak hours, which occur three times a day: between 7am and 9am, 1pm and 2pm and most of the evening from 6pm onwards. The worst congestion is around the approaches to Al-Maktoum and Al-Garhoud Bridges and along Al-Ittihad Rd towards Sharjah.

It is compulsory to wear seatbelts in the front and it is illegal to use a hand-held mobile phone while driving.

As you can imagine, Dubai is not short on petrol stations. Petrol is sold by the imperial gallon (an imperial gallon is just over

---

Dubai Rail

Dubai is planning to build the Gulf's first urban railway network. Construction is scheduled to begin in 2003.

One line will start at Dubai international airport and run to Al-Ittihad Square (Map 4) in front of the Dubai Municipality headquarters on the Deira shore of the Creek. The line will then cross the Creek and run south-west along Sheikh Khalifa bin Zayed Rd and Sheikh Zayed Rd, as far as Interchange No 1 (Defence Roundabout). The second line will start on Al-Nahda Rd, in Al-Qusais on the northern side of the airport (Map 3), and meet with the other line at the main station at Al-Ittihad Square.

At the time of writing, it hadn't been announced when the first section of the rail system was expected to open, or whether it would be a surface or underground network. But the Dubai Municipality did say that some time in the future the network would be extended to Sharjah and perhaps the emirates further north, as well as to Abu Dhabi.

4.5L). Regular petrol costs Dh4 per gallon and premium is Dh4.56.

It is not possible to hire motorcycles in Dubai – probably just as well. Before you drive in Dubai, read the boxed text 'Dangerous Drivers' over the page for some important safety messages.

Rental

As seems to be the case with most things in Dubai, you must have a credit card to be able to hire a car. There are few exceptions to this. If you do find a car-rental company that will take a cash deposit instead, you will probably have to leave your passport with them as security. This could be difficult, as most hotels require you to leave your passport in their safe for the duration of your stay. Some agencies insist on a credit card deposit as well as your passport. Find another agency if this is the case. You do not have to leave your passport with them. A photocopy of it is sufficient. The reason for all this security is to protect themselves against people who run up traffic violations and then leave town without paying them.

For tourists, most foreign driving licences are accepted in Dubai so long as you are either a citizen or a resident of the country that issued the licence. Some companies insist on an international licence, however, so it's worth getting one of these before you leave home.

At large international agencies, small cars such as a Mazda 626 start at about Dh120 per day with another Dh20 to Dh25 for collision damage waiver (CDW) insurance. These rates fall to about Dh120 per day including insurance for a week's hire, and around Dh85 to Dh95 per day with insurance for a month. If you have taken out CDW, the larger agencies do not charge an excess in the case of an accident that is your fault. Always call the police if you are involved in an accident (see the boxed text 'Accident Alert' for more details).

At the smaller agencies, you should be able to negotiate a net rate of around Dh120 per day, including CDW insurance. With these agencies, no matter what they tell you, you may still be liable for the first Dh1000 to Dh1500 of damage in the event of an accident that is your fault, even if you have CDW. Sometimes this excess is only Dh200 if you have paid CDW. Ask questions and read the small print on the contract carefully.

The first 100km or 150km per day are usually free with additional kilometres costing 40 or 50 fils each. If you rent a car for more than three days you should be given unlimited mileage.

Most agencies have free pick-up and delivery within Dubai, either to/from a hotel or the airport. They also offer a chauffeur service, but you'll pay around Dh180 per eight hours for this privilege. If you are just moving around Dubai for the day it is much cheaper to use taxis.

Although smaller agencies are generally cheaper than the larger chain companies, it's worth considering the convenience of being able to contact the local office of a reliable company if you are driving out of Dubai and something goes wrong. It's also worth ensuring complete insurance cover (zero liability).

Dangerous Drivers

If you're going to drive in Dubai, be careful. Most drivers seem oblivious to other cars around them, and courtesy on the road is rare. Although it's not as bad as in other parts of the UAE, people tend to cut in front of you, turn without indicating, race each other and take up two parking spaces or double park next to your car. They have a tendency to wander across lanes at roundabouts and try to turn out of them from inside lanes. Drivers sitting behind you at a red traffic light have an annoying habit of beeping you impatiently the minute the light goes green. Also, be very careful crossing the road. Not all drivers seem to understand the purpose of a pedestrian crossing and will not slow down, let alone stop, unless there are lights. Finally, don't drive in the fast lane unless you're intending to really speed. On highways out of the city, this lane is the preserve of expensive cars doing extraordinary speeds. Not getting out of their way can provoke intimidating road-rage tactics.

The UAE has one of the world's highest rates of road deaths per capita. Speeding and reckless driving are the major causes. The worst thing about all this is that there doesn't seem to be a sufficient incentive not to drive badly. Although speeding fines are meted out, it doesn't stop most of the population from driving way too fast. Causing a death through an accident requires the payment of blood money (dhiyya) to the victim's family. Although this is a large sum (about Dh160,000), nationals are insured against it. This often means that the only punishment for causing death or injury through reckless driving is an increased insurance premium. Licences are not even cancelled. Overall, the message doesn't seem to be getting through. One motoring magazine launched an anti–road toll campaign over several months, and in response its circulation halved!

Accident Alert

All accidents, no matter how small, must be reported to the traffic police. If it's a serious accident, call ☎ 999, otherwise in Bur Dubai call ☎ 345 0111 and in Deira call ☎ 266 0555. Unless your car is causing a traffic jam, do NOT move it until the traffic police get there. If there has been an injury, or it's not blindingly obvious who was at fault, don't move the vehicles at all. For insurance claim purposes you must have a police report and if you move your car, the police may not be able to issue a complete report. Outside Dubai you should leave your car exactly where it is, no matter how bad an obstruction it is causing, and call the police immediately. If you are driving a hire car and you have a crash, your insurance may not cover any damage unless a police report is written. One reader tells of such an experience:

I hired a car from Avis. I backed into a post in the hotel car park and I even had to call the police for that! If I had not done so, Avis would not have paid for the damage, even though I had taken out full insurance.

Caroline Williams

There are dozens of car-rental firms in Dubai, including all the major international chains as well as plenty of local companies. The highest concentrations of local companies are on Abu Baker al-Siddiq Rd (Map 5), just north of the Clock Tower Roundabout, and on Omar ibn al-Khattab St (Map 3). They are also found opposite the minibus and taxi station (Map 5, #30) on Omar ibn al-Khattab St in Deira, on the Bur Dubai side of the creek on Sheikh Khalifa bin Zayed Rd, just north of Al-Adhid Rd (Map 6), and on Kuwait St in Karama (Map 6).

Avis (Map 5, #43; ☎ 295 7121, W www.avis .com) Al-Maktoum Rd, Deira ● (☎ 224 5219) Airport arrivals hall (24 hrs)
Budget (Map 5, #16; ☎ 282 3030) Airport Rd, just before Cargo Village ● (☎ 224 5192) Airport arrivals hall (24 hrs)
Diamondlease (Map 3, #53; ☎ 331 3172; W www.diamondlease.com) Sahara Towers, Sheikh Zayed Rd

Europcar (☎ 352 0033) Desks at the Crowne Plaza, Dubai Inter-Continental, Al-Bustan Rotana and Hyatt Regency Dubai hotels
Hertz (Map 5, #17; ☎ 282 4422; W www.hertz-uae.com) Airport Rd, just before Cargo Village ● (☎ 224 5222) Airport arrivals hall (24 hrs)
Patriot Rent-A-Car (Map 5, #20; ☎ 294 0294; e patriot@emirates.net.ae) Abu Baker al-Siddiq Rd, Deira ● (☎ 224 4244) Airport arrivals hall
Thrifty (☎ 355 6732; e thrifty@emirates.net .ae) Desks at Golden Sands 3, Hilton Dubai Jumeirah hotels ● (☎ 224 5404) Airport arrivals hall (24 hrs)

Road Rules

Drive on the right in Dubai. The speed limit is 60km/h on city streets or 80km/h on major city roads. On Sheikh Zayed Rd and on other dual-lane highways around the UAE the official speed limit is 100km/h on some sections, but otherwise it's 120km/h. If you are caught speeding, you will be fined, but in some cases you will simply be sent a bill by the police. For this reason, many car-rental companies require customers to sign a statement acknowledging that they are aware of this and authorising the rental company to charge their credit card for any tickets that turn up after they have left town. There are also speed cameras on the major highways.

Increasingly the busier city streets have a strictly enforced four-hour limit on parking. Tickets must be purchased from one of the numerous orange ticket-dispensing machines, and displayed on your dashboard. Rates start at Dh2 for an hour. Parking rates apply from 8am to 1pm and from 4pm to 9pm Saturday to Thursday. Parking in the centre of Dubai is free on Friday and holidays. Fines for not buying a ticket start at Dh100, and you can't re-register your car until you've paid up.

TAXI

Dubai has a large, modern fleet of taxis with meters, and you can usually find one without difficulty. The starting fare is Dh3 plus Dh1.43 per kilometre, rising to Dh3.50 plus Dh1.70 per kilometre between 10pm and 6am. Drivers rarely carry much change so, to save the drama of finding a shop to break a note, it helps to keep coins and Dh10 and Dh5 notes handy.

There are still a few taxis without meters, but these are slowly disappearing as their licences expire and are not renewed. The minimum fare is Dh5, rising to Dh12 or so if you cross the Creek.

Dubai Transport Corporation has women taxi drivers and if you book in advance it can provide wheelchair-accessible taxis.

Taxi companies include the following:

Cars Taxis (☎ 800 4825)
Dubai Transport Corporation (☎ 208 0808)
Metro Taxis (☎ 267 3222)
National Taxis (☎ 336 6611)

ABRA

Scores of *abra*s (small motorboats) cross the Creek from early morning until around midnight, taking two routes (Map 4). One route links Bur Dubai abra station near the Bank of Baroda Building with the Deira Old Souq *abra* station at the intersection of Old Baladiya St and Baniyas Rd. The other route, further up the creek, connects the Dubai Old Souq *abra* station (at Dubai Souq) with the Sabkha *abra* station on the Deira side, at the intersection of Al-Sabkha and Baniyas Rds.

Like shared taxis, *abra*s leave when full, but it never takes more than a few minutes for one of them to fill up. The fare of 50 fils is collected once you are out on the water.

It can be quite tricky getting on and off the *abra*s – not something to attempt wearing high heels. The municipality plans to install floating pontoons to make boarding easier.

BICYCLE

You can't hire bicycles in Dubai and we don't recommend that you cycle here. With an abundance of bad drivers who are not accustomed to sharing the road with cyclists, there's a high chance you'll be knocked down. It has been done though, so if you want to bring your bike to tour Dubai remember it's always hot and humid here: drink plenty of water. And always yield to car drivers. Don't think they're going to watch out for you.

Also, bear in mind that the only bikes found here tend to be old-fashioned models used by labourers. Getting any repairs done on a modern mountain bike is likely to be difficult, so take plenty of spare parts and be prepared to be your own mechanic.

WALKING

The older parts of Dubai, with their souqs, fascinating architecture and museums, can be covered on foot as long as it's not too hot. A walk along the Creek to see the dhows is a pleasant way to spend half a morning. The rest of Dubai is very spread out, though, and getting from a shopping centre to a beach, for instance, is impossible by foot. See the Things to See & Do chapter for two walking tours that take in the best sights on both sides of the Creek.

ORGANISED TOURS

There is a huge range of different tours you can take, both within Dubai and outside. Basically, the tours are all pretty similar, but though prices don't vary much it's still worth shopping around. Most companies can arrange individually tailored tours so if you want to go bird-watching or mountain biking, or even get married in the desert Bedouin-style, it can be arranged. These specialist tours can be very pricey.

For a complete list of tour operators in Dubai, see *What's On* or *Time Out* magazine or the 'Tourist Guide' section at the beginning of the phone book. Brochures for tour companies can also be picked up from the reception desks of most hotels. When you book a tour with one of these companies you will usually be picked up from your hotel. Some of them require a deposit which is non-refundable if there is less than 24 hours' notice of cancellation.

For details of tours involving activities such as desert safaris and sand-skiing, see Activities in the Things to See & Do chapter.

Dubai City Tours

Arabian Adventures (*Map 2, #30;* ☎ *343 9966;* **w** *www.arabian-adventures.com; Emirates Holidays Bldg, Interchange No 2, Sheikh Zayed Rd, Dubai*) has a half-day city tour, including Jumeira Rd, the Jumeira Mosque, the Dubai Museum and the Gold and Spice Souqs in Deira, for Dh110 per person. It also has half-day shopping tours of the Gold and Spice Souqs as well as Karama for the same price. Children under 14 go for free.

Arabian Dream Tours *(Map 5, #2; ☎ 221 1129; w www.adtdubai.com; Suite 201, 2nd floor, Al-Burj Offices, Omar ibn al-Khattab Rd, Deira)* has a half-day city tour, which covers Jumeira, Sheikh Saeed al-Maktoum House, Bastakia, the Dubai Museum and the Gold and Spice Souqs. It costs Dh110 per person for adults, Dh55 for kids under 14.

Net Tours & Travels *(Map 5, #12; ☎ 266 8661; w www.nettoursdubai.com; Al-Bakhit Centre, Abu Baker al-Siddiq Rd, Hor al-Anz)* has a half-day tour with an itinerary virtually identical to the Arabian Dream Tours excursion, but it costs Dh95.

If it's within your budget, you can take a 45-minute Fly By Dubai tour with **Desert Air Tours** *(Map 3, #7; ☎ 299 4411; e desair@emirates.net.ae; Terminal 2, Dubai International airport)* in a six-seater Cessna 207 for Dh250 per person. Alternatively, you can charter the plane for Dh1900 per hour.

Aerogulf Services *(Map 3, #8; ☎ 282 3157; e aerogulf@emirates.net.ae; Terminal 1, Dubai international airport)* offers 10-minute helicopter tours of Dubai for Dh700 for a group of up to four people.

Bird-watching tours for small groups can be arranged through Colin Richardson, who heads the Emirates Bird Records Committee and is author of *Birds of the United Arab Emirates* and the Shell *Bird-Watching Guide to the UAE*. A half-day tour of Emirates Golf Course and Khor Dubai Wildlife Sanctuary costs Dh200 per person. Tours to other hot spots around the UAE can also be arranged. For more information, contact **Colin** *(☎ 650 3398, 050-650 3398; e colinr@emirates.net.ae)*.

Tours Outside Dubai

The following tour prices are per person and generally you need a minimum of four people to fill a 4WD. Bear in mind that you could hire a car for two or three days and take yourself to lots more places in your own time for the same price as a tour.

Arabian Adventures *(see Dubai City Tours)* has a Grand Canyons tour for Dh340 per person that takes in Masafi market and Dibba, then goes off-road through wadis in the Hajar Mountains and on to Ras al-Khaimah via a camel farm. One of the overnight tours (Dh425 per person) it offers takes you to a camel race, then over sand dunes by 4WD to a camp site in the desert where you have a barbecue meal. You return to Dubai the next day through the Hajar Mountains.

Arabian Dream Tours *(see Dubai City Tours)* has tours of Sharjah for Dh110 for adults, the east coast for Dh175 and Al-Ain for Dh175. Children pay 50% of the adult price.

Net Tours & Travels *(see Dubai City Tours)* offers a tour of Sharjah and Ajman for Dh100 and an Al-Ain city tour for Dh210. It also has a full-day east-coast tour, including Dibba, Bidiya, Khor Fakkan and Fujairah, for Dh210, and a full-day jaunt to the Hatta rock pools for Dh310.

Orient Tours *(Map 3, #13; ☎ 282 8238; w www.orienttours.co.ae; Al-Garhoud Rd, Deira)* has a one-day east-coast tour every Tuesday that takes in Masafi market, Dibba, Bidiya Mosque, Khor Fakkan Souq and Fujairah for Dh175/85 adults/children.

Things to See & Do

WALKING TOURS

If you only have one day, and you don't want to spend it shopping, then a walking tour around the older parts of Bur Dubai and Deira should be the first thing on your list. These areas lend themselves well to walking tours as they are quite small and the things worth seeing are all fairly close together. The rest of Dubai does not have as many sights and they are all spread out anyway, making a walking tour impossible.

We've included two walking tours in this section – Walk 1 takes in the sights of Bur Dubai and Walk 2 takes you round the

sights of Deira. Both tours can be done within half a day, broken up with an *abra* (boat) ride and a stop for refreshment. If you are in Dubai when it is hot, you might want to do one walking tour in the early morning and the other in the early evening.

Most things to see on these walking tours are discussed more fully later in this chapter, so just flick ahead a few pages for more information.

Walk 1: Bur Dubai (Map 4)

Begin this walking tour at the **Dubai Museum** *(Map 4, #55; Al-Fahidi St)*; the entrance

---

Dubai Highlights

The following is a list of our favourite things to see and do in Dubai.

- **Deira Souqs (p88)** No-one should miss out on a wander through the Spice Souq, the Deira Covered Souq or the Gold Souq. This maze of alleys bustles with commercial vigour; turn one corner and find a street lined with glittering jewellery, turn down another and your olfactory senses will alert you to the vast array of Eastern spices on sale in the Spice Souq. It adds up to one of Dubai's classic experiences.

- **Dubai Museum (p83)** This offers a great introduction to the culture of the emirates and the history of Dubai. There is a reconstruction of a souq; displays on ecology, pearling and fishing; traditional arts and crafts; and an audiovisual presentation depicting the city's development.

- **Abra Ride on the Creek (p83)** For only 50 fils you can jump on an *abra* (boat) at any time of the day and evening. It's the best way to view the city, with its incongruous mixture of old and new architecture. For around Dh40 you can hire a boat for a 30-minute cruise along the city's maritime artery.

- **Sheesha by the Creek (p121)** The Kanzaman restaurant and Fatafeet Café are the best places to sit, admire the cityscape and watch a variety of boats trundle up and down the Creek. Enjoy a puff of apple-flavoured tobacco from your *sheesha* (traditional smoking implement) and sip a cup of Arabic coffee. The best time is just before sunset.

- **Taking in the Al-Dhiyafah Street Scene (p121)** Come Thursday and Friday night this palm-lined boulevard of shops and cafes is buzzing, with young bucks showing off their wheels, à la American Graffiti. Relax with a *sheesha* pipe or an ice cream and watch the world's finest automobiles cruise by.

- **Bastakia Quarter (p86)** Stroll around the narrow lanes of one of Dubai's oldest and most interesting neighbourhoods, full of merchants' villas with shaded courtyards and wind towers, then stop by the wonderful Majlis art gallery.

- **Nad al-Sheba Club (p125)** On race nights the grandstands of this superb modern racecourse fill with spectators from all of Dubai's communities. Even if horse racing isn't usually your thing, the chance to mingle with sheikhs, jockeys and punters shouldn't be missed.

CHRIS MILLOR

TONY WHEELER

CHRISTINE OSBORNE

Dubai Museum occupies the old Al-Fahidi Fort (top left). The original wooden door of the fort (top right) and traditional wind towers and pearling boats in the courtyard (bottom) evoke a vision of Dubai's past.

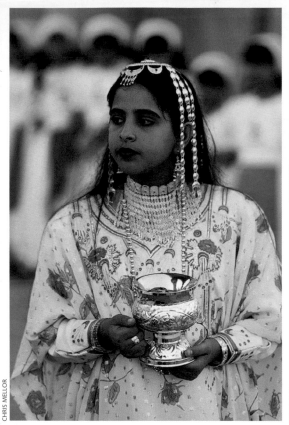

Arabic coffee

Laden with gold, a girl carries an incense burner during celebrations

A *khanjar* or dagger

An *oud*

Drums set the tempo for a traditional display of song and dance

to the museum is on 76A St. Before you enter the museum you might like to make a small diversion to an interesting backstreet of the Dubai Souq. Walk north from the museum's entrance down 76A St for a closer look at the multidomed **Grand Mosque** *(Map 4, #57)*. When you visit the Sheikh Saeed al-Maktoum House later on this walk you will be able to see old photos of Dubai showing the original Grand Mosque.

Walk past the mosque on its right-hand side and in the alley directly behind the mosque is a Hindu temple, the **Shri Nathje Jayate Temple** *(Map 4, #58)*, also called the Krishna Mandir (*mandir* is Hindi for temple). You'll recognise it by the racks for shoes outside. It's usually closed outside prayer times, which are at 6.30am, 8.30am, 10.15am, 5pm and 6pm. These last for about half an hour, accompanied by some spirited *bhajans* (hymns). Visitors are welcome, as long as you take off your shoes and don't take photos. Leaving the temple by its front door, head back, then take a left, go under an old archway, then turn left into a narrow lane. Along here you will notice vendors selling Hindu religious paraphernalia – baskets of fruit, garlands of flowers, gold-embossed holy images, sacred ash, sandalwood paste and packets of *bindis* (the little pendants Hindu women stick to their foreheads). You may also notice lots of shoes at the base of a flight of stairs. This is the way up to the **Sikh Gurdwara** *(Map 4, #59)*. You must cover your head before entering the Sikh shrine (there are headscarves kept in a box near the stairs). Inside is a copy of the Sikh holy book, the Granth Sahib, covered by a canopy.

From here continue along this side street then turn right and you will be in the **Dubai Souq**, surrounded by dozens of colourful fabric stores. You can either make your way back to the Dubai Museum, or you can do a shortened version of the walk by skipping the next few paragraphs, picking it up again at the souq.

After you have spent an hour or two inside the museum, you'll emerge from the exit on Al-Fahidi St. Turn left and continue along this street until you get to the next

roundabout. This is Al-Fahidi Roundabout; Al-Musalla post office (Map 4, #53) should be across the road on your right.

You are now standing on the edge of the **Bastakia Quarter**, which features a number of old wind-tower houses (for more information on these, see the special section 'Architecture' in the Facts about Dubai chapter), which were once the homes of wealthy Dubai merchants from the Bastak district in southern Iran. On your left you will see a white building; this is the **Majlis Gallery** *(Map 4, #54)*, which is housed in a restored wind-tower house. Walk inside to get a good look at this fine example of traditional Gulf architecture, featuring a courtyard with a number of rooms coming off it.

Wend your way northwards through the small streets that wrap around the wind-tower houses towards the **Creek**. Once you reach the Creek, turn left and walk along the front of the Creek past the impressive **Diwan** *(Map 4, #56)*, with its traditional wind towers, modern sculptures and black cast-iron fence. The Diwan is the highest administrative body of the Dubai government. It is also Sheikh Maktoum's office and so it is often referred to as the Ruler's Office. Look over to the other side of the Creek and you'll notice some other wind towers. These form part of Deira Old Souq, which you can explore on Walk 2.

Once past the Diwan you will come to an open area on the Creek waterfront. You won't be able to walk any further here (unless you want a swim) so turn left into the **Dubai Souq**. Before you pass through the wooden pillars of the souq entrance look to your right and notice the restored **waterfront houses**.

Once you have wandered through the souq, which sells mainly materials from Asia, you will come out at its western entrance. The **Bur Dubai *abra* station** will be ahead of you and to your right. Walk past the *abras* and continue along the waterfront to the **Shindagha Tower** *(Map 4, #13)*. This watchtower was built in 1910 and differs from other watchtowers in the emirates as it is square rather than round. It once marked the boundary between the culturally mixed trading community of Bur Dubai and the purely Arab settlement of Shindagha, where Sheikh Saeed al-Maktoum lived.

The rest of the walking tour takes you further along this peaceful stretch of waterfront towards the mouth of the Creek. The next place of interest along here is the **Bin Suroor Mosque** *(Map 4, #8)*. It is a tiny, restored mosque that was originally built in 1930 and is mainly used by the people working nearby. Next to this is the **Sheikh Saeed al-Maktoum House** *(Map 4, #6)*; once the residence of the ruling family of Dubai, it has now been turned into a museum featuring a photographic history of the city. The **Sheikh Juma al-Maktoum House** *(Map 4, #7)* nearby is another noble old Shindagha house, currently being restored.

Next door to Sheikh Saeed's House are the **Diving Village** *(Map 4, #3)* and **Heritage Village** *(Map 4, #4)*. Inside you will find displays on pearl diving and village life, a museum featuring archaeological relics found in Dubai, and a small souq. One sign of Dubai's development is that the authorities actually had to bring in sand to give the area that authentic look. Fifty years ago this area was all sand. A little further on, past the Kanzaman restaurant, is a small sandy park called **Arabian Bedouin Life** *(Map 4, #1)*. It features a donkey, a horse and a camel or two, employed to give kids a short ride. This is where your walking tour of Bur Dubai ends. Now you'll probably feel like stopping for a drink at the **Kanzaman restaurant** *(Map 4, #2)*, where you can sit and watch the Creek life float by.

If you have the stamina, you can make your way back to the *abra* dock, cross the Creek and begin a walking tour of Deira.

Walk 2: Deira (Map 4)

Begin this walking tour at the *abra* station on the corner of Baniyas and Al-Sabkha Rds. Walk north along Al-Sabkha Rd and turn left onto Al-Suq al-Kabeer St, just past Al-Khaleej Hotel (Map 4, #81), which will be on your right. Turn right into 67 St then left onto 20D St. This will bring you into the hustle and bustle of Deira. As you head west along here you will pass shops selling

various goods such as textiles, clothes, rugs and luggage. This area is known as the **Murshid Souq**. There is probably not a lot of merchandise here that you will want to buy, but the ethnic diversity here – shoppers from East Africa, Iran and the old Soviet Union, street peddlers from Afghanistan, shopkeepers from India and Pakistan – give it a unique commercial verve.

When you get to Suq Deira St turn left and then immediately right back on to Al-Suq al-Kabeer St. This will bring you to the wooden entrance of the **Deira Old Souq**, also known as the Spice Souq. This is where things get more interesting. You will know you are here when your nose is bombarded with the pungent aromas of cardamom, cloves and cinnamon. The alleyways here are narrow and intricate and there is no set route you should take. Just wander around at will and enjoy the many exotic sights.

If you continue in a southwesterly direction you will eventually come out on Al-Abra St. Turn right then turn left onto Al-Ras St, the next main street. Walk along here until you get to Al-Hadd St, where you turn right. Al-Hadd St is lined with shops selling sacks of spices, nuts and pulses. When you get to the end of this street turn right into Al-Ahmadiya St. About 50m along you will come to a restored house called the **Heritage House** *(Map 4, #9)*. Behind this is the restored **Al-Ahmadiya School** *(Map 4, #10)*. Built in 1912, it was once a school for the sons of Dubai's wealthy merchants. The building is spacious and airy and is decorated with arches along a veranda on the ground floor.

Continuing along Al-Ahmadiya St, turn right into Old Baladiya St; ahead you will see the wooden latticed archway of the entrance to Dubai's famous **Gold Souq** where you will be dazzled by the expanse of glittering gold. When you come out at the other end of the souq, continue in the same direction along Sikkat al-Khail St and you will pass the **Perfume Souq**, a string of shops selling Arabic and European perfumes. Try them out, though be aware that Arabic perfumes are extremely strong and you only need a little dab. After passing through the

Perfume Souq, you will come to a round-about. Turn right into 107 St where you will find trinket shops selling kitsch souvenirs.

Tucked behind the shops lining the east side (left side) of Al-Soor St is the **Deira Covered Souq**, which sells everything from *sheeshas* (smoking implements) to henna. Turn left and head through the souq. You will come out onto Al-Sabkha Rd near the bus station. Turn left here then turn right into Naif Rd.

Follow Naif Rd and turn right into 9A St. As you round the corner you will see an **old fort** *(Map 4, #99)* on your left, which is now a police station. A little further along you will come to **Naif Souq**. This small, covered souq is frequented almost exclusively by women, as it sells *abeyya*s (the full-length black robes worn by Arab women), head-scarves, materials, perfumes and children's clothes. A walk through here will bring you to Deira St on the souq's south side. Turn left into Deira St and walk to Al-Musalla Rd. Turn left into Al-Musalla Rd and on the next corner is **Naif Park**, which is a nice place to rest and end your walking tour of Deira.

THE CREEK (Map 4)

If you do only one touristy thing in Dubai, make it a visit to the Creek. Dubai's waterfront epitomises the city's personality, and the best way to see any great trading port is from the water. Instead of booking an expensive cruise (see Creek Cruises later in this chapter), you can hire an *abra* for an hour or so from any of the *abra* stations on the Creek. For around Dh40 (for the whole boat) the captain should take you to Al-Maktoum Bridge and back. For Dh60 he ought to extend that route to include a trip to the mouth of the Creek and back. These prices take a bit of bargaining to achieve. The shorter trip takes just over half an hour, the longer one takes 45 to 60 minutes.

Also take some time to walk along the **dhow wharfage** on the Deira side of the Creek to the west of the *abra* dock. Dhows bound for every port from Kuwait to Mumbai dock here to load and unload all sorts of cargo. You'll see tyres, air-conditioners, jeans, kitchen sinks, cars and probably just about anything else you can imagine.

MUSEUMS
Dubai Museum (Map 4, #55)

This museum (☎ 353 1862; Al-Fahidi St; bus No 25; adult/child Dh3/1; open 8.30am-8.30pm Sat-Thur, 3pm-9pm Fri) occupies Al-Fahidi Fort on the Bur Dubai side of the Creek, next to the Diwan. The fort was built in the early 19th century and is thought to be the oldest building in Dubai. For many years it was both the residence of Dubai's rulers and the seat of government, before it became a museum in 1971.

The impressive front door came from the house of Sheikh Saeed al-Maktoum, grandfather of the current ruler. In the entrance is a display of **aerial photographs** showing the growth of Dubai over the years. As you enter the fort's courtyard, you'll see a big tank which was used to carry fresh water on pearling boats. Several small **boats** are also in the courtyard, including a *shasha*, a small fishing boat made of palm fronds, still used by fishermen around Khor Kalba on the east coast of the UAE. There is also a *barasti house* with a wind tower (see the special section 'Architecture' in the Facts about Dubai chapter for more information on *barasti* houses).

The hall along the right-hand side of the courtyard has a display on the fort itself and another display featuring *khanjars* (curved daggers) and other **traditional weapons**. The hall to the left of the courtyard has a video of traditional Emirati dances, a display of musical instruments and more weapons.

The tower at the far corner of the courtyard leads down to a large underground area where the rest of the museum's exhibits are. The first is a very slick multimedia presentation of the city's development. Then you come to very detailed re-creations of a **typical souq**, a home and school as they would have looked in the 1950s. These come complete with disturbingly lifelike dummies of people. This is followed by a display on water and how it used to be conserved in the desert.

There is also an **interactive display** on the flora and fauna of the UAE, a display of seafaring life and another on the archaeology of the area, including a complete grave from the Al-Qusais archaeological site. Another room features finds from the digs at both Al-Qusais and Jumeira (2500 to 500 BC and 6th century AD, respectively).

To get to the museum if you've come across the Creek by *abra*, walk inland from the dock for about 100m then turn left onto Al-Fahidi Rd. You'll see the museum on your left. Alternatively, head inland through the Dubai Souq and out the other end through the narrow streets and lanes and you'll eventually come to the museum. If you are catching a taxi, the Arabic word for museum is *mathaf*.

All displays in the museum have explanations in Arabic and English. Photography is not permitted.

Sheikh Saeed al-Maktoum House (Map 4, #6)

The house of Sheikh Saeed (☎ 393 7139; Al-Shindagha Rd; bus Nos 8, 16, 19 & 20; adult/child Dh2/1; open 8.30am-9pm Sat-Thur, 3pm-10pm Fri), the grandfather of Dubai's present ruler, has been restored as a museum of pre-oil times. It sits along the Creek waterfront, next to the Heritage and Diving Villages, on the Bur Dubai side in the Shindagha area. The 30-room house was built in 1896 during the reign of Sheikh Maktoum bin Hasher al-Maktoum. For many years it served as a communal residence for the Al-Maktoum family, in keeping with the Arabian tradition of having several generations living in separate apartments within the same house or compound. Sheikh Saeed lived here from 1888 until his death in 1958. The house was re-opened as a museum in 1986 and houses an **exhibition of photographs**, mainly from the 1940s, '50s and '60s, documenting the history and development of Dubai. It is amazing to see how different the place looked only a few decades ago and makes you realise just how quickly Dubai has developed from a sleepy Gulf fishing village into the leading metropolis of the region.

Some of the photos go back to the late 19th century and there are some fascinating shots of traditional life in Dubai taken in souqs and at celebrations such as Tawminah,

the festival carried out on completion of the recitation of the Quran by schoolchildren. Traditional Bedouin life is also represented, and there are models of the different sorts of dhows used in Dubai. There is also a model of Bur Dubai from the 1950s.

There is a display of **coins** that were once used in the region, which were sometimes given unusual new names. Coins featuring Edward VII were known as *umm salaah*, meaning the 'bald headed'. Until 1965 the Indian rupee (both the British Raj version and the Republic of India version) was the official currency, whereas between 1966 and 1973 Dubai and Qatar issued their own currency, called the riyal. The UAE dirham was adopted in 1973. There is also a small display of postage stamps, too – before the oil economy got going the sale of stamps to overseas collectors was a handy little earner for the sheikhs of the future UAE.

The two-storey house, built around a courtyard, has a wind tower at each corner and is divided into four wings. Near the entrance is the main *majlis* (reception area or meeting room) and a room that was once set aside for the sheikh's clerk. The house is built of coral quarried from the Gulf and then covered with lime and plaster. Until recently this was a common building method along both the Gulf and Red Sea coasts of Arabia and you can see more examples of it around Bastakia in Dubai and in the Heritage Area of Sharjah (see the Excursions chapter).

The gift shop sells some souvenirs as well as a guide to the house (Dh5).

Heritage & Diving Villages (Map 4, #4 & #3)

These villages (Al-Shindagha Rd; bus Nos 8, 19, 20 & 25; admission free; open 7.30am-2pm & 3pm-9pm daily) are on the Creek in the heart of the old Shindagha area.

The Diving Village (☎ 393 9390) has displays on pearl diving, once the livelihood of the city, and scale models of various types of dhows and pearling boats. There are also a couple of diving schools based here (see Diving later in this chapter).

You will notice some signs along the waterfront here offering **boat cruises** for

Dh100 per hour. If you want to take a boat ride it's better to make a deal with one of the many skippers who cruise up and down this area; you should only pay Dh40 for half an hour or Dh60 for one hour.

The Heritage Village (☎ 393 7151) recreates traditional Bedouin and coastal village life, complete with *barasti* homes, a traditional coffeehouse and a small souq where you can buy freshly made *dosa* (a flat, grilled bread made of flour and water) from Emirati women for Dh1. There are also some traditional pottery and weaving workshops. The folks working here are very hospitable; it's well worth stopping by and chatting over a coffee. The other shops in the souq sell rather nice traditional handicrafts, Bedouin jewellery and pottery, as well as some tacky and rather overpriced souvenirs from India, Africa and Asia.

There is also a small **museum** here displaying artefacts and diagrams from archaeological sites at Al-Qusais, on the northeastern outskirts of town; Jumeira; and Al-Sufouf, near Hatta. Finds from the Al-Qusais site (2500-550 BC) include human skeletons, bronze arrowheads, stone vessels, daggers, hooks, needles and pottery collected from around 120 graves. At Al-Sufouf, a circular, collective tomb was discovered much like the one at the Hili Archaeological Gardens in Al-Ain. It suggests that this society belonged to the Umm an-Nar culture, which rose near modern Abu Dhabi. Little is known about them except that they were probably part of the Bahrain-based Dilmun empire, which was then the ascendant power in the central and northern Gulf. More than 50 individual tombs were discovered, most of which were looted over the centuries. Finds from those found intact include jars, jewels, beads and weapons.

ART GALLERIES

Dubai has a small but growing fine-arts scene, showing an intriguing synthesis between Western art forms and Arab and Islamic themes. The exhibition season lasts from October until March or April. Admission is free to all the galleries listed here.

Majlis Gallery (Map 4, #54)

This gallery (☎ 353 6233; Al-Fahidi Roundabout; bus No 19; open 9.30am-1.30pm & 4pm-7.30pm Sat-Thur), in an old house in Bur Dubai's Bastakia neighbourhood, exhibits the paintings of local artists. There are also some handicrafts on display, such as cushion covers and bags, ceramics, glassware and sculpture. Most, but not all, of the paintings have some sort of local connection – Islamic calligraphy or desert scenes, for example. The owner has lived here for almost 20 years and has a wealth of knowledge of the local arts scene.

Green Art Gallery (Map 3, #48)

One of Dubai's finest galleries, the Green Art Gallery (☎ 344 9888; 51 St, behind Dubai Zoo, Jumeira; bus No 8; open 9.30am-1.30pm & 4.30pm-8.30pm Sat-Thur) occupies two villas on a suburban street. It holds regular exhibitions in classic 'white-cube' galleries, and also sells limited-edition prints and handcrafted items. If you can't fork out a few thousand dirhams for an original oil painting, their range of greeting cards featuring exhibited works makes a useful alternative.

Total Arts at the Courtyard (Map 2, #22)

This gallery (☎ 228 2888; Road 6, Al-Quoz Industrial Zone; bus No 12; open 10am-1pm & 4pm-8pm Sat-Thur) is just off Sheikh Zayed Rd, about 15km south of the Creek. Turn off at Intersection No 3 and take the first right; the building has a high arched window. Total Arts is a strikingly modern commercial gallery with a range of international abstract art, as well as pieces that appeal to local tastes (desert scenes, calligraphy, horses etc). The other shops in the complex include a florist, an Art Deco furniture maker and a photographic studio. An arts-oriented café is set to open here.

Hunar Gallery (Map 2, #36)

This gallery (☎ 286 2224; Villa 6, 49 St, off Nad al-Hamar Rd, Rashidiya; bus Nos 4, 11, 15, 33 & 44; open 9.30am-1.30pm & 4.30pm-8pm Sat-Thur) is a small place run by an

Emirati woman from a house in a well-to-do neighbourhood. When asked if Dubai was a cultural desert, she replied 'Yes, you have to brush away a little sand to find the art underneath'. The gallery holds regular exhibitions of works by Emirati artists, as well as works by foreign artists on Arabian and Islamic themes.

Dubai International Arts Centre (Map 3, #43)

This centre (☎ 344 4398; 4A St, Jumeira; bus No 8; open 8.30am-7pm Sun-Wed, 8.30am-4pm Thurs & Sat), off Jumeira Rd opposite McDonald's, is a nonprofit, membership organisation, which means it exhibits only the works of its members, all of whom are UAE locals, who represent over 60 nationalities. Some of the more interesting works are by Abdul Wahed al-Mawlawi, Susan Walpole, Fay Lawson, Alem Goshime and Shakeel Siddiqui. The fairly basic premises also host courses for members in everything from pottery to framing and photography.

HERITAGE & ARCHAEOLOGICAL SITES

Majlis Ghorfat Um-al-Sheef (Map 2, #26)

It is unusual to find a traditional building still standing so far from the Creek, but this one, south of Jumeira Beach Park, has been well restored and is worth a visit. The two-storey Majlis Ghorfat Um-al-Sheef (17 St; admission Dh1; open 8.30am-1.30pm & 3.30pm-8.30pm Sat-Thur, 3.30pm-8.30pm Fri) was built in 1955 and was attended in the evenings by Sheikh Rashid bin Saeed al-Maktoum. Here he would listen to his people's complaints, grievances and ideas. It was a place of open discussion and exchange. A former British political resident of Dubai, Donald Hawley, saw the Majlis as 'an Arabian Camelot' and Sheikh Rashid as 'King Arthur'.

The majlis also provided a cool retreat from the heat of the day. It is made of gypsum and coral rock, traditional building materials of the Gulf, and the roof is made of palm fronds (areesh). The ground floor is an open area surrounded by columns and the

The Majlis

Majlis translates as 'meeting place' or 'reception area'. The majlis was a forum or council where citizens could come and speak to their leaders and make requests, complaints or raise any issues. In Dubai the majlis system was preserved until the 1960s. In its domestic sense, a majlis is a reception area found in all older buildings in Dubai (such as Al-Fahidi Fort, now the Dubai Museum, and the Heritage House in Al-Ahmadiya). Its Western cousin is probably the lounge room. The majlis is still an important room in an Arab household and is usually the domain of the male members of the family. It's a place where they can get together and talk without disturbing the women of the house. Some traditional houses had a separate majlis for women.

floor above consists of a veranda on one side and the enclosed majlis on the other. The columns, windows and doors are all made of teak from India. The majlis is decorated with cushions, rugs, a coffeepot, pottery and food platters, and is pretty close to the way it would have looked in Sheikh Rashid's day. Windows surround the room and, in the summer heat, the breeze circulates freely around the house, keeping it relatively cool.

A garden of date palms and fig trees has been constructed around the majlis, and a traditional barasti café sits in one corner of the enclosure. The garden, with its falaj (traditional irrigation system), needs to mature a little, but the sound of running water is very soothing and, though it's in the middle of a residential area, it's very peaceful. The majlis is on 17 St, which runs off Jumeira Rd, on the inland side, just past the Jumeira Beach Park. You can catch bus No 8 and get off just south of Jumeira Beach Park.

Bastakia Quarter (Map 4)

This district, on the waterfront east of the Dubai Souq and the Diwan, features a number of traditional old wind-tower houses. Built at the turn of the 20th century, these houses were once the homes of wealthy

Persian merchants lured to Dubai by its relaxed trade tariffs. Most came from the Bastak district in what is now southern Iran, hence the name Bastakia. Wind towers were a traditional form of air-conditioning whereby cool air was funnelled down into the house (for more details, see the special section 'Architecture' in the Facts about Dubai chapter).

The quarter has been declared a conservation area and restoration work is being carried out. As you wander through the narrow, peaceful lanes you can easily imagine the life of the merchant residents at the turn of the 20th century. Notice the original carved wooden doors that remain on some of the houses.

Some of the wind-tower houses have been fully restored and are private homes. If you pass one of the houses under restoration ask the workmen if you can have a look around. One restored house is home to the Majlis Gallery (see Art Galleries earlier in this chapter), which is well worth visiting to see some local artwork. There are plans to turn another Bastakia villa into a café, while another will be the premises of the Sheikh Mohammed Centre for Cultural Understanding.

Al-Ahmadiya School (Map 4, #10)

This school (Al-Ahmadiya St), behind the Heritage House in the souq area of Deira, will eventually be turned into a museum detailing early education in Dubai. The classrooms of the school lead off a central courtyard and inscriptions from the Quran sit above each doorway. The school was built by a philanthropic pearl merchant in 1912 and was attended by Sheikh Rashid bin Saeed al-Maktoum, the prime mover behind the development of modern Dubai. By the middle of the century the building fell into disrepair and it wasn't until the early 1990s that restoration work began.

The small area around the school is home to a number of traditional houses that have been restored of late, including some courtyard houses (see the special section 'Architecture' in the Facts about Dubai chapter). They are made of gypsum, sea rock, coral,

wood (from East Africa) and the trunks of date palms. At the time of writing the houses were not officially open to the public, but if the doors are open you can wander inside and have a look. You can catch any of the buses that go along Baniyas Rd and around the Al-Ras district to get here, including Nos 4, 5, 11, 14, 15, 19, 20, 22, 25 and 31. You'll need to get off at the public library (Map 4, #12) and walk from there.

Heritage House (Map 4, #9)

This restored traditional house, next to Al-Ahmadiya School in the souq area of Deira, was built in 1890 and was once home to a wealthy Iranian merchant. It differs from the old houses in the Bastakia Quarter on the other side of the Creek as it has no wind towers. The house is characterised by many wooden shutters at street level and a balcony railing along the roof. Once inside, you find yourself in a large courtyard surrounded by rooms, with a veranda at one end.

As you move around the courtyard you pass a *majlis*, a cattle pen, kitchen, bedrooms, the ladies' *majlis* and a bride's room. This last room was where a young bride-to-be would prepare for her wedding day with the help of other women of the harem. It is decorated with mattresses, pillows and Persian rugs.

Jumeira Archaeological Site (Map 3, #63)

This site is considered one of the biggest and most significant archaeological sites in the UAE. Remains found here date from the 6th century AD and can be seen in the small museum at the Heritage Village in Shindagha. The settlement is particularly interesting in that it spans the pre-Islamic and Islamic eras. Surrounded by modern villas and shopping centres, this settlement was once a caravan station on a route linking Ctesiphon (in what is now Iraq) to northern Oman.

Remains at the site link it with the Persian Sassanid empire, the dominant culture in the region from the 3rd to the 6th century AD. The Sassanids were wiped out by Arab tribes, notably the Umayyad dynasty, with the coming of Islam in the 7th century. The Umayyads extended and restored many of the original buildings and the site continued to exist until at least the 10th century.

Excavations have revealed a series of stone walls that surrounded a souq made up of seven shops and a storage room. There are also the remains of a few houses, including a large courtyard house with decorative plaster work that was most likely the governor's palace (this kind of decoration can still be seen on restored houses in Dubai, such as in the Al-Ahmadiya district and along the waterfront in Bur Dubai).

There is no public access to the site. If archaeologists are working, you may be able to have a look inside, otherwise you'll just have to make out parts of the site through the fence.

To reach the site, head south down Jumeira Rd and do a U-turn when you get to the Jumeira Beach Park, just past the Jumeira Beach Club. Take the first street on the right, which is 27 St, and continue straight to the end, then turn right; you will see a large fenced-in area about 50m along on your left. You can also catch bus No 8 as far as the Jumeira Beach Park; the site is a five-minute walk from there.

SOUQS (Map 4)

Compared with how it would have been only 20 or 30 years ago, not much of the old covered souqs remain, but they still operate in the early morning and in the evening from around 5pm to 8pm. The **Deira Covered**

Watch This Space

The speed with which new projects in Dubai are approved and get off the ground is legendary. The ruling family wastes no time when someone comes up with a bright idea, no matter how bold. These are just a few of the projects set to transform Dubai's landscape.

Palm Islands Project

This one is truly amazing. Two artificial islands formed in the shape of palm trees, 8km long with 14 peninsula-like 'fronds' plus a protective barrier island, will give Dubai an extra 120km of beach frontage. Each frond will be lined with boutique hotels and luxury villas, while the trunks will include a water park and shopping areas. The first island is being built near Al-Mina al-Seyahi, and the whole project is due to be finished by 2004.

Dubai Marina City (Map 2, #10)

This is a vast new housing complex for 150,000 people being built around an artificial harbour near Al-Mina al-Seyahi. This will include the first residential properties that foreigners will be able to own outright.

Souk al-Nakheel (Map 2, #15)

Snowboarding in the desert? By 2004 a local company plans to build a 320m indoor ski slope complete with real snow, an ice-skating pond and an alpine village where children can throw snowballs and make snowmen. The bulk of the complex on Sheikh Zayed Rd will have a Moroccan theme, and will also include 60,000 sq metres of retail space and a Carrefour hypermarket.

Dubai Festival City (Map 3)

Stretching for 4km along the Deira side of the Creek, east of Al-Garhoud Bridge, this residential, retail and leisure complex will include a marina and skyscraper. The complex will be the base for the Dubai Shopping Festival.

Madinat Jumeirah (Map 2, #17)

Relatively modest by comparison, this will be a new shopping and leisure complex just south of the Jumeira Beach Hotel, featuring a waterfront boardwalk, cafés and an auditorium.

Souq, off Al-Sabkha Rd, sells just about everything, though it has more of an Indian feel than an Arabic one. Textiles, spices, kitchenwares, walking sticks, *sheeshas*, clothes and a lifetime's supply of henna are all available here.

The **Deira Old Souq** (Spice Souq) is a wonderful place to wander around and take in the smells of spices, nuts and dried fruits. The spices are mainly found at the souq's eastern end, nearest the Creek. There are sacks brimming with frankincense, dried lemons, ginger root, chilli and cardamom, to name but a few. Other shops in this souq sell tacky trinkets, kitchenware, shoes, rugs, glassware and textiles.

Deira's **Gold Souq**, on and around Sikkat al-Khail St, between Suq Deira and Old Baladiya Sts, is probably the largest such market in Arabia and attracts customers from all over the Middle East and the subcontinent. If you don't spot the glittering gold in the windows you'll recognise this souq by the wooden lattice archways at the entrances.

At the eastern end of the Gold Souq, on Sikkat al-Khail St, is the **Perfume Souq**. A number of shops here sell a staggering range of Arabic and European perfumes. The European perfumes are a mixture of designer originals and copies. The Arabic perfumes are much stronger and spicier than Western perfumes.

At Dubai's famous **Electronics Souq**, near the corner of Al-Sabkha and Al-Maktoum Hospital Rds, dozens of shops are packed together, all selling virtually the same stock. They do a roaring trade, especially with visitors from the former Soviet Union.

The **Dubai Souq** in Bur Dubai has been beautifully reconstructed to appeal to tourists, but most of the shops here target Indian expat shoppers. It sells mostly materials and shoes, with very little in in the way of Arabic antiques or souvenirs. If you want to have a sari made, however, this is the place to come.

For more on what to buy at these souqs and how much it costs, see the Shopping chapter later in this guide.

MOSQUES

The multidomed **Grand Mosque** (Map 4, #57) in Bur Dubai, just north of the Dubai Museum, boasts Dubai's tallest minaret. This mosque might appear to be a beautiful example of restoration work but it was in fact built in the 1990s. Maintaining the style of the original Grand Mosque, which dated from 1900 and was knocked down to make way for another mosque in 1960, its sand-coloured walls and wooden shutters blend in perfectly with the surrounding old quarter of Bur Dubai. As well as being the centre of Dubai's religious and cultural life, the original Grand Mosque was also home to the town's *kuttab* school where children learnt to recite the Quran from memory.

Jumeira Mosque (Map 7, #25; Jumeira Rd) is the best known mosque in Dubai due to its size and elaborate design. The best time to see it is at night when it is spectacularly lit up. You can catch bus No 8 or 20 along Jumeira Rd to get there.

It's worth a quick drive to Satwa to see the stunning **Iranian Mosque** (Map 7, #24; Al-Wasl Rd) and, opposite it, the Iranian Hospital (Map 7, #23). The incredibly detailed design of the brilliant blue mosaic work is typical of Iranian building design. Bus Nos 7 and 12 go along Al-Wasl Rd.

Ali bin Abi Taleb Mosque (Map 4, #19; Ali bin Abi Taleb St), at the rear of Dubai Souq, is notable for its sensuous bulbous domes and gently tapering minaret. Its outline is probably best appreciated from Baniyas Rd in Deira, on the opposite side of the Creek.

Non-Muslims are not permitted to enter mosques in the UAE. However, during events such as the Dubai Summer Surprises, the Sheikh Mohammed Centre for Cultural Understanding (see Cultural Centres in the Facts for the Visitor chapter) organises tours inside Jumeira Mosque.

OTHER ATTRACTIONS
Dubai Zoo (Map 3, #46)

This zoo (Jumeira Rd; bus Nos 8 & 20; admission Dh2; open 10am-6pm Wed-Mon) is due to close and a new one is planned to open next to Mushrif Park on the outskirts of Dubai. The old zoo is a rather grim place;

the animals are well cared for, but there just isn't enough room. The zoo was originally a private collection, but more and more cages and enclosures have been crammed in to accommodate the animals. If the sight and smell of animals in poor conditions upsets you, give this place a miss.

Dubai World Trade Centre (Map 7, #19)

The World Trade Centre tower (☎ 331 4200; Sheikh Zayed Rd; bus Nos 6, 61, 90 & 98) was once Dubai's tallest building. Although it has now been overshadowed by taller skyscrapers, it is still an important landmark in the city. There is a **viewing gallery** (admission Dh5) on the 37th floor for those who want a bird's-eye view of the city, but can't afford to hire a helicopter. You can only visit the gallery as part of a tour. These leave daily from the information desk in the tower lobby at 9.30am and 4.30pm.

Dhow-Building Yard (Map 3, #38)

On the Creek waterfront, about 1km south of Al-Garhoud Bridge in the Jaddaf district, is a yard where huge dhows are built in the traditional style. This means that the planks are curved and fitted, one on top of the other, and then the frame is fitted on the inside. (In the West, the frame of a boat is generally built first, and the planks are fitted to it.) The enormous vessels are all built by hand, using just the most basic of tools – a hammer, saw, chisel, drill and plane. Teak, because it's so sturdy, and shesham are the most commonly used woods. Both are imported from Asia. These days, of course, dhows are powered by engines rather than sails.

To get to the dhow yard from the Bur Dubai side of the Creek, head along Al-Qataiyat Rd towards Al-Garhoud Bridge. Take the first exit to the right after the Dubai Police Club. Go past the nursery and turn left onto a gravel track just before the Dubai Docking Yard. Follow this track for about 700m as it bends around to the left and you will come to a string of dhow-building yards. You can't miss the enormous hulls of these dhows. If you are coming from the

Dhows

Dhows are just as much a characteristic of Dubai now as they were centuries ago. The dhow wharfage along the Creek, piled with assorted goods from Iran, India, Pakistan and East Africa, gives the city an exotic flavour. Despite the glistening steel and glass buildings that now dominate the Creek waterfront, the dhows give the place an unmistakably oriental feel.

Dubai was once one of the most important dhow-building centres on the Gulf coast. The dhow builders (al-galalif in Arabic) used basic materials and methods to construct the enormous vessels. The development of Dubai's maritime culture is reflected in the large number of different boats they constructed for different purposes. The larger dhows used for long-distance journeys were called al-boom, al-bateel and al-baglah and were up to 60m in length. Some of them have now been turned into cruise vessels and floating restaurants. The sambuk was a smaller boat, never more than 30m long, which was used mainly for fishing. It was characterised by its single mast and square stern, which had decorative wings protruding from it. Pearling boats (baggara) were larger and had no mast. The abra is still used to ferry people across the Creek.

Deira side you will have to cross over Al-Garhoud Bridge then do a U-turn at the next roundabout to be on the other side of the road. Bus No 14 goes as far as the Dubai Docking Yard from where it's a five-minute walk to the dhows.

Al-Boom Tourist Village (Map 3, #37)

This is really just a nice place to go for a coffee and sheesha in traditional barasti surroundings or to have a meal at the Fishmarket Floating Restaurant. This enormous restaurant dhow is permanently moored here. The rest of the 'village' is just made up of function rooms. The sheesha café livens up in the evenings. The village lies next to Al-Garhoud Bridge on the Bur Dubai side of the Creek. Bus No 44 goes past here.

PARKS
Safa Park (Map 2)
This park (cnr Al-Wasl Rd & Al-Hadiqa St, Safa; bus Nos 7 & 12; admission Dh5; open 8am-11pm daily, women & children only Tues) stretches for 1km from Al-Wasl Rd to Sheikh Zayed Rd. It is one of the most colourful parks in Dubai and is very popular with local residents. Lots of cricket gets played on the wide grassy expanses at weekends. One attraction is its small-scale models of famous landmarks from around the world, such as the Taj Mahal, the Colosseum and the Leaning Tower of Pisa. There is a lake where you can hire paddle boats, tennis courts, a soccer pitch, barbecues and an artificial waterfall. Bus No 12 runs along Al-Wasl Rd and past the park.

Creekside Park (Map 3)
This park (admission Dh5; open 8am-11pm Sat-Wed, 8am-11.30pm Thur, Fri & public holidays, women & children only Wed) is the largest of Dubai's parks and runs for 2.6km from Al-Garhoud Bridge on the Bur Dubai side towards Al-Maktoum Bridge. It has children's play areas, dhow cruises, kiosks, restaurants, an amphitheatre and beaches (though it's not advisable to swim in the Creek). It's one of the most scenic parks, in a delightfully artificial sort of way – fancy there being woodlands in the middle of a desert city. The park also features a 2.5km-long cable-car ride (tickets Dh5), 30m above the shore of the Creek, but the ride does start to pall after a while. Another feature is the Al-Aflaj section of the park, with a reconstruction of a villa from Hatta, Dubai's mountain enclave, and gardens watered with a falaj channel system. Bus Nos 3, 5, 6, 14, 16, 23, 33 or 44 will get you close to the park, but you will have to cross a couple of major roads to get to the entrance.

Al-Mamzar Park (Map 2)
This park (bus No 22; person/car Dh5/30; open 8am-9.30pm Sat-Wed, 8am-10.30pm Thur, Fri & public holidays, women & children only Wed) covers a small headland on the northern outskirts of Dubai at the mouth of Khor al-Mamzar. Across this inlet lies Shar-jah. It has plenty of open space and a wooden castle for kids to play on. There are beaches, jet skis for hire, a swimming pool, children's play areas, barbecues and kiosks. Lifeguards are on duty between 8am and 6pm on at least one of the small beaches. At the northern tip of the park there are 15 **chalets** (booking office ☎ 296 7948; open 9am-10pm daily), which can be hired for the day. Each has a kitchen, bathroom, barbecue and a small sitting room. The booking office near the tennis courts told us that the chalets are booked weeks in advance for weekends. The five big chalets cost Dh200 each per day to hire, the 10 smaller ones Dh150 each per day. Bookings are taken once you've paid (cash only).

Wednesday is for women and children only, unless there is a special event, in which case it's open to everyone.

Mushrif Park (Map 2)
This park (person/car Dh2/10; open 8.30am-10.30pm Sat-Wed, 8.30am-11pm Thur, Fri & public holidays) is the largest of Dubai's parks and is on the eastern outskirts of the city, about 15km from the centre. Except for a core area with irrigation-fed greenery, most of the park is rolling scrubland and dunes. To get here, continue along Airport Rd, past the airport, until it becomes Al-Khawaneej Rd. You will see signs for the park. The biggest attraction here is the 'World Village', which is a miniature reconstruction of buildings from around the world, including a Dutch windmill, Tudor cottages and Thai stilt houses. Kids are welcome to crawl around the models. Another cute feature is the Smurf statues scattered around the place. There are camel and pony rides, a miniature train (Dh2 per ride), swimming pools (separate ones for men and women) and barbecues. Dubai's new zoo will be located here.

You can catch bus No 11 or 15 along Al-Khawaneej Rd, from where it's a few minutes' walk into the park.

BEACHES
The coast around Dubai boasts miles of broad, sandy beaches. Most of the beaches are the private domains of the five-star beach

hotels; if you're staying at one of these, you'll have free access to the beach. If not, you can pay for the use of the hotel's facilities, but it's generally very expensive. The average cost for a day visit varies from Dh60 to up to Dh200 (with Dh100 redeemable on food and drinks on the latter). Some are only open to hotel guests and members. For the day charge you get changing rooms, showers, beach chairs, and the use of at least one swimming pool (often several). If you need to splash around with a cocktail handy, this can be arranged. Hotel beaches are generally spotlessly clean as well.

Otherwise, your best option is the beach park at Jumeira or the few nice stretches of public beach, though oglers can be a problem at these for women, especially women on their own.

Jumeira Beach Park (Map 3; Jumeira Rd; bus No 8; person/car Dh5/20; open 8am-11pm daily, women & children only Sat & Mon) fronts onto Jumeira Beach and a walk on the grass is a real treat. There is a children's play area, barbeques, picnic tables, walkways and kiosks. The long stretch of beach is clean and lined with date palms for shade. Lifeguards are on duty here between 8am and 6pm. We highly recommend this beach for women who don't want to pay a small fortune to use one of the beach clubs at the five-star hotels, but also don't want to risk the unwanted male attention they may receive at other public beaches.

Next to the Dubai Marine Beach Resort & Spa just off Jumeira Rd, more or less opposite the Jumeira Mosque, there is a stretch of **public beach** (Map 7) with facilities, including showers, shelters and toilets, and plenty of date palms. A little further away from town, north of the Jumeira Beach Hotel, there is the **Umm Suqeim public beach** (Map 2), with hardly any facilities apart from a couple of rudimentary shelters. There are patches of beach between the hotels south of here, but they're quickly being filled up with more hotels and developments.

On the Deira side of the Creek there is a public stretch of beach running along the bank of the **Khor al-Mamzar** (Map 2), which looks out over Sharjah. Follow the signs for

Al-Mamzar Park and you'll see the beach about 50m past the entrance to the park. There are no sun shelters or lifeguards here, only rubbish bins; watch out for jet-skiers.

ACTIVITIES

Dubai offers a wide range of activities and sports clubs – too many to list here. *Dubai Explorer* and *Time Out* are the best sources for this sort of information; both have alphabetical listings of all the activities available in Dubai, where to do them and how much it will cost you. *What's On* also has information on clubs and leisure activities in Dubai.

Golf

It costs a fortune to maintain grass courses in this part of the world. And yes, this cost *is* reflected in exorbitant green fees. There are currently four courses in Dubai, and the upcoming Emirates Hill Golf Resort development near the Emirates Golf Club will add three more.

There is a 10% discount on the first three of these courses if you have United Arab Emirates Golfers' Association (UGA) membership, which costs from Dh200. To play at these courses, men must be wearing a shirt with sleeves and a collar and trousers. Jeans and 'beach wear' are not allowed. For more information about the Emirates and Dubai Creek courses, go to their website (**W** www .dubaigolf.com).

Emirates Golf Club (Map 2; ☎ 347 3222; Interchange No 5, Sheikh Zayed Rd) is one of the sites of the Dubai Desert Classic, part of the European PGA Tour. The clubhouses, designed to resemble Bedouin tents, are a local landmark. Green fees are Dh370 (Dh425 Thursday to Saturday) for the 18-hole Majlis course and Dh330 (Dh365 Thursday to Saturday) for the 18-hole Wadi course, plus a compulsory Dh50 for cart rental. Men must have a handicap under 28 and an official certificate to prove it, while for women the maximum handicap is 45. Bus No 90 goes along Sheikh Zayed Rd, as far as the golf club, but you'd have to cross Sheikh Zayed Rd which is likely to be fatal. Catch a taxi, for about Dh45, instead.

Dubai Creek Golf & Yacht Club *(Map 3, #19; ☎ 295 6000)*, near the Deira side of Al-Garhoud Bridge, hosted the Dubai Desert Classic in 1999 and 2000. The weekend rate (Thursday to Saturday) to play the 18-hole course is Dh425, or Dh370 on weekdays, plus Dh50 for cart rental. The same handicap restrictions as for the Emirates Golf Club apply for the main course, or anyone can hack away on a nine-hole, par-three course for Dh180 plus cart rental. At night the nine-hole course is floodlit and costs only Dh30 per round. No bus route passes the club entrance, but bus Nos 4, 11 and 15, which travel along Al-Maktoum Rd, go close.

Nad al-Sheba Club *(Map 2, #32; ☎ 336 3666; bus No 16)* is on the outskirts of town. It has a floodlit 18-hole course, nine of which are within the racecourse. The course is usually closed during horse races, so call to see what time you can tee off on race days. Green fees are Dh220 during the day or Dh295 at night (it's open until 10pm). Head down Oud Metha Rd, as if you were driving to Al-Ain or Hatta, then follow the signs for Nad al-Sheba.

Dubai Country Club *(Map 2, #39; ☎ 333 1155; Ras al-Khor Rd)* saves on expenses by saving on grass – there isn't any. Instead this nine-hole course has brushed sand around each hole ('browns' rather than greens), and golfers are given a little piece of grass to slide under the ball on the fairways. Nonmembers are charged a very reasonable Dh65 to play a round. Bus Nos 16 and 61 run close to the club.

Water Sports

Water sports are big business in Dubai, as the tourism industry increasingly promotes the city as a winter 'sea & sun' destination. Most water-sports facilities are based either at a big hotel with huge fees or at a private club, and therefore are not generally accessible to budget travellers.

Jet-Skiing There are jet skis based at the Oasis Beach Hotel, the Ritz-Carlton, the Hilton Dubai Jumeirah, the Metropolitan Resort & Beach Club and the Royal Mirage. If you really want to express your hatred for

the environment, you can pay for the use of a hotel beach club for the day plus Dh100 for 20 minutes jet-skiing on top of that.

You can also go jet-skiing on Dubai Creek (Map 3, #18), just south of the Al-Garhoud Bridge on the Deira side. It costs around Dh100 for 30 minutes. To get here from the Deira side of the Creek, take Al-Garhoud Rd past the bridge and follow the signs to Al-Rashidiya. Turn right at the first set of lights after the bridge and follow the track to the shore. From the Bur Dubai side, take the right-hand exit just over the bridge, then turn right at the next set of lights. There are no buses running close to here so if you don't have your own transport, you'll need to take a taxi. This area has been earmarked for development, however, so it's not clear how much longer the jet skis will operate from this spot. Given the pollution in the Creek, it's probably no great loss.

Another spot where there are jet skis for hire on calmer waters than the Gulf is on the Khor al-Mamzar (Map 2, #17), south of Al-Mamzar Park, which looks cleaner. Bus No 22 runs along the shore of this lagoon.

Remember that jet-skiing can be a dangerous, as well as environmentally unfriendly, activity, so take care and let other jet-skiers have plenty of room. There was a particularly nasty accident several years ago, which led to a British woman being jailed.

Water-Skiing If you are staying at a five-star hotel with a beach club, it costs Dh100 for a half-hour of water-skiing. If you are not a guest at one of these places you will also have to pay the daily admission fee to the beach club (usually about Dh60 to Dh200).

The only place to water-ski other than hotel beach clubs is at the **Dubai Water Sports Association** *(Map 3, #39; ☎ 334 2031; admission Dh15 Mon-Fri, Dh30 Sat & Sun; open 9am-dusk daily)* on the Bur Dubai side of the Creek. The admission fee is to get into the club and use the pool, deck chairs or Jacuzzi, or hang out at the bar and restaurant. If you want to water-ski it will cost you Dh45 for a 10- to 15-minute tow. There is no water-skiing on Sunday.

To get here from the Deira side of the Creek, head along Al-Qataiyat Rd towards Al-Garhoud Bridge. Take the first exit on the right after the Dubai Police Club. Continue past the nursery and turn right just before the Dubai Docking Yard. The tarmac road ends here, but continue along a sand track for 1.4km as it skirts around a large fenced-in compound. At this point you'll see the club ahead and to your right. You can get bus No 14 as far as the fenced-in compound, but you will have about a 10-minute walk from here.

Diving Although the waters around Dubai are home to some coral reefs, marine life and a few modern shipwrecks, visibility in the water is not very good. Most dive companies take you up to the east coast to dive in the waters between Khor Fakkan and Dibba and off the east coast of the Musandam Peninsula, which is part of Oman. Not including equipment hire, a day's diving (with two dives) costs between Dh200 and Dh500. Dives are offered to people at all levels of expertise. If you are uncertified you might want to take a diving course (see Courses later in this chapter).

The Emirates Diving Association is the official diving body for the UAE and takes a strong interest in environmental matters. The association has a useful and detailed website at W www.emiratesdiving.com. Another handy resource is the 180-page *UAE Underwater Explorer* (Dh65), which has information on 30 dive sites.

Al-Boom Diving *(Map 7, #33;* ☎ *342 2993; Al-Wasl Rd, Jumeira)*, just south of the Iranian Mosque, is linked to the Sandy Bay Diving Centre on the East Coast (see Bidiya in the Excursions chapter for details), and many of its dives start from there.

Scubatec Diving Centre *(Map 6, #38;* ☎ *334 8988; Sana Bldg, cnr Sheikh Khalifa bin Zayed & Al-Adhid Rds, Karama)* offers a two-dive trip off Khor Fakkan for Dh525 (including equipment), as well as dives on wrecks in the Gulf from Dh250. With a few days notice they can also arrange a dive on the pearling beds in the Gulf.

Scuba Dubai *(Map 7, #21;* ☎ *331 4014; Block C, Dubai World Trade Centre Apart-*

---

ments, Sheikh Zayed Rd) organises daily dives off the west and east coasts. It costs from Dh300, including equipment. This is also Dubai's biggest diving equipment store.

Inner Space Diving Centre *(Map 4, #3;* ☎ *331 7775; Diving Village, Shindagha)* will arrange a dive off the Dubai coast if you really want, although it will warn you that it's not the best diving in the country. It also arranges dives off the Musandam Peninsula for Dh500.

Scuba International *(Map 4, #3;* ☎ *393 7557; Diving Village, Shindagha)* offers dives off Dibba on the east coast for Dh300, including equipment. Diving on wrecks off the coast costs from Dh200 per day (two dives).

Fishing This is not allowed in the Creek and, given the amount of pollution released by the endless number of boats plying the waterway, you wouldn't want to fish here anyway. As for deep-sea fishing, there are a few options, all of which are very expensive. If luck is on your side and the weather conditions are right, you're likely to catch flying fish, tuna, barracuda, kingfish and sailfish. The best time to fish off the coast of Dubai is from September to April when the water is not as warm as during the summer months. You will probably have to leave a deposit, usually about Dh50 per person, when you book a fishing trip.

Dubai Creek Golf & Yacht Club *(Map 3, #19; ☎ 205 4646)* rents out a 10m boat with skipper for up to six passengers. It costs Dh1500 for four hours or Dh2200 for eight hours, which includes fishing tackle, bait, lunch and drinks.

Prices are similar with **Bounty Charters** *(Map 2, #7; ☎ 348 3042; Dubai International Marine Club, Al-Sufouh Rd)*, 21.5km south of the centre. It charges Dh1500 for four hours and Dh1800 for six.

A fishing trip with **Fenikia Marine** *(Map 2, #21; ☎ 348 6838; Jumeira Beach Hotel Marina, Jumeira Rd, Umm Suqeim)* costs Dh1500/2000 for four/six hours.

A somewhat pricier fishing trip can be arranged on the *Discovery*, which is operated by **Creek Cruises** *(Map 5, #52; ☎ 393 7123; Quay 2/3, Dhow Wharfage, Deira)* from the docks just east of the Sheraton Dubai. This 12m yacht can accommodate up to seven passengers. It's more expensive than the others, however, at Dh2500 for a four-hour trip.

Wild Wadi Waterpark (Map 2, #19)

This 5-hectare water park *(☎ 348 4444; bus No 8; adult/child Dh95/75; open 11am-7pm daily Sept-May, 1pm-9pm daily June-Aug)*, next to Jumeira Beach Hotel, opened with a great fanfare in 1999. Two million gallons of water are pumped through the park's various tunnels, tubes, slides, caves and pools daily. The 24 rides are all interconnected so that you can get off one and jump straight onto another. Some of the hairier rides reach speeds of 80km/h, while the Jumeira Sceirah is the highest and fastest free-fall water slide

outside North America. The Tunnel of Doom ride is pretty cool as well. There are wave pools for swimmers and surfers as well as more sedate rides for younger kids and slightly nervous adults, and plenty of lifeguards on duty.

The design of the park, with its sand- and stone-coloured structures, is based around a legend in which the Arabic adventurer Juha and his friend, Sinbad the sailor, are shipwrecked on a lush lagoon, beyond which lies a magical oasis. The design blends in with the natural surroundings fairly well. There are two restaurants and a few kiosks where you can buy food and drinks with a special credit card attached to your wrist. The balance is refunded when you leave. Towels and lockers can be rented for Dh5, and body boards and tubes are free.

Creek Cruises

Coastline Leisure *(Map 5, #56; ☎ 398 4867)*, in front of Sheraton Dubai in Deira, offers one-hour guided tours of the Creek by dhow daily at 11.30am, 1.30pm, 3.30pm, 5.30pm and 7.30pm for Dh35 per person. It also offers dinner cruises on Tuesday and Sunday for Dh240, and the charter of larger boats.

Danat Dubai Cruises *(Map 4, #50; ☎ 351 1117; Al-Seef Rd, Bur Dubai)* offers a sundowner cruise (Dh95/35 for adults/children) from 6.30pm to 8pm Sunday to Friday, and a dinner cruise (Dh195/130) from 8.45pm to 11.15pm Sunday to Friday. Both cruises include free beer and wine.

For Dh270 with **Arabian Adventures** *(Map 2, #30; ☎ 303 4888; Sheikh Zayed Rd)*, next to Metropolitan Resort & Beach Club, or Dh210 with **Orient Tours** *(Map 3, #13; ☎ 282 8238; Al-Garhoud Rd, Al-Garhoud)*, you can take a dhow dinner cruise along the Creek. Both companies will pick you up from your hotel and drop you back.

Creek Cruises *(Map 5, #52; ☎ 393 3333; Quay 2/3, Dhow Wharfage, Deira)* has a fleet of boats for hire, including the *Malika al-Khor*, which can accommodate 125 people. Contact them for prices and cruise timings.

For something different, take a ride on *Seascope* to see some of the marine life around Dubai. This semisubmersible lives

THINGS TO SEE & DO

at the Diving Village (Map 4, #3) in Shindagha and can take up to 24 people for a 45-minute cruise along the Dubai coast. The cost is Dh55 per person. Contact **Sam Tours** (☎ 393 8904) for bookings.

Ice Skating

Believe it or not, Dubai has two ice rinks and a junior ice hockey club – indoors of course. There is one at the **Hyatt Galleria** (Map 3, #1; ☎ 209 6550; off Al-Khaleej Rd; bus Nos 8, 16, 19 & 20); sessions cost Dh25/15 with/without skate hire and the times are from 10am to 1.30pm, 2pm to 5.30pm and 6pm to 9.30pm Saturday to Thursday. It closes at 8pm on Friday. Wearing socks is mandatory and unless you bring your own you will have to pay an additional Dh5 to buy some.

There is another rink at **Al-Nasr Leisure-Land** (Map 3, #27; ☎ 337 1234; off Oud Metha Rd; bus No 14), in Oud Metha. Admission costs Dh10 plus a Dh10 skating fee. Sessions last two hours, starting at 10am, 1pm, 4pm and 7.30pm.

Horse Riding

Given the deep interest of the ruling Al-Maktoum family in all things equestrian, it's perhaps no surprise that Dubai has a world-class riding school. The **Dubai Equestrian Centre** (Map 2, #31; ☎ 336 1394), near the Nad al-Sheba racecourse, has dressage arenas, a floodlit main arena, training facilities and stables for 150 horses

Five one-hour lessons cost Dh525/475 for adults/children. Children can also take five 30-minute lessons for Dh150. Lessons are held from 6.30am to 9.30am and 4.30pm to 7pm daily.

Club Joumana (☎ 883 6000) is at the Jebel Ali Hotel (see Jebel Ali in the Excursions chapter), about 30 minutes by car from central Dubai. Tuition is good value at Dh60 for 30 minutes or Dh115 for one hour. Lessons are given daily except Monday, but not between June and September.

Health Clubs

All five-star and most mid-range hotels have health clubs, which are free for guests. The

facilities of the larger places include a gym, sauna, swimming pool, squash courts and tennis courts. Generally, if you are not a guest at the hotel you must be a member or a member's guest to use the facilities. A few, however, accept day visitors for a fee. **The Creek Health Club** (Map 5, #57; ☎ 207 1712; Sheraton Dubai) charges Dh50 per day. **Le Mirage Dubai** (Map 3, #9; ☎ 702 2430; Le Meridien Dubai) charges Dh55 per day Saturday to Wednesday and Dh77 Thursday and Friday, while the **Griffins Health Club** (Map 5, #10; ☎ 607 7755; JW Marriott Hotel) is slightly more expensive at Dh66 for the day Saturday to Wednesday and Dh85 on Thursday and Friday. **Inter-Fitness** (Map 4, #60; ☎ 222 7171; Dubai Inter-Continental) charges Dh50 for the day Saturday to Wednesday and Dh75 on Thursday and Friday. If you decide to use one of the hotel beach clubs for the day you will have access to their gym facilities as well. This is not cheap, though, and the average day fee is Dh60 to Dh200. The most lavish health club is the **Assawan** at the Burj al-Arab (Map 2, #18) – annual membership is a breathtaking Dh20,000 and the day fee is Dh700!

If you are going to be in Dubai for a week or more you can join the exclusive **Pharaohs Club** (Map 3, #34; ☎ 324 0000), part of the Wafi City complex. This place is truly awesome, from the sphinxes and hieroglyphic columns at the entrance to the artificial beach and 'lazy river' on the rooftop. A week's membership costs Dh250, which is cheaper than paying Dh50 per day at the hotels or Dh200 per day to use the facilities at the beach clubs. Massages, spas and beauty treatments are available for men and women in luxurious surroundings – for a price of course. It has even got a climbing wall. If you are in the area, it's worth dropping in just to have a look at the facilities or to have lunch at one of the restaurants in the complex.

Desert Safaris

Desert safaris are popular activities for tourists and expats alike and a great way to experience the rugged terrain of the UAE. Driving over the dunes is exhilarating and sometimes quite frightening – it's easy

The exclusive Dubai Creek Golf & Yacht Club is one of three real-grass golf courses in Dubai

The Dubai World Cup is the world's richest horse race, with prize money of US$6 million

Once used to transport goods across the desert, camels are now bred for racing, a major sport in Dubai

Falconry is a traditional desert sport (top right) and Dubai even has its own falcon hospital (middle right). Today, however, you're more likely to go sandboarding (top left) or dune driving (bottom).

Dune Driving

It's not a good idea to drive on the dunes unless you know what you are doing, or you are accompanied by an experienced desert driver. Even if you are experienced, you should always travel with another vehicle in case you get seriously stuck in the sand and need help getting out. If you do go dune driving yourself, remember these basic tips:

• Always let someone know where you are going and how long you expect to be. Take a mobile phone with you.

• Deflate your tyres by one-third to a half (to between 15 and 20 psi). Check the condition of the tyres, and the spare tyre as well.

• Always engage low 4WD.

• Descend the slope of a dune straight down, not diagonally.

• Don't use your brakes – they'll dig the tyres into the sand. You need just enough momentum to get the car over the crest of the dune, no more and no less.

• If the tyres are spinning on a relatively flat area of sand, try driving slightly forward and slightly back a few times. This can compress the sand beneath the tyres enough to get traction.

• Always carry a spade, at least two flat pieces of wood or mats (to stick under the tyres if you get stuck), a tow rope, a tyre pump, a jack and spare petrol and water (for you and the car).

• If you're really stuck, don't leave your car. Your chances of being found are much lower if you're trying to walk out of the desert alone.

enough to roll down the side of a dune if you are an inexperienced driver. There are dozens of off-road 4WD jaunts from Dubai that take in amazing desert and mountain scenery, wadis (seasonal river beds), ruins, archaeological sites and remote villages. Having said this you should keep in mind that 'bashing' around the place in a 4WD is potentially damaging to the environment (see the Responsible Tourism section in the Facts for the Visitor chapter).

The best way to enjoy a desert or wadi drive is to book a trip with one of the many tour operators (see Organised Tours in the Getting Around chapter for a list of operators). Generally speaking, a half-day desert safari or wadi drive with lunch/dinner costs around Dh250 per person. They usually leave Dubai in the afternoon so that you can see the sun set over the desert. Overnight desert trips cost Dh350 to Dh450. This will get you some dune driving, a camel ride, a barbecue dinner (maybe with a belly dancer for entertainment) and a night at a Bedouin-style camp site.

You could also rent a 4WD, but at around Dh900 a day, this option is out of reach of most travellers' budgets. Also, unless you are an experienced desert driver, it's not a good idea to take to the sands on your own. Desert driving courses are available, however. If you do know what you're doing and want to do some off-road driving, the *UAE Off-Road Explorer* is the best guide available.

There are a number of desert driving rallies throughout the year, including events organised by the **Emirates Motor Sports Federation** (☎ 282 7111; W *www.emsf.org .ae*). The most popular event is the *Gulf News* Overnight Fun Drive, held annually in late January. In 2002 there were 750 participating vehicles (the maximum number allowed) in a two-day drive over the dunes from Dubai to Hatta. If you are interested in the Fun Drive, call ☎ 344 7100; you'll need to get your tickets well in advance.

Sandboarding

This sport involves a monoski and an arduous climb up the highest dune you can find. Alas, there are no ski lifts.

Arabian Adventures (Map 2, #30; ☎ 343 9966; Emirates Holidays Bldg, Interchange No 2, Sheikh Zayed Rd) charges Dh195 for a half-day of sand-skiing and camel riding. The camels take you to the top of the dune, then you plane down.

Orient Tours (Map 3, #13; ☎ 282 8238; Al-Garhoud Rd, Al-Garhoud) will also take you sand-skiing and camel riding for Dh180/ 125 for adults/children. They'll pick you up and drop you back at your hotel.

Go-Karting

The best facilities in Dubai Emirate, and in the Middle East for that matter, are at **Go-Karting** (☎ 349 7393; open 2pm-dusk Mon, noon-dusk Tues-Sun), in Jebel Ali, just beyond the main entrance to the Jebel Ali Hotel. It costs Dh75 for 15 minutes and floodlit functions can be arranged.

Dubai Kart Club (☎ 050-651 5945) is based at the same place as Go-Karting. Membership costs Dh850 per annum, and competition days are held 14 times a year, culminating in the UAE championship. If you are catching public transport, minibuses only go as far as Jebel Ali Port so you will have to catch a taxi the rest of the way. Alternatively, it costs around Dh65 one way in a metered taxi from the centre of Dubai.

Formula One (Map 2, #25; ☎ 338 8828; Sheikh Zayed Rd; open 10am-10pm daily), near the Oasis Centre at Interchange No 2, charges Dh40 for 10 minutes, or Dh60 for 30 minutes. They also have an 'endurance race', which costs Dh140 per person with a minimum of eight drivers. To get there, turn left at the interchange, then immediately right at the sign that says 'Oasis Centre'. Turn right at the first street then left and continue along this road for 2.1km.

Chevrolet Grand Prix Karting (Map 3, #36; ☎ 334 1222; admission Dh10 Thur-Sat, Dh20 Fri; open noon-8pm daily), at the Wonder-Land amusement park near Al-Garhoud Bridge on the Dubai side of the Creek, has a 450m outdoor go-kart track. It costs Dh35 for 10 minutes, in addition to the entrance fee.

COURSES
Language Courses

Most language courses on offer are for English. There are only a few places where English speakers can study Arabic. This is because of the great demand by national students and expats from the subcontinent who want to improve their employment opportunities in the world of business, which is dominated by the English language.

Polyglot Language Institute (Map 4, #61; ☎ 222 3429; e polynet@emirates.net.ae; Al-Masaeed Bldg, Al-Maktoum Rd, Deira) offers beginner courses and conversation classes in Arabic, French, German and English. A 10-week Arabic course with three classes per week costs Dh1000.

Arabic Language Centre (Map 7, #19; ☎ 308 6036; e laura@dwtc.com; Dubai World Trade Centre, Sheikh Zayed Rd) offers five courses a year in Arabic from beginner to advanced levels.

British Council (Map 3, #24; ☎ 337 1540; w www.britcon.org/uae), on the Dubai side of the Creek just to the right of the entrance to Al-Maktoum Bridge, has intensive courses in Arabic for beginners. Eight sessions of three hours each costs Dh750.

Berlitz Language School (Map 3, #47; ☎ 344 0034; Jumeira Rd) offers courses in a number of languages, including Arabic and Urdu. The latter is useful to know to some extent as this is the language of so many of the Pakistani expats in the UAE.

Diving

There are half a dozen or so companies in Dubai offering diving courses. The companies listed here offer Professional Association of Divers International (PADI) certified courses, ranging from beginner to instructor level.

Al-Boom Diving (Map 7, #33; ☎ 342 2993; Al-Wasl Rd, Jumeira) offers open-water courses for Dh1600; advanced courses cost Dh900. It has two classrooms and a swimming pool for training.

Scubatec Diving Centre (Map 6, #38; ☎ 334 8988; Sana Bldg, cnr Sheikh Khalifa bin Zayed & Al-Adhid Rds, Karama) charges between Dh1500 and Dh2000 for an open-water course, and Dh800 for an advanced open-water course.

Inner Space Diving Centre (Map 4, #3; ☎ 331 7775; Diving Village, Shindagha) is another PADI diving school, which also caters to divers with a disability. Prices are available on request.

Scuba International (Map 4, #3; ☎ 393 7557; Diving Village, Shindagha) has a beginner's course for Dh1600 that takes about four days to complete. If you don't have your own mask, fins and snorkel you can hire them for Dh100.

Time Out and *Dubai Explorer* have full listings of the diving courses on offer in Dubai.

4WD Desert Driving

Driving over dunes is a thrill, but it takes a certain amount of practice and skill.

Voyagers Xtreme *(Map 7, #5;* ☎ *345 5770; Piva Travel, Dune Centre, Al-Dhiyafah Rd)* runs a 'Dune Driving Academy'. A one-day course costs Dh690, including one Land Cruiser for three people, a lead vehicle, instructor, lunch and soft drinks. It requires a minimum of three people. It also offers a two-day course for Dh1750 (minimum six people) which ventures deep into the dunescape of the Empty Quarter, south of Abu Dhabi.

Sahara Tours *(*☎ *06-552 1153)* in Sharjah offers private desert driving tuition for people with their own vehicles. Prices are available on request.

Places to Stay

With around 450 hotels and more on the way, Dubai doesn't lack for accommodation options; except, alas, for cheap and cheerful independent backpacker hostels. The area around the Deira souq (Map 4) has the only real budget hotels. It's handy because of its central location, although it's Dubai's most densely packed neighbourhood and can be quite noisy. Bur Dubai (Map 4) and Rigga (Map 5) are also fairly central, though there are not as many cheap hotels. Bur Dubai has plenty of hotel apartments, which can be the best value if you're planning to stay for longer than a fortnight or so. The luxury beach hotels down past Umm Suqeim (Map 2) are perfect for a beach holiday, but they are a long way from the centre.

The hotel prices we've quoted are inclusive of municipal tax (10%) and service charge (10%). Keep in mind that these are the hotels' rack rates. This means they are the standard, published, high-season rates. They only apply when people walk in off the street and are willing to pay any price to get a room, and the hotel is nearly full. Discounts are almost always offered on the rack rates so make sure you ask. We were generally offered a 30% discount, and often it was more like 50%. The trick is, don't look too desperate (don't drag in your luggage), and don't be afraid to walk away; at that point rates will often drop. Having business cards to show means you can qualify as a corporate client, which earns a substantial discount. During summer the tourist traffic really drops off so from mid-May to mid-September hotels drop their rates, often by between 50% and 70%. Throughout Ramadan (for dates, see Public Holidays in the Facts for the Visitor chapter) and on weekends during the Dubai Shopping Festival (March) most hotels drop their rates by about 50%.

All mid-range and top-end hotels require you to leave your passport in their safe for the duration of your stay. They also require you to leave a credit-card authorisation of about Dh500 per night. If you don't have a credit card you will have to leave a cash deposit. This can make things difficult if you don't have a lot of cash with you, or if your credit card is nearly at its limit.

PLACES TO STAY – BUDGET
Camping
There are no official camp sites in or around Dubai. Camping in the desert or on beaches is quite common outside Dubai, but this is usually done in the more mountainous areas around the east coast. The best time to camp is November to March, when it's not too hot.

Hostels
Dubai Youth Hostel *(Map 3, #6; ☎ 298 8161; e uaeyha@emirates.net.ae; Al-Nahda Rd; dorm beds Dh35-50, singles Dh60-80, doubles Dh120-145)* has the cheapest accommodation in town. To get there from central Deira take Salahuddin Rd to Al-Giyada Intersection, turn left into Al-Ittihad Rd, and then right onto Al-Nahda (Qusais) Rd. The place on the left with a stadium is the Al-Ahli Club, the hostel is another 100m along on the same side of the road. The hostel has an old wing with two- and three-bed dorms, and a new wing with very comfortable single and double rooms. Rooms in the new wing have air-con, TVs, minifridge and bathrooms and are as good as a three-star hotel. Breakfast is available for Dh10 and lunch and dinner for Dh15. Women, as well as men, can be accommodated and there are separate rooms for families.

If you don't have a Hostelling International (HI) card, the dorm beds and rooms cost an extra Dh15 per night. Membership cards are available from the hostel and from DNATA outlets around town and at the DNATA Airline Centre (Map 5, #19) on Al-Maktoum Rd. There is no age limit.

Bus No 13 runs from the Deira bus station to the hostel every 10 minutes from 6am until 11.45pm. The fare is Dh1. A taxi from central Deira will cost about Dh14.

Hotels

Dubai's hotels are scattered over a wide area. The cheapies are concentrated in the Deira souq area (Map 4), particularly along Al-Sabkha Rd and in the side streets off Suq Deira St. All the hotels listed have rooms with fridges and TVs.

The budget hotels bottom out around Dh70 to Dh80 for a single and Dh100 to Dh120 for a double. There are places with quasi-permanent male guests that are Dh10 to Dh15 cheaper, but they're pretty grim and we wouldn't recommend them.

Quite a few hotels and hotel residences in Deira and Bur Dubai are bases for prostitution. However, this business is often restricted to the hotel bar. If there's a billboard advertising a nightclub featuring nothing but women in garish make-up, that's probably the deal. For solo male travellers, the staff may assume you're staying there to take advantage of the ladies' hospitality. Single women travellers staying at these places run the slight risk of being mistaken for a prostitute, but that's as far as the problem goes. It is unlikely you will suffer any harassment beyond a misguided solicitation. It's better to stay at places that advertise themselves as 'family hotels'. This means that they will not accept single men but will usually accept single women and couples, and have strict policies about visitors in guests' rooms. If you are a single man, you may be accepted at the family hotels, as long as you do not bring home company.

Deira The following hotels are very similar so if money is your only concern, simply go with the cheapest. Solo women might want to try the first four listed.

Al-Khayam Hotel (Map 4, #94; ☎ 226 4211; e khayamh@emirates.net.ae; Suq Deira St; singles/doubles Dh150/180) is a respectable 'family' hotel (so no 'night visitors') with only 26 rooms, which are smallish but clean.

Gold Plaza Hotel (Map 4, #96; ☎ 225 0240, fax 225 0259; Suq Deira St; singles/doubles with balcony Dh125/150), a family hotel, is right at the entrance to the Gold Souq. The rooms are small and have tiled

floors. Some of the bathrooms need renovating, but otherwise it's not bad.

Hotel La Paz (Map 4, #95; ☎ 226 8800; e lapazhtl@emirates.net.ae; Suq Deira St; singles/doubles Dh120/170) is a clean family hotel with friendly English-speaking staff, but the rooms are only average quality.

Deira Palace Hotel (Map 4, #92; ☎ 229 0120, fax 225 5889; 67 St; singles/doubles Dh130/150) is a large family hotel, with clean rooms but somewhat uncomfortable beds.

Al-Khail Hotel (Map 4, #91; ☎ 226 9171, fax 226 9226; Naif Rd; rooms Dh100) is one of the cheaper hotels in Deira, but the rooms are only just OK.

Metro Hotel (Map 4, #98; ☎ 226 0040, fax 226 2098; 32 St; singles/doubles/triples Dh80/100/130) in an alley between Sikkat al-Khail and Al-Soor Sts, has OK rooms, but accepts families only.

New Avon Hotel (Map 4, #86; ☎ 226 1233; e avongrp@emirates.net.ae; Al-Sabkha Rd; singles/doubles Dh140/180) is a cheapie with pretty ordinary rooms and bathrooms. The clientele is predominantly male.

Vienna Hotel (Map 4, #88; ☎ 221 8855, fax 221 2928; Al-Sabkha Rd; singles/doubles Dh120/150) is a spartan budget hotel without much to recommend it other than it isn't a base for prostitution, as far as we know.

Bur Dubai This area, strictly speaking, runs north–south from the Creek to Khalid bin al-Waleed Rd and west–east from Al-Khaleej Rd to Sheikh Khalifa bin Zayed Rd, although the entire area on this side of the Creek is often also referred to as Bur Dubai.

Hyde Park Hotel (Map 4, #24; ☎ 393 9373; e hydepark@emirates.net.ae; 38 St; singles/doubles Dh165/220) is one of the very few cheap hotels on this side of the Creek. It is basic but clean and comfortable (with strange dark cane furniture) and it is well located near the Bur Dubai bus station.

Time Palace Hotel (Map 4, #20; ☎ 353 2111; 34 St; singles/doubles Dh180/240), the only other cheap hotel in Bur Dubai, is on the edge of Dubai Souq. The rooms are small and slightly musty, but the sheets and bathrooms are kept clean. The entrance is in an alley just off 34 St.

Panorama Hotel *(Map 6, #2; ☎ 351 8518;* e *panhotel@emirates.net.ae; Al-Mankhool Rd; singles/doubles Dh250/350)* is a rather old building but it's in a good location and the rooms are quite large, though not noise-proofed. It used to be a hotel apartment building. The hotel bar is frequented by the Dubai demimonde – approach with caution.

PLACES TO STAY – MID-RANGE

Unless otherwise stated, all hotels in this price range have business centres with Internet access and secretarial services. Most offer courtesy buses to and from the airport.

Deira

Victoria Hotel *(Map 4, #85; ☎ 226 9626, fax 226 9575; 20 St; singles/doubles Dh200/250)* is a decent, if dull, place, in an alley near the intersection of Al-Sabkha and Al-Maktoum Hospital Rds. The hotel doesn't have business facilities.

Hotel Delhi Darbar *(Map 4, #100; ☎ 273 3555, fax 273 3737; Naif Rd; singles/doubles Dh175/250)*, as its name indicates, is an Indian-oriented establishment. It's better than most of the hotels in this area, featuring spacious clean rooms with decent bathrooms, minifridge and TV. There's an Indian restaurant on the ground floor.

Hotel Florida International *(Map 4, #89; ☎ 224 7777;* e *floridai@emirates.net.ae; Al-Sabkha Rd; singles/doubles Dh300/400)* is a new hotel in the heart of Deira, opposite the Al-Sabkha Rd bus station. The rooms are on the small side but nicely furnished. We were offered a 50% discount quite quickly.

St George Hotel *(Map 4, #11; ☎ 225 1122;* e *stgeorge@emirates.net.ae; Al-Ahmadiya St; singles/doubles Dh590/710)* is a large establishment in the Al-Ras district, behind the public library. The views are great but the rooms are looking shabby, and there were prostitutes in the ground-floor coffee shop. It would be a good place if the management picked up its act.

Landmark Hotel *(Map 4, #78; ☎ 228 6666;* e *land1@emirates.net.ae; Baniyas Square; singles/doubles Dh550/660)*, on the north side of the square, is the best hotel in the area. Members of staff are efficient and keen to please and the hotel has parking for guests. Guests staying on business can get discounts of around 50%. There's a small swimming pool on the roof.

Ramee International Hotel *(Map 4, #77; ☎ 224 0222;* e *rameedxb@emirates.net.ae; 9C St; singles/doubles Dh250/350)*, a busy hotel off Baniyas Square, is good value, given the standard of rooms.

Phoenicia Hotel *(Map 4, #75; ☎ 222 7191;* e *hotphone@emirates.net.ae; Baniyas Square; singles/doubles Dh220/330)* is a large establishment in a central location. The rooms are quite nice, but the hotel's bars seemed a bit sleazy.

Riviera Hotel *(Map 4, #65; ☎ 222 2131;* e *riviera@emirates.net.ae; Baniyas Rd; singles/doubles Dh500/625)* is somewhat overpriced for what you get, but the rooms overlooking the Creek have a great view of the bustling dhow docks.

Rigga

This area runs west to east from Omar ibn al-Khattab Rd to Abu Baker al-Siddiq Rd and south to north from Al-Maktoum Rd to Al-Muraqqabat Rd. There are lots of restaurants and shops around here. You're just a short stroll from the Creek front as well as being close to Al-Maktoum Bridge, so getting to places on the other side of the Creek is quick and easy.

Lords Hotel *(Map 5, #33; ☎ 228 9977;* e *lords@emirates.net.ae; Al-Jazeira St; singles/doubles Dh495/605, executive suite Dh1440)* has spacious rooms and bathrooms and is quite good value.

Orchid Hotel *(Map 5, #45; ☎ 295 6999;* e *orchidsl@emirates.net.ae; 40C St; singles/doubles/triples Dh420/480/550)* is off 37 St, near the Clock Tower Roundabout, between Al-Rigga and Al-Maktoum Rds. It seems to be popular with Russians and Arab travellers, and has some colourful bars and nightclubs.

Sun and Sand Hotel *(Map 5, #41; ☎ 223 9000;* e *sshtl@emirates.net.ae; 37 St; singles/doubles Dh450/550, suite 2000)* is a boldly decorated place – the suite with the mirrored walls and ceilings would only appeal to some. However, it's a respectable establishment, with clean rooms.

Nihal Hotel (Map 5, #44; ☎ 295 7666; e nihalhtl@emirates.net.ae; 40 St; singles/doubles Dh390/540, executive suite Dh780), near the Orchid Hotel, is a good option for women travellers. The suites each have a small sitting room, enormous bathroom, bedroom and a kitchen with all the trimmings. The hotel is starting to age a bit, however.

Sheraton Deira (Map 5, #5; ☎ 268 8888; e shedeira@emirates.net.ae; Al-Mateena St; singles/doubles Dh462.50/500), situated on the outskirts of the interesting part of Deira, is very much geared towards business

guests. It is rated as a five-star hotel, so it's rather good value. It has a business and conference centre, and is fairly close to the airport. It's not to be confused with the Sheraton Dubai, which is on the Creek (see Places to Stay – Top End for details).

Quality Inn Horizon (Map 5, #25; ☎ 227 1919; e qualitin@emirates.net.ae; Al-Rigga Rd; singles/doubles Dh540/660) is a comfortable three-star hotel with decent-sized rooms. There's a small rooftop swimming pool.

Mayfair Hotel (Map 5, #40; ☎ 228 4444; e mayfair@emirates.net.ae; 42A St; singles/doubles Dh650/750), just north of Al-Maktoum Rd, is starting to look tired but is well set up for business travellers.

The Call to Prayer

If you haven't visited a Muslim country before, be prepared to be awoken at about 4.30am each morning by an inimitable wailing. This is the azan, the call to prayer. At the first sign of dawn, you'll hear a cacophony of droning sounds as muezzins chant the call to prayer through speaker phones positioned high up on the minaret of each mosque. Before speaker phones were used to tear people from their beds, the muezzins used to climb the minarets and call out from the top.

There are five prayers each day: at dawn; when the sun is directly overhead; when the sun is in the position that makes the shadow of an object the same length as that object; at the beginning of sunset; and at twilight when the last light of the day disappears over the horizon. Of course, things are worked out a little more technically than this and exact times are printed in the daily newspapers.

Once the call has been made, Muslims have half an hour in which to pray. There is an exception for the dawn prayer; after the call they have about an hour and 20 minutes in which to wake up and pray, before the sun has risen. The sixth time printed in newspapers indicates this sunrise deadline.

If Muslims aren't near a mosque, they can pray anywhere, so long as they face Mecca. You'll find a qibla (a niche that indicates the direction of Mecca) in every hotel room in Dubai.

If someone cannot get to a mosque, they will stop wherever they are to pray – by the side of the road, in hotel lobbies, in shops – so you may have to step around people occasionally. This is OK, just be as unobtrusive as you can, and if possible don't walk in front of them. All public buildings, such as government departments, libraries, shopping centres, airports etc, have prayer rooms or designated areas where people can pray.

The phrase that you will be able to make out most often during the call to prayer is Allah-u-akbar which means 'God is Great'. This is repeated four times at the start of the azan. Next comes Ashhadu an la illallah ha-Illaah = 'I testify there is no god but God'. This is repeated twice. So is the next line, Asshadu anna muhammadan rasuulu-ilaah, 'I testify that Mohammed is His messenger'. Then come two shorter lines, also sung twice; Hayya ala as-salaah (Come to prayer) and Hayya ala al-falaah (Come to salvation). Allah-u-akbar is repeated two more times, and then comes the last line Laa ilaah illa allah – 'There is no god but God'.

The only prayer call with a difference is the one at dawn. In this azan, after the exhortation to come to salvation, comes the gently nudging extra line, also repeated, As-salaatu khayrun min al nawn, which translates as 'It is better to pray than to sleep'.

Bur Dubai

Admiral Plaza Hotel *(Map 4, #32;* ☎ *521 111;* e *admplaza@emirates.net.ae; Al-Nahda St; singles/doubles Dh240/350)* offers well-appointed but rather cramped rooms.

New Penninsula Hotel *(Map 4, #25;* ☎ *393 9111;* e *pennin@emirates.net.ae; Al-Raffa St; singles/doubles Dh420/540),* next to the Bur Dubai bus station, is handy for the *abra* (water taxi) station. The rooms are on the small side, but nicely furnished.

Ambassador Hotel *(Map 4, #22;* ☎ *393 9444;* e *ambhotel@emirates.net.ae; Al-Falah Rd; singles/doubles Dh312.50/475)* is one of the oldest hotels in Dubai (it was established in 1968), and has some very groovy '60s decor. The deluxe rooms (Dh480) are very spacious and have modular chairs that recall *A Clockwork Orange.*

Astoria Hotel *(Map 4, #26;* ☎ *353 4300;* e *reserve@astamb.com; Al-Nahda St; singles/ doubles Dh360/480)* is a large, rather ugly place, which has been around forever and a day. It's popular with groups from Russia and the subcontinent.

Regal Plaza Hotel *(Map 4, #44;* ☎ *355 6633;* e *rameedxb@emirates.net.ae; Al-Mankhool Rd; singles/doubles Dh600/700)* is near the corner with Khalid bin al-Waleed Rd. When we visited we were quoted a discounted price of Dh200 for a double, which is excellent value for the recently renovated rooms. Run by a reputable Indian hotel company, the hotel has a pub on the ground floor as well as a swimming pool. Definitely worth a try.

Four Points Sheraton *(Map 4, #45;* ☎ *397 7444;* e *fpshrdxb@emirates.net.ae; Khalid bin al-Waleed Rd; singles/doubles Dh720/840)* is a smallish hotel oriented towards business travellers, which has got good reports from several readers. The rooms are standard habitation cuboids, but it's a friendly place and the Viceroy bar on the 1st floor has leather couches to relax in.

Regent Palace Hotel *(Map 6, #24;* ☎ *396 3888;* e *rameedxb@emirates.net.ae; Sheikh Khalifa bin Zayed Rd; singles/doubles Dh720/ 840),* opposite the Bur Juman Centre, is a quiet hotel with a relaxing and leafy lobby area. Discounts are easily negotiated.

Capitol Hotel *(Map 7, #1;* ☎ *3460 111;* e *caphotel@emirates.net.ae; Al-Mina Rd, Satwa; singles/doubles Dh770/907.50)* is a subtly tasteful hotel, popular with flight crews and business travellers from the US. The huge rooms are beautifully furnished, and the neo–Art Deco lobby is stunning.

PLACES TO STAY – TOP END

Unless otherwise noted, all hotels in this category have business centres, conference facilities and swimming pools.

Deira

These two five-star hotels, although in an enviable position on the Creek, are a bit past their prime. With the proliferation of so many other top-end hotels in the city with better rates and newer furnishings, you're not really getting your money's worth here.

Dubai Inter-Continental Hotel *(Map 4, #60;* ☎ *222 7171;* e *intercon@emirates.net .ae; Baniyas Rd; singles/doubles Dh1416/ 1536)* is a huge hotel overlooking the Creek. It's a well-established hotel with a number of excellent restaurants, and it's enduringly popular with business travellers.

Sheraton Dubai *(Map 5, #57;* ☎ *228 1111;* e *sheradxb@emirates.net.ae; Baniyas Rd; rooms Dh1200)* has the best position in Deira, right on the edge of the Creek.

Hilton Dubai Creek *(Map 5, #51;* ☎ *227 1111;* e *hiltonck@emirates.net.ae; Baniyas Rd, Rigga; rooms from Dh1440)* is a classy boutique hotel with a stunning interior – all glass, chrome, stainless steel and wood. The rooms feature curved wooden wardrobes and black leather armchairs. Some rooms overlook the bustling dhow wharfage.

The Airport

Distances are all fairly small around Dubai, although traffic can be an issue during rush hour. If you really want to be sure you don't miss your plane, the following hotels are only three minutes from the airport by taxi.

Le Meridien Dubai *(Map 3, #9;* ☎ *282 4040;* e *lmdxb@emirates.net.ae; Airport Rd; singles/doubles from Dh1200/1320, suites from Dh1600)* is opposite the airport. Built around a grassy courtyard, the hotel has

14 different bars and restaurants, but the rooms are somewhat cramped. At these prices, you could stay somewhere better.

Al-Bustan Rotana *(Map 3, #12; ☎ 282 0000;* e *albustan.hotel@rotana.com; 16 St; singles/doubles Dh1080/1320)* backs on to Le Meridien and has a very impressive range of services. It's certainly one of the nicer hotels in Dubai and better value than Le Meridien.

Rigga
This district has the best range of three- and four-star hotels.

Avari Dubai Hotel *(Map 5, #46; ☎ 295 6666;* e *avarigst@emirates.net.ae; 45C St; singles/doubles Dh847/957, 2-room suite Dh1320)* is an average-standard hotel, most of whose clientele are Asian business travellers. It is set back off the west side of Abu Bakr al Siddiq Rd, near the Clock Tower Roundabout. The suite is good value compared with suites at other hotels in this price range.

Holiday Inn Downtown *(Map 5, #23; ☎ 228 8889;* e *hidowtwn@emirates.net.ae; 37 St; singles/doubles Dh550/650, suite Dh1260)* is north of Al-Rigga Rd is a fairly subdued business-oriented hotel but the rooms are large and luxurious. You could do a lot worse in this price range.

Hyatt Regency Dubai *(Map 3, #1; ☎ 209 1234;* e *hyattbus@emirates.net.ae; off Al-Khaleej Rd; singles/doubles Dh1164/1254, suites from Dh2100)* is the great brute of a building you'll have trouble ignoring between Al-Khaleej Rd and the Corniche. Rooms here have great views over the Gulf, Dubai and Sharjah. It has business and conference facilities for up to 2000 people, as well as two cinemas.

JW Marriott Hotel *(Map 5, #10; ☎ 262 4444;* e *marriott@emirates.net.ae; Abu Baker al-Siddiq Rd; rooms from Dh1260, executive suites Dh3000)* is one of the most impressive five-star hotels in Dubai. It's beautifully decorated and standard rooms are very luxurious and spacious. It also has a Royal Suite, which will set you back a mere Dh18,000.

Renaissance Dubai Hotel *(Map 5, #4; ☎ 262 5555;* e *rendubai@emirates.net.ae;* *Salahuddin Rd; rooms from Dh1050, executive suite Dh2400)* is a plush business hotel run by the Marriott chain, in a not very interesting part of Rigga. It offers substantial discounts to corporate clients; up to 70% off the rack rates we've quoted.

Metropolitan Palace Hotel *(Map 5, #34; ☎ 227 0000;* e *metpalace@emirates.net.ae; Al-Maktoum Rd; singles/doubles Dh1260/ 1440, suites from Dh2040)* is a rather tacky five-star hotel (the building is a true architectural carbuncle) which serves mostly business clients.

Taj Palace Hotel *(Map 5, #37; ☎ 223 2222;* e *tajdubai@emirates.net.ae; 23D St, Rigga; singles/doubles Dh1100/1200, suites Dh2300)* is a vast new luxury hotel in the heart of Rigga. Interestingly, it's the only five-star hotel of its type without a liquor licence. The rooms are very elegant, and there's an apartment complex attached to the hotel.

Bur Dubai
Ramada Hotel *(Map 6, #4; ☎ 351 9999, fax 352 1033;* e *rhddxb@emirates.net.ae; Al-Mankhool Rd; singles/doubles Dh960/1080)* has an eye-catching 1970s stained-glass mural stretching the height of the atrium. The rooms are decent, if a bit dated, but the hotel has a good location.

Seashell Inn Hotel *(Map 4, #34; ☎ 393 4777;* e *sshellinn@emirates.net.ae; Khalid bin al-Waleed Rd; singles/doubles Dh840/ 960)* has nicely furnished rooms, but no swimming pool. It's centrally located, on a very busy road. The rates here seemed very optimistic for what you get; with a bit of bargaining you should be able to get mid-range prices.

The World Trade Centre Hotel *(Map 7, #20; ☎ 331 4000;* e *info@twtch-dubai.com, Sheikh Zayed Rd; rooms Dh1200)* was opened back in 1978, so while it isn't the flashiest hotel in town, it would suit people who have business at the adjacent Dubai World Trade Centre. Guests have access to the Jumeira Beach Club.

Crowne Plaza Hotel *(Map 3, #49; ☎ 331 1111;* e *hicpdxb@emirates.net.ae; Sheikh Zayed Rd; singles/doubles from Dh1100/ 1200, Royal Suite Dh11,100)* is part of an

PLACES TO STAY

enormous complex which includes bars, restaurants and a shopping centre. It's popular with business travellers as it is well set up for conferences and meetings. The executive floors are especially plush, in a kind of French Restoration style.

Rydges Plaza Hotel *(Map 7, #10;* ☎ *398 2222;* e *rydges@emirates.net.ae; cnr Al-Dhiyafah & Al-Mankhool Rds, Satwa; standard rooms Dh850, executive suites Dh1000)* is part of an Australian chain of hotels. The exterior belies the fine refurbishing job they've done on the rooms. Rates are highly negotiable (around Dh300 per night if you stay a week), and this place has been recommended as a good business hotel in a handy location.

Emirates Towers *(Map 3, #51;* ☎ *330 0000;* e *eth@emirates-towers-hotel.com; Sheikh Zayed Rd; doubles from Dh1440, Royal Suite Dh7200)* is the tallest hotel in the Middle East, a slick, ultramodern monument to Dubai's self-confidence. But they still play a muzak version of 'Candle in the Wind' in the lobby, which slightly detracts from its supercool Armani-meets-Tokyo design motifs. It's in the smaller of the two towers.

Dusit Dubai *(Map 3, #59;* ☎ *343 3333;* e *ddd@dusit.com; Sheikh Zayed Rd; rooms Dh850)* is the startling blue-clad edifice shaped like an upside-down letter 'Y'. The rooms are exceptionally comfortable with luxurious Thai furnishings, and there's a spectacular view from the rooftop pool on the 36th floor.

Beach Hotels

If you come to Dubai on a package holiday, you will probably stay at one of the five-star hotels along the beach on the way south from Dubai to Jebel Ali. These luxurious hotels are about 30km from the centre of Dubai; getting into town costs about Dh50 in a taxi. All the hotels provide shuttle buses to major shopping centres and to Baniyas Square, which operate two or three times a day. All have beach clubs and pools and offer a variety of water sports. The hotels in this section are listed from the Dubai side towards Jebel Ali.

Dubai Marine Beach Resort & Spa *(Map 7, #27;* ☎ *346 111;* e *dxbmarine@emirates .net.ae; Jumeira Rd, Jumeira; singles/doubles Dh1000/1200)* has villa-style rooms set in attractive tropical gardens, with lots of small fountains and ponds. However, the resort's beach is rather meagre and the rooms could use a revamp. The resort puts more effort into its many bars and restaurants – you certainly won't lack for nightlife if you stay here.

Jumeira Beach Club *(Map 3, #64;* ☎ *344 5333;* e *info@jumeirahinternational.com; Jumeira Rd, Jumeira; suites from Dh2880)* is a small, intimate resort with suites in pavilions separated by lush tropical gardens. It's in the heart of Jumeira, but the city feels far away. The suites have a Southeast Asian feel to them – lots of wood and broad balconies. The swimming pool and the stretch of beach here are lovely.

Jumeira Beach Hotel *(Map 2, #20;* ☎ *348 0000;* e *reservations@jumeirahinternational .com; Jumeira Rd, Umm Suqeim; singles/ doubles Dh1560/1650)* is the broad wave-shaped building at the foot of the Burj al-Arab. With 618 rooms it's one of the biggest hotels in Dubai, and has 19 bars, cafés and restaurants plus a shopping arcade.

Burj al-Arab *(Map 2, #18;* ☎ *301 7777;* e *reservations@jumeirahinternational.com; Jumeira Rd, Umm Suqeim; singles/doubles Dh3200/6700)* is perhaps a bit expensive as far as a place to lay your head goes, but that's probably not why you'd stay here. If the idea of paying a huge sum of money to stay in a suite with your own private butler appeals, go for it. The hotel is 320m high, on an artificial island 280m offshore from the Jumeira Beach Hotel. It comprises 202 suites, includes a helipad, and has an extraordinary, almost cartoonish interior; everything that looks gold is gold.

Royal Mirage *(Map 2, #9;* ☎ *399 9999;* e *royalmirage@royalmiragedubai.com; Al-Sufouh Rd; singles/doubles Dh1950/2160)* is the closest rival to the Burj al-Arab. Built as a fantasy image of an Arabian palace, the gold statues of sheikhs on camels at the entrance set the tone. The hotel also features a beachfront date-palm oasis, burbling canals and a spectacular lobby. Cynics might say it's Disney meets Arabia, but it's actually quite beautiful, and much more restrained than the Burj. Suffice to say, staying here isn't cheap.

Le Meridien Mina Seyahi Resort *(Map 2, #8; ☎ 399 3333; e reservations@lemeridien-minaseyahi.com; Al-Sufouh Rd; rooms without/with sea view Dh1200/1400)* is a resort hotel with all the five-star accoutrements. The hotel is less oppressively large than some, and has an elegant Art Deco–influenced interior.

Metropolitan Resort & Beach Club *(Map 2, #6; ☎ 399 5000; e metbeach@emirates.net .ae; Al-Sufouh Rd; singles/doubles Dh1250/1350)* is a leafy low-rise resort with tropical gardens and a pleasantly relaxed atmosphere. The rooms are fairly modest compared with some of the other resorts.

Le Royal Meridien Beach Resort *(Map 2, #5; ☎ 399 5555; e reservations@leroyal meridien-dubai.com; Al-Sufouh Rd; singles/ doubles Dh1200/1440)* is a massive three-towered resort complex with the ambience of a financial centre. It has a wide range of bars and restaurants.

The Ritz-Carlton *(Map 2, #4; ☎ 399 4000; e rcdubai@emirates.net.ae; Al-Sufouh Rd; rooms from Dh2050)* is one of the most luxurious hotels in Dubai, with a design that looks like a meeting of Beverley Hills and Spanish Mission style. The gardens are unusually attractive, and the rooms are furnished in a comfortable clubbish style, with lots of overstuffed armchairs and Liberty prints.

Oasis Beach Hotel *(Map 2, #3; ☎ 399 4444; e oasisbeachhotel@dutcohotels.com; Al-Sufouh Rd; singles/doubles Dh840/960)* is a step down from its neighbours, with tacky tropical decorations and unexceptional rooms. Still, if it's beach and sunshine you want, it's as good as any of its neighbours.

Hilton Dubai Jumeirah *(Map 2, #2; ☎ 399 1111; e hiltonjb@emirates.net.ae; Al-Sufouh Rd; singles/doubles Dh1250/1350)* only opened in 2000 and is one of the nicer hotels on this strip. Over three-quarters of the rooms have beach views, and there's a spacious stretch of beach frontage.

Sheraton Jumeirah Beach Resort & Towers *(Map 2, #1; ☎ 399 5533; e sheraton .jumeirah.dxb@starwoodhotels.com; Al-Sufouh*

Rd; singles/doubles Dh1200/1320)* is a modern resort hotel and the nearest beach hotel to the DEWA power station, which doesn't do much for the view. Nevertheless, the beachfront is nicely landscaped and the hotel is perfectly comfortable.

Ecotourism

Al-Maha Resort *(☎ 303 4224; w www.al-maha.com; Margham; 2-person suite US$1210 Oct-May, US$770 May-Sept)*, for something very different and very exclusive, is an eco-tourism resort about 65km southeast of Dubai off the Dubai–Al Ain highway. The resort has 30 standard suites and three ultra-luxurious ones; each suite is assigned a guest relations coordinator and wildlife field guide. The price includes meals and activities, such as dune driving, camel trekking and falconry. It is set in a 27-sq-km wildlife reserve surrounded by a 165-sq-km buffer zone, a beautiful desert landscape area of peach-coloured dunes. Each guest room is a luxurious, tent-style suite complete with Bedouin antiques and a private plunge pool. The main building is in the style of a Hatta nobleman's house, while the bar resembles a colonial-era safari lodge.

The area is home to endangered species such as the scimitar-horned oryx (*al-maha* in Arabic) and slender-horned gazelle, Arabian foxes and caracals. The resort uses recycled paper and packaging, biodegradable products and solar energy. There are also permanent exhibitions of paintings, sculptures and handicrafts by UAE artists. Children under 12 are not allowed at the resort.

LONG-TERM RENTALS

The Bur Dubai and Mankhool areas are riddled with suites and residences that rent rooms by the day, week, month or year. These places offer larger rooms than normal, with kitchens complete with cooking utensils. They also have pool and gym facilities. Most places will offer discounts on the rates we've quoted for stays of more than a week. The largest concentration of these residences is found between Al-Mankhool and Sheikh Khalifa bin Zayed Rds, just south of Khalid bin al-Waleed Rd.

PLACES TO STAY

This neighbourhood is often called Golden Sands, after the chain of hotel residences, though officially it is Mankhool, a name unfamiliar to every taxi driver.

Golden Sands 3 *(Map 6, #5;* ☎ *355 5551;* e *gldnsnds@emirates.net.ae; 10B St, Mankhool; rooms from Dh322)* and its neighbouring building, **Golden Sands 5** *(Map 6, #6)*, offers accommodation for short-term (less than three months) visitors. There are 10 Golden Sands buildings, mostly apartments leased out for six months or longer, and several more Silver Sands complexes owned by the same company. An apartment in Golden Sands 3 is much like a three-star hotel room, except that it also has an oven, a washer/dryer and basic kitchenware. If you stay longer than a week, rates can be negotiated down to about Dh150 per day.

Dubai World Trade Centre Apartments *(Map 7, #21;* ☎ *331 4555;* e *hotelapartments@dtwc.com; Sheikh Zayed Rd; rooms from Dh622)* is an older collection of apartment buildings near (you guessed it) the Dubai World Trade Centre. The rooms are looking a bit dowdy, but staying here gets you into the large sports club behind the complex, which features tennis courts, squash courts, a swimming pool etc.

Rolla Residence *(Map 4, #37;* ☎ *359 2000;* e *rollabus@emirates.net.ae; Al-Rolla Rd; rooms Dh600)* is a mid-range apartment complex in a fairly central location.

Capitol Residence *(Map 4, #35;* ☎ *393 2000;* e *capres@emirates.net.ae; 14A St, rooms Dh500)* is a new hotel residence complex in a slightly downmarket neighbourhood, just off Khalid bin al-Waleed Rd. The rooms are unusually large, big enough for three adults.

Savoy Residence *(Map 6, #8;* ☎ *355 3000;* e *savoy@emirates.net.ae; 12A St; rooms Dh440)* is rather luxurious and has the added bonus of a washing machine in each room.

Pearl Residence *(Map 6, #9;* ☎ *355 8111;* e *pearlres@emirates.net.ae; 18B St; rooms Dh450)* is one of the smarter places in the area. Rooms are large, but very bland. There is a washing machine in each room.

Al-Hina Residence *(Map 6, #7;* ☎ *355 5510;* e *hinarest@emirates.net.ae; 7 St; rooms Dh300)* has rooms which are spacious and have washing machines.

Places to Eat

The cultural mix of people in Dubai is reflected in the city's restaurants and cafés. Cheap Indian and Pakistani restaurants are everywhere, catering to the huge expat population. Filipino food is also very common, especially around the Karama shopping district. Chinese food is widely available, although its authenticity is sometimes open to question; often Chinese food tastes suspiciously like the national cuisine of the cook, usually Indian or Filipino. Lebanese and Iranian food is easy to find in all price ranges. At the top end of the market, you can satisfy just about any craving, from Mexican to Thai, Japanese to French. Fast-food chains have successfully infiltrated the streets of Dubai – you'll find them all over the city.

FOOD
There isn't much in the way of local cuisine in Dubai. Middle Eastern dishes are largely borrowed from other countries in the region, in particular Lebanon and Iran. The diet of the Bedouin who inhabited the area that is now Dubai consisted only of fresh fish, dried fish, dates, camel meat and camel milk. Traditional Emirati cuisine doesn't lend itself to tantalising interpretations of these ingredients.

Muslims do not eat pork, as it is *haram*, or forbidden by Islam. Sometimes, as an alternative to pork bacon, supermarkets sell beef bacon and turkey bacon. Dishes containing pork generally only appear on the menus of top-end restaurants. Meat consumed by Muslims must be *halal*, meaning religiously suitable or permitted. The animal must be killed by having its throat cut and the blood drained out before it is butchered. This is why much of the red meat slaughtered and sold locally is very pale in colour. If you are a red-meat eater you might find the taste of your steak a little bland here.

Indo-Pakistani
Indo-Pakistani fare in Dubai is tasty, cheap and available all over the city. Broadly speaking, there are two main cuisines. North Indian and Pakistani restaurants serve meat dishes and bread made of wheat, whereas South Indian restaurants tend to be vegetarian and serve breads or pancakes made from rice. Dishes such as biryani (rice with chicken or meat, flavoured with cardamom and other spices) are ubiquitous, but you'll also find *kima* (minced meat with peas and tomato) served with salad and *paratha*, an Indian bread; dhal (lentils); and roti (Indian breads). *Puri bhaji*, another common dish, is a delicious Indian breakfast dish of curried vegetables and flaky bread, usually served with a coconut dipping sauce, which you can only get before 10.30am. For lunch most South Indian restaurants offer a *thali*, a mini-smorgasbord served on a steel plate with different dishes in little metal bowls. It includes dry and wet vegetable dishes, rice, pickle, curd, a sweet, and lots of crispy pappadams (wafers made from dhal). The waiters will bring more rice until you've had enough. At the end of the meal, you'll be brought a little dish of hot water to wash your fingers. A *thali* lunch can be as cheap as Dh6. Another South Indian speciality is a *masala dosa*, a pancake made from fermented rice, rolled up with a spicy potato filling and eaten with *sambar* (a thin, spicy dipping 'soup'). They're cheap, filling and quite addictive. Many Indo-Pakistani restaurants have adopted a number of Arabic staples into their menus such as *moutabel* (eggplant and sesame-seed dip) and *fuul* (mashed and stewed broad beans).

In general, the small Indian-run places that call themselves 'cafés' serve only sandwiches, fruit juices and snacks such as samosas and *pakora* (bite-size pieces of vegetable dipped in chickpea-flour batter and deep-fried). The term 'sandwich' covers a variety of snacks. If you ask for a chicken or mutton sandwich, you're usually asking for a *shwarma* (strips of grilled meat). Sometimes, you'll get the meat served in a European-style roll or you may even get a chicken or mutton burger with chips. If you want to be sure of what you're getting, just look around at what other people are eating, or ask to be shown the bread. Omelette sandwiches make a great snack or breakfast. One- or two-egg omelettes are wrapped in Indian *paratha* bread with tomato, cucumber, onion and chilli. You can ask for the less greasy Arabic bread instead, if you prefer. The staff in these places are not scared to make a sandwich out of anything – you can also have a *kima* sandwich, *fuul* sandwich, *moutabel* sandwich or even a samosa sandwich if you ask for it.

Lebanese

Lebanese cuisine in Dubai is slightly different to Lebanese cuisine elsewhere, as it has adopted some of the traditional aspects of cooking from this part of the Arabian Peninsula. Lebanese restaurants are found all over Dubai and in all price ranges. All Lebanese dishes are served with pickles, piles of Arabic bread and a big plate of fresh salad, so you really get value for money.

Shwarma and felafels are the favoured snack and are available from most street cafés for about Dh3 each – just look for the huge grills outside restaurants. They always come with a small serve of pickled cucumbers and radishes. Lebanese appetisers are known as mezze. They include hummus (chickpea and garlic puree), which is also available with pine nuts mixed through it and/or small pieces of lamb; *arayes* (minced meat with spices, spread inside Arabic bread then fried); *fatayer* (baked pockets of pastry filled with minced meat, cheese or spinach); and *kibbeh* (delicious deep-fried balls of minced meat, with pine nuts, onion and cracked wheat), which is also served raw. A thick and creamy, cheesy yogurt called *labneh* is very popular among Arabs as a dip at the beginning of a meal, but it can also be bought in a slightly less viscous form as a drink. *Fattoush* is a salad of lettuce, tomato, cucumber, fried Arabic bread, and a lemon, garlic and olive-oil dressing. Another well known Lebanese salad is tabouleh, which is made from finely chopped parsley, tomato, cracked wheat and mint.

Main dishes include *kofta* (a grilled skewer of spicy minced lamb), various incarnations of shish kebab (pieces of grilled meat on a skewer) and shish *tawouq* (delicious spiced pieces of char-grilled chicken). If you want a little taste of everything, you should order a mixed grill, which is found on every menu.

Iranian

Though there are similarities with Lebanese cooking, Iranian food has its own style and flavours. The Iranians are big on *berenj* (spicy rice dishes, which are usually topped with nuts and raisins) and *koresh* (meat stews with vegetables). Kebabs are also a staple of Iranian cuisine, but the Iranian kebab is bigger, flatter and generally more substantial in texture and size than a Lebanese kebab, and it is served in many different ways. You'll find *chelow kebab* on every menu. It is a grilled kebab served on top of rice (*chelow* means a dish in which the rice has been cooked separately from the other ingredients). There are many different types of kebab, for instance *chelow kebab barg* is a kebab that is thinner than usual, *chelow kebab makhsous* is one that is thicker than usual, *bakhtari kebab* is served with grilled capsicum and a *lari kebab* is marinated and cooked in yogurt.

An Iranian-style biryani is called *Istanboli polow* and consists of rice with haricot beans and chicken or mutton on top. Other Iranian dishes include *baghleh polow* (rice with dill, broad beans and chicken or mutton) and *zereshk polow* (rice mixed with barberry and chicken).

A favourite in Iranian cooking is the buttery crust left at the bottom of the pan after rice is cooked. Anyone who doesn't serve this part of the rice dish to guests is considered either a bad cook or a bad host.

Iranian food is usually served with a plate of lettuce, cabbage, tomato and onion, with a minty yogurt sauce on the side. Naan (Iranian bread) is baked in different ways, but the most common variety in Dubai is *lavash*, which is thin, square and somewhat elastic.

DRINKS

Nonalcoholic drinks are widely available in Dubai; there are drink vending machines on just about every street corner. Mineral water and soft drinks cost Dh1 while most fruit juices cost Dh1 to Dh2. Freshly squeezed (and usually sweetened) juice is available from Indian and Lebanese cafés, which are plentiful in the souq areas of Bur Dubai and Deira. A glass costs Dh5.

For a really refreshing pick-me-up, try a cup of *chai* (tea) from any Indian café or restaurant. For 50 fils you get a cup of Lipton's with a good dash of Rainbow milk (sweetened milk) and loads of sugar. It'll really get you going. Western-style tea is also available in most hotels, restaurants and European-style cafés.

Coffee

In Arabic, coffee is called *qahwa*. Arabic coffee is flavoured with cardamom, which makes it green, or sometimes greenish-brown, in colour. The version served in Dubai is fairly tame, but should you ever find yourself out in the desert with Bedouin, be prepared for an extremely bitter taste. Arabic coffee is served in tiny handleless cups that hold only two or three sips worth. In many offices and in the lobbies of some hotels you'll see a thermos of coffee and a few cups. This is not for display so help yourself if you feel like it.

In restaurants and hotels in Dubai it is most likely that you will be offered Turkish coffee. This will usually be served *mazboot* (with medium sugar), unless you specify otherwise. If you only want a little sugar ask to have the coffee *areeha*; *khafeef* means with a lot of sugar and *saada* with no sugar at all. Turkish coffee is very thick and strong; even if you usually drink coffee without sugar, you will probably want to have at least some sugar in your Turkish coffee. Turkish coffee is served in small cups similar to those used for espresso. Don't drain your cup – you'll find a thick layer of grounds in the bottom of the cup.

There are a growing number of cafés in Dubai that offer a world-class caffeine fix of espresso, cappuccino and *caffe latte* but

equally there are quite a few places that serve a weak and watery Italian-style cup.

Alcohol

Alcohol can only be sold in restaurants and bars attached to hotels (in practice, three-star hotels or better). The selection is what you would expect to find in any well-stocked bar. The prices are pretty outrageous – expect to pay around Dh18 for a pint of beer or a glass of wine, and more like Dh22 at a nightclub. Even the most ordinary table wine will cost you at least Dh85 a bottle.

In an Arab Home

If you are invited into someone's home, the following tips may be useful:

- It is appropriate to take a small gift such as sweets or pastries.
- Do not sit in such a way that the soles of your feet are pointing at someone else.
- Do not eat or offer things with your left hand.
- It is considered polite to let your host set the pace in any conversation.
- Be careful of openly admiring any of your host's ornaments or other such things. It is an Arab custom to make a gift of anything that a guest admires.
- It is polite to take a second or third helping, but don't leave your plate completely empty. This implies that you are still hungry and that your host has not been attentive to your needs.
- It is considered very impolite to refuse an offer of coffee or tea in any social or business setting. After finishing your coffee hold out the cup in your right hand for more. If you have had enough, rock the cup gently back and forth to indicate that you're through. It is generally considered impolite to drink more than three cups, unless the conversation drags on for an extended period of time.
- Don't overstay your welcome. If you are dining at someone's house it's best to leave soon after coffee is served.

Non-Muslim expatriates must obtain an alcohol licence (with the permission of their sponsor) to buy takeaway booze. These licences allow the holder to spend a limited amount on alcohol each month, depending on their salary. In the small emirates of Ajman and Umm al-Qaiwain there are several 'holes in the wall' where alcohol is sold to those without licences. Umm al-Qaiwain even has a liquor store, at the Barracuda Beach Resort just off the main highway to Ras al-Khaimah. In Dubai some expats buy liquor from boats at the dhow docks on the Creek, but the risks of being ripped off, or worse, being caught, are a deterrent.

RESTAURANTS – BUDGET
Deira
Cafeteria al-Abra *(Map 4, #83; snacks Dh5-10)*, next to the Sabkha *abra* (water taxi) station in Deira, at the intersection of Al-Sabkha and Baniyas Rds, is ideal for a snack while watching the activity on the Creek. It has good *shwarma* and samosas, along with fruit juices and sodas.

Popeye *(Map 4, #67; Baniyas Rd; snacks Dh5-15)* has *shwarma*, burgers and other snacks. It has a pretty good offer of two *shwarma* and one drink for Dh5, and an intriguing caviar sandwich for Dh15.

Al-Burj Cafeteria *(Map 4, #93; snacks Dh5-15)*, near the entrance to the Gold Souq, is a stand-up affair offering excellent *shwarma*, fresh fruit juices, soda and popcorn.

Golden Fork *(Map 4, #74; ☎ 224 3834; Baniyas Square; mains Dh5-15)* has an odd combination of Asian (mainly Filipino) and Western fast food. The Western food is cheaper and better; for Dh10 you can get three pieces of fried chicken with fries and bread, or a burger, salad and fries.

Entezary Restaurant *(Map 4, #76; Al-Maktoum Hospital Rd; meals Dh15)* also offers good-value food. A typical dinner here consists of servings of kebab, rice, soup, salad, hummus, bread and tea. Judging by the signs and menus in Russian, this place is very popular with tourists from the former Soviet Union.

Hatam Restaurant *(Map 4, #68; Baniyas Rd; meals Dh14-25)* is a place we can highly recommend. It serves excellent Iranian food at very reasonable prices. A traditional *chelow kebab* (which appears on the menu as 'sultan kebab') costs Dh17, including soup and salad. Most full dinners cost under Dh20.

Gulf Restaurant & Cafeteria *(Map 4, #87; cnr Al-Sabkha Rd & Deira St; meals Dh8-18)* is a good Indo-Pakistani restaurant. Generous serves of chicken, lamb or fried fish on a pile of rice with salad cost Dh12. You can also get freshly squeezed fruit juice for Dh5.

Bur Dubai
Pars Iranian Kitchen *(Map 7, #11; ☎ 398 4000; Al-Dhiyafah Rd, Satwa; mains Dh17-20)*, an Iranian restaurant behind Rydges Plaza Hotel, is also a sweet shop and bakery. It has a varied menu of traditional Iranian cuisine, including stews, seafood and caviar as well as the ubiquitous kebabs.

Istanbouli Restaurant *(Map 7, #14; ☎ 345 0123; Al-Dhiyafah Rd; mains from Dh15)*, just west of Satwa Roundabout, is a long-established little Lebanese restaurant with a cosy stucco interior. Mezzes cost Dh7 to Dh12 apiece.

Ravi Restaurant *(Map 7, #12; ☎ 331 5353; Al-Satwa Rd, Satwa; meals around Dh15)* is a Pakistani restaurant close to Al-Dhiyafah Rd, which comes highly recommended by readers. Women and mixed couples will be directed to the Ravi Palace section, next door to the main building. Both restaurants are stark and clean, and a meal consisting of a curry, biryani, or chicken tikka with bread, salad, raita and a drink comes to about Dh15. Chinese dishes are also served.

Mini Chinese *(Map 7, #17; ☎ 345 5635; Al-Dhiyafah Rd; mains Dh20-30)* has groovy diner-style booths and bright modern decor. The servings of Chinese standards, such as Manchurian chicken (Dh27), are generous but a little bland. It's a good place for people-watching on the Al-Dhiyafah Rd strip, though.

Kwality *(Map 4, #33; ☎ 393 6563; Khalid bin al-Waleed Rd; mains Dh12-20)* is a branch of a reputable Indian chain of restaurants. You can't go wrong with dishes such as chicken *makhani* (butter chicken) or

Vegetarian Restaurants

With the proliferation of Indian restaurants, vegetarians will have no trouble finding places to eat, and they are all terrific value. Vegetarians can also enjoy plenty of dishes from any Lebanese and Iranian restaurant, for example hummus, *labneh*, tabouleh, spinach and cheese mezze and salads.

There is a strong selection of all-vegetarian Indian restaurants in Bur Dubai just north of Khalid bin al-Waleed Rd and in Karama.

Emirates House Restaurant *(Map 4, #29;* ☎ *352 2597; Al-Esbij St, Bur Dubai; mains Dh3-7)* specialises in South Indian vegetarian dishes, such as *thalis* and *dosas*. It's simple, but clean and comfortable, and it's certainly easy on your pocket.

Dasaprakash *(Map 4, #30;* ☎ *352 7429; Al-Esbij St, Bur Dubai; mains Dh3-9)* is a simple but friendly little place serving South Indian vegetarian cuisine. Try the *masala dosa* for only Dh4, or a special *thali* for Dh9. For dessert there's the irresistible chocolate ring-a-ding (Dh7), an ice cream and chocolate concoction.

Bhavna Deluxe Restaurant *(Map 4, #27;* ☎ *353 0707; 25C St, Bur Dubai; mains Dh6-15)* is a well-known establishment where vegans are also catered for (no egg or dairy products). The all-you-can-eat *thalis* are great value at Dh9.

India House *(Map 4, #28;* ☎ *352 6006; Al-Hisn St, Bur Dubai; meals Dh15-20)* has a great selection of North and South Indian vegetarian dishes and a more upmarket interior than most restaurants around here. It also serves Chinese dishes, Indian style.

Chhappan Bhog *(Map 6, #28;* ☎ *396 8176; Sheikh Khalifa bin Zayed Rd, Karama; mains Dh8-12)* serves mainly North Indian dishes. It is very popular with the local Indian population and has a fast-food counter and sweets shop downstairs.

Kamat *(Map 6, #23;* ☎ *396 7288; 2A St, near Bur Juman Centre, Karama; mains Dh10-15)* is another good-value Karama restaurant. Service is speedy, and the menu spans the subcontinent from Punjab to South India. A lunch-time *thali* costs Dh14.

Sarovar Restaurant *(Map 4, #97;* ☎ *225 5549; 39 St, Deira; mains Dh4-8)*, just off Sikkat al-Khail St in the Gold Souq, is one of the best places in Deira for a quick, cheap meal. It's a very small, basic, all-vegetarian restaurant serving North and South Indian dishes.

rogan josh (lamb curry). It also has lots of vegetarian options.

Fiesta Filipino *(Map 6, #36;* ☎ *334 4121; 45B St; mains Dh12-15)*, near Al-Karama Shopping Centre, offers friendly service and the food is good value. Try *ginateen manok* (coconut chicken curry), or *lapu-lapu*, a baked fish dish, usually served with *sinigang*, a kind of tamarind soup.

Chef Lanka *(Map 6, #35;* ☎ *335 3040; 27A St; mains Dh8-15)*, near Karama Park, serves up spicy Sri Lankan curries, plus some Chinese dishes for the less adventurous.

RESTAURANTS – MID-RANGE
Deira

Cibushi Cafe *(Map 4, #63;* ☎ *220 0111; 18 St; mains Dh20-30; open 8am-midnight daily)*, near the Inter-Continental Hotel, is a groovy little café in a utilitarian lane parallel to Baniyas Rd. Popular with office workers for lunch, it offers thin-crust pizza for Dh20 to Dh30, antipasto for Dh20 and a sushi platter for Dh30.

Hana *(Map 4, #65;* ☎ *222 2131; Riviera Hotel; mains Dh30-50; open noon-3pm & 7pm-11pm daily)*, an enormous place, offers three different menus: Japanese, Thai and Chinese. The sushi platter (Dh45) is delicious. The food is authentic and reasonably priced, but alcohol is not served.

The Pub *(Map 4, #60;* ☎ *222 7171; Dubai Inter-Continental Hotel; sandwiches Dh20-30, mains Dh30-50)* is about as good an imitation of the real thing as you'll find in the Gulf. It serves a varied menu of sandwiches and 'traditional pub food' (ie, shepherd's pie, roast beef etc).

Automatic Restaurant *(Map 5, #24; ☎ 227 7824; Al-Rigga Rd; mezze Dh12-15, mains Dh25-45)* is clean, comfortable and not as over-brightly lit as many restaurants in Dubai. Fish dishes are a little pricier than other mains such as the mixed grill. There are two branches of the Automatic chain of restaurants along here. This one is closer to Omar ibn al-Khattab St. There is also a branch *(Map 4, #40; ☎ 355 0333)* in the Al-Khaleej Shopping Centre on Al-Mankhool Rd.

Little Italy *(Map 5, #55; ☎ 223 1000; Al-Khaleej Palace Hotel, Al-Maktoum Rd; meals Dh25-30)* is a rustic little bistro serving tasty Italian fare at reasonable prices. Beef carpacchio costs Dh20, gnocchi with spinach Dh30.

Barrio Fiesta *(Map 5, #28; ☎ 221 1872; Omar ibn al-Khattab Rd; mains Dh18)*, near the Deira minibus and taxi station, has reasonably priced Filipino food, with an emphasis on seafood. Soups and rice dishes cost Dh12. The menu also offers some Chinese and Indonesian dishes, as well as the good old Arabic grill for Dh20.

Bur Dubai

Lebanese Village *(Map 4, #41; ☎ 352 2522; Al-Mankhool Rd; mains Dh20-38)* is a popular new place between Spinney's and the Ramada Hotel on Al-Mankhool Rd. It has an open air-terrace and an air-con section indoors. Generous serves of shish *tawouq*, tabouleh and hummus together will cost about Dh 50.

Al-Borz *(Map 3, #50; ☎ 331 8777; Al-Durreh Tower, Sheikh Zayed Rd; kebabs Dh30-45)* is a charming Iranian restaurant in a tower block next to the Crowne Plaza Hotel. The kebabs (lamb, chicken and fish) are deliciously tender and flavoursome, and the service is exceptionally welcoming. We highly recommend it. Soups and salads come free.

Arabian Pavilion *(Map 6, #27; ☎ 351 3888; Spinney's, Sheikh Khalifa bin Zayed Rd; mains Dh24-42)* is a spacious, modern Lebanese restaurant with some outdoor terrace seating. All the usual Lebanese dishes are available, fresh and tasty, but it's worth asking for their daily specials. The service

is attentive and cheerful. A flavoured *sheesha* costs Dh15.

Japengo *(Map 7, #26; ☎ 345 4979; Palm Strip Shopping Centre, Jumeira Rd; mains Dh25-50)* is a cheerfully trendy little place, serving coffee, noodles and sushi in a casual environment.

Bento-Ya *(Map 3, #57; ☎ 343 0222; Al-Kawakeb Bldg D, Sheikh Zayed Rd; mains Dh40-80)* is a quiet and moderately priced Japanese eatery. The sushi platter prepared from local fish (Dh65) is delicious, as are the salads and the miso soup. They also have a wide range of bento boxes for around Dh50. The restaurant is on the ground floor of a nondescript tower block close to the Dusit Dubai (the fourth one along from the hotel), facing away from Sheikh Zayed Rd.

Kowloon *(Map 4, #38; ☎ 359 8777; Al-Rolla Rd; mains Dh20-30)*, next to the Rolla Residence, is highly recommended. It serves excellent Chinese food at very reasonable prices. The place has a nice, friendly atmosphere. Alcohol is not served.

Kitchen Restaurant *(Map 7, #8; ☎ 398 5043; Satwa; starters around Dh8, mains Dh18-25)*, behind Al-Dhiyafah Rd, is an atmospheric little Indian restaurant, which also serves Chinese dishes and Arabic-style grills. Main dishes include fish tikka; it also has lots of offerings for vegetarians for around Dh15.

Thai Terrace *(Map 6, #29; ☎ 336 7356; Sheikh Khalifa bin Zayed Rd, Karama; mains Dh28-33; open noon-2.30pm & 7pm-11pm daily)* is a favourite for fans of authentic and interesting Thai food. The food is a little expensive, but the servings are generous and the dishes are excellent. Especially good is the crispy fish salad – try it. As the restaurant is not part of a hotel, alcohol is not served.

RESTAURANTS – TOP END

At the top end of the market almost any kind of cuisine can be found in Dubai, but in most cases 'top-end' food means eating at the five-star hotels. In the last few years lots of new competition has hiked up the standards of cuisine and service but not, alas, lowered prices much. If you want to splurge, there are world-class restaurants representing nearly every style of cooking, and more opening all the time. With the high import duties on alcohol, a bottle of wine or two can raise the bill considerably.

Deira

Boardwalk (Map 3, #19; ☎ 295 6000; Dubai Creek Golf & Yacht Club; mains Dh28-70) has tables perched over the Creek, where you can enjoy the fresh breezes off the water. The menu is mostly a modern Australian-style fusion of Asian and European influences; the fillet of beef costs Dh55, while Thai salmon cakes cost Dh28. The food doesn't quite match up to the prices, but the setting is terrific. Vegetarians and children are catered to, and there's a bar. You can also ogle the stunning array of luxury vehicles in the golf club's car park.

Casa Mia (Map 3, #11; ☎ 282 4040; mains Dh50-85; open 12.30pm-3pm & 8pm-11.30pm daily), behind Le Meridien Dubai, is ably run by an Italian couple – he commands the kitchen and she, with lots of charm, commands the dining room. The menu is interesting and the carefully chosen wine list is unlike any other in Dubai. For our money it's the best Italian restaurant in town.

Blue Elephant (Map 3, #12; ☎ 282 0000; Al-Bustan Rotana; mains Dh45-60) serves excellent Thai food. The restaurant is decked out like a Thai village, complete with a pond and bridge.

Topkapi (Map 5, #37; ☎ 223 2222; Taj Palace Hotel, 23D St, Rigga; mains Dh40-70) is a top-class Turkish restaurant with a warm, cosy atmosphere. It serves a range of hot and cold mezzes (try the patlican, or eggplant, dishes) along with salads, warm Turkish bread and hearty kebabs. The hotel has a no-alcohol policy.

Al-Dawaar (Map 3, #1; ☎ 209 1100; 25th floor, Hyatt Regency Dubai; buffet lunch/dinner Dh140/160) is a rotating restaurant. As it spins you get fantastic views of the Gulf, Sharjah, Port Rashid and Deira. The restaurant is buffet only and the food on offer is international – salads, seafood, meats and soups.

Bur Dubai

Fakhreldine (Map 3, #29; ☎ 336 6000; Holiday Inn Bur Dubai, 19 St, Oud Metha; mains Dh40-80) gets our vote for Dubai's best restaurant. All the classic Lebanese dishes are represented; they simply taste better here than anywhere else. The decor is a brilliant blend of chrome, carpets and subtle lighting. For the budget-conscious, the **Liwan Fakhreldine** is a separate outdoors section of the restaurant, with tents to relax in and grills for around Dh30 and mezzes between Dh10 and Dh15, as well as sheesha pipes.

Kanzaman (Map 4, #2; ☎ 393 9913; Heritage & Diving Villages, Shindagha; starters Dh10-15, mains Dh30-50) translates as 'once upon a time', which gives a sense of the Arabian traditions this popular café, restaurant and sheesha bar evokes. There's seating inside a heritage building but the real atmosphere is outside overlooking the Creek. The menu offers a long list of mezzes, grills, steaks and seafood. The breezes off the Creek offer cool relief most of the year, but can be chilly on a winter's night.

Al-Mahara (Map 2, #18; Burj Al-Arab, Jumeira Rd, Umm Suqeim; mains Dh120-200; open noon-3pm & 7pm-11.30pm daily) is the signature restaurant in Dubai's landmark hotel, and costs a bomb. Seeing as you're sitting next to a giant fish tank, it figures that the menu concentrates on seafood. A bottle of wine could push the bill for two to over Dh1000. Dress up and worry about the bill later.

El Malecon (Map 7, #27; ☎ 346 1111; Dubai Marine Beach Resort & Spa, Jumeira, mains Dh50-80) is a funky Cuban restaurant with a band that plays until 2am. The food is a delicious mix of seafood (mariscada, seafood, casserole Dh70) and spicy Caribbean dishes (pollo à la Cuban, a chicken dish, Dh55). Diners can write their names on the walls. Other restaurants here include **Capanna Nuova** (Italian), and **Al-Qasr** (Lebanese), with similar prices.

JW's Steakhouse (Map 5, #10; ☎ 607 7977; JW Marriott Hotel, Abu Baker al-Siddiq Rd, Rigga; mains Dh100-150) is an upmarket restaurant with fabulous leather seats and an American steakhouse-style menu. The steaks here are cooked to perfection.

Beach Bar & Grill *(Map 2, #9; ☎ 399 9999; Royal Mirage, Al-Sufouh Rd, Al-Mina al-Seyahi; mains Dh80-120)* is an attractive building perched by the sea in the midst of the gardens of this lavish hotel. Be prepared to spend about Dh200 per person for three courses, which might include oysters, a Greek salad and a seafood grill.

Verre *(Map 5, #51; ☎ 227 1111; Hilton Dubai Creek, Baniyas Rd, Rigga; mains Dh80-120)* is a franchise owned by British celebrity chef Gordon Ramsay. The emphasis is on elegant, fresh food without the frills, so the restaurant is of starkly modern design with lots of chrome and glass. For the full gastronomic experience, the seven-course menu costs Dh275 per person. In the same hotel there is also the **Glasshouse Brasserie** *(Map 5, #51; ☎ 227 1111; mains Dh50-80)*. It's not quite as expensive as Verre, but offers wonderful modern cuisine and excellent breakfasts for Dh70.

Trader Vic's *(Map 3, #49; ☎ 331 1111; Crowne Plaza Hotel, Sheikh Zayed Rd; mains Dh60-90)* is a curious Polynesian/Asian/European hybrid, which actually works. The emphasis is on seafood, such as salmon steak with lemongrass sauce (Dh69) or lobster salad with avocado (Dh66). The restaurant also has a long list of 'tropical' cocktails.

CAFÉS

Lime Tree Café *(Map 7, #28; ☎ 349 8498; Jumeira Rd, Jumeira; coffee Dh10, snacks Dh10-20)* is our favourite Dubai café, hands down. A converted villa near the Jumeira Mosque, the Lime Tree has an outdoor terrace, tables in the garden and comfortable chairs inside. Along with excellent coffee, the kitchen serves up an ever-changing range of muffins, sandwiches and quiches. There's always a selection of magazines and newspapers to read.

Gerard *(Map 7, #30; ☎ 344 3327; Magrudy's Shopping Centre, Jumeira Rd, Jumeira; coffee Dh10)* is a cheerfully snooty little café in the open-air atrium of this small shopping centre. Seating is in wicker chairs, and

there's always an intriguing mix of customers: Emiratis juggling cigarettes and cell phones; ladies who lunch (the 'Jumeira Janes') and a few sunburned tourists, all relaxing over coffees. There's another branch in Al-Ghurair Centre *(Map 5, #27)*.

Costa *(Map 3, #16; ☎ 286 9216; Century Village, Deira; coffee Dh9-12, cakes Dh10)*, an Italian coffeehouse next to the Irish Village, is another decent café. It offers regular coffee (Dh9), as well as a 'French Bowl' (Dh12) and delicious-looking cakes.

Cafe Mozart *(Map 4, #66; ☎ 221 6565; 18 St, Deira; coffee Dh8-12, pastries Dh5)* is a slightly faded but pleasant re-creation of a Viennese coffeehouse, authentic down to the change purse carried by the waitress. The pastries and croissants are very good and both the regular coffee and cappuccino are excellent.

Shakespeare & Co *(Map 3, #55; ☎ 331 1757; Kendah House, Sheikh Zayed Rd; coffee Dh8)* is a comfortable, even homely, café at the base of a towering office block. It has a long menu including pasta, seafood, vegetarian dishes and some Moroccan recipes as well, and the service is charming and efficient.

Dôme *(Map 6, #12; ☎ 355 6004; Bur Juman Centre, Khalid bin al-Waleed Rd, Rigga; coffee Dh9-13, snacks around Dh25)* is a popular place for people-watching, and good for recharging after a shopping spree. The coffee is consistently drinkable, but the range of snacks is a little overpriced (Dh25 for a large sandwich).

La Marquise *(Map 4, #64; ☎ 224 7606; Twin Towers Shopping Centre, Baniyas Rd, Deira; coffee Dh10, snacks Dh10-25)*, on level 3, serves sandwiches, salads, pastries and coffee. It has an outdoor terrace with fine views over the Creek. There's another branch at the Palm Strip Shopping Centre *(Map 7, #26)* on Jumeira Road.

FAST FOOD

Fast food has become as popular with Emiratis as it is with Westerners, and all the multinational junk-food chains are represented here. The fast-food invasion is blamed for many social problems (such as young people spending more time away from their families) and health problems in Dubai, including obesity and diabetes. Of course, there are other contributing factors to these problems, such as a lack of exercise in a very sedentary society, but fast food is at the top of the list.

There are various fast-food chains along major roads and shopping centres around the city. Along Al-Rigga Rd in Rigga (Map 5) you'll find **Wendy's**, **KFC**, **Pizza Hut** and the English fish-and-chip chain, **Harry Ramsden's** (Map 5, #26). On Al-Dhiyafah Rd in Satwa (Map 7) there are plenty of fast-food eateries, including **Burger King**, **Hardees** and **Round Table Pizza**.

There are branches of **McDonald's** on Jumeira Rd (Map 7), next to the Crowne Plaza Hotel (Map 3) on Sheikh Zayed Rd, at Al-Khaleej Shopping Centre (Map 4, #40) on Al-Mankhool Rd in Bur Dubai and at Al-Ghurair Centre (Map 5, #27) on the corner of Al-Rigga and Omar ibn al-Khattab Rds in Rigga. There are **Subway** outlets at Wafi City (Map 3, #33), Deira City Centre (Map 3, #21) and Al-Rigga Rd (Map 5) in Rigga.

Many of the shopping centres also have a **food court**, usually with an Indian, Chinese and Thai outlet serving steam-tray fare, plus a pizza joint and a Lebanese shwarma stall. The biggest food courts are at Deira City Centre (Map 3, #21), the Bur Juman Centre (Map 6, #25), Wafi City (Map 3, #34) and Al-Ghurair Centre (Map 5, #27).

BAKERIES & SWEET SHOPS
One of the great pleasures of eating in Dubai are the delicious Lebanese, Iranian and Indian delicacies on offer at the many bakeries and sweet shops around town. The best time to go to a bakery is early in the morning (they usually get going at about 4am) when everything is warm and fresh and the smell is marvellous. Most bakeries make Western-style loaves of bread, but they are usually laden with sugar. French-style bread sticks and croissants are your best bet as they are usually pretty authentic. Bakeries and sweet shops are usually open long hours, from early morning to midnight Saturday to Thursday, as well as Friday evening.

The best place to go for Indian sweets is Sheikh Khalifa bin Zayed Rd between Khalid bin al-Waleed Rd and Kuwait St. **Puranmal** (Map 6, #30), one of the sweet shops, has delicacies such as milk cake, cream chum chum and delicious chocolate barfi.

Feras Sweets (Map 7, #6; Al-Dhiyafah Rd, Satwa) specialises in very sticky Jordanian sweets and pastries. A 250g bag of sinfully sweet and sticky baklava costs Dh15.

King Pastries (Map 5, #22; Al-Rigga Rd, Rigga; coffee Dh6-8) is a bakery and coffee shop serving European and Lebanese pastries and sweets. A serve of sweets is Dh5.

Al-Sindbad Bakery (Map 4, #46; Khalid bin al-Waleed Rd, Bur Dubai; coffee Dh6) is a neon-lit landmark, serving coffee and a range of Lebanese and European pastries and sticky cakes.

Iranian Sweets (Map 5, #29; Omar ibn al-Khattab St, Deira), next to the minibus and taxi station, is a good place for coffee and sweets. Coffee and a selection of sweets for two people costs around Dh12.

SELF-CATERING
Those interested in self-catering will find plenty of small grocery stores around Deira, Bur Dubai, Karama, Satwa and Rigga. They sell a good range of basic groceries as well as a small selection of fruit and vegetables, although these are not always of the best quality.

For fresh fruit and vegetables the best place to go looking is the enormous **Fruit & Vegetable Market** (Map 4) in Deira, just past the Shindagha Tunnel. Food is exported from here to Qatar, Oman and Bahrain. A huge range of fruit and vegetables is available, imported from Europe, Asia and the Middle East. Another part of the complex houses the **Fish & Meat Market** – collectively it's often called the Shindagha Market. It's open from 7am to 11pm daily. There are no fixed prices, so bargaining is the order of the day.

Further up Al-Khaleej Rd, near Hamriya Port, the **Wholesale Market** (Map 2, #33; open 7am-11pm daily) is even cheaper, but most sales are in bulk quantities. Again, haggling is the norm. The huge parking area is usually filled with trucks bringing in produce from Oman.

The biggest supermarket is **Carrefour** *(Map 3, #21; Deira City Centre)* with 100 checkouts, but it gets so crowded in the late afternoon and evening, it's just not worth it. If you can get there early you'll be treated to a great selection of fresh seafood. **Spinney's** is the most popular supermarket with Western expats, though it is a little more expensive than the rest. It's the only supermarket to serve ready-made meals. There are branches on Abu Baker al-Siddiq Rd, Deira *(Map 5, #7)*; on Al-Mankhool Rd *(Map 4, #42)*, opposite Al-Rolla Rd; on Sheikh Khalifa bin Zayed Rd *(Map 6, #27)*, near the corner with Kuwait St; on Jumeira Rd *(Map 7, #29)*; and on Al-Wasl Rd *(Map 2, #24)*, in Safa. All are open from 8am to midnight daily.

Choithrams targets the Indian and Pakistani community more than Western expats, but it has much the same stuff as Spinney's at considerably lower prices. Along with Spinneys, Choithrams sells pork products. You'll find a **Choithrams** *(Map 4, #39; cnr Al-Rolla & Al-Mankhool Rds)* next to Al-Khaleej Shopping Centre. There's another on Al-Wasl Rd, Jumeira *(Map 2, #27)* near Safa Park.

Safestway *(Map 3, #61; Sheikh Zayed Rd)*, near Interchange No 1, has a better bakery and delicatessen section than Choithrams, but it is a little out of the way for most people. **Union Co-op Society** has a good selection of cheap groceries, but no pork products. There is one shop on Al-Wasl Rd near Safa Park *(Map 2, #27)* and a second on Sheikh Khalifa bin Zayed Rd in Mankhool *(Map 6, #37)*.

Entertainment

Dubai is easily the most fun city in the Gulf, with a wide and growing range of pubs, clubs, cinemas and sporting events. There's no shortage of after-hours social life – they don't call Dubai the party capital of the Gulf for nothing. A night out, however, is not going to be cheap. If you're drinking, plan on spending well over Dh150 and even non-drinkers could easily go through half that in cover charges and overpriced soft drinks.

Dubai's licensing laws require venues serving alcohol to be attached to hotels or private clubs. Sometimes the connection can be pretty tenuous but usually a bar is ensconced on the ground floor of a hotel. It's slightly disconcerting to walk out of a rowdy bar into a sombre marble-clad foyer. The entertainment scene in the big hotels is constantly changing. The best way to keep up is to get a copy of *Time Out* magazine. Almost everything – lounge acts, rock, techno or a quiet piano bar – is available somewhere. The problem is that, with the exception of a few perennials, the hotels keep changing the theme in their clubs in an attempt to keep everything contemporary. For example, you might have karaoke night, football night, quiz night, ladies' night, happy night (whatever that means) and teachers' night, all in one week.

As befits a port city, Dubai's nightlife has its seamy side. Plenty of hotels in Deira and near Port Rashid host nightclubs and cabaret where women offer fee-based hospitality. They're often ethnically based (eg, 'Dhaka by Night, the Bengali Disco Inferno') and are advertised with posters showing women in lurid spangled clothing and heavy make-up. Quite a few popular watering holes turn sleazy late at night, or have one night a week when working girls appear.

Pubs and clubs don't last for long as the trendiest spot in town. Generally, the advertising and media crowd are the first to adopt a new club or pub, which often reaches the peak of its popularity when airline crews follow their lead. Then, almost overnight, the focus shifts elsewhere.

PUBS & BARS

Dubai has many pubs and bars. Don't be surprised to see Gulf Arabs enjoying a pint just as much as non-Muslims. Yes, it's illegal for them to purchase alcohol, but who cares? This is Dubai.

Pubs and bars in Dubai are open until 1am or 2am. They are well stocked with spirits and all the major beers are available. The wines are invariably the same as the wines at licensed restaurants – mostly table wines from France, Italy, Australia and California. Expect to pay about Dh18 to Dh20 for a pint of beer or a glass of wine. The posher pubs at the five-star hotels charge around Dh22 plus tax and a 20% service charge for each drink. Most bars and pubs have a happy hour where all drinks are around Dh10 to Dh12. Happy hour times vary from place to place. Most pubs and bars serve meals as well. Many places hold a 'ladies' night', when those of the right sex get two free drinks. Not surprisingly, ladies' nights tend to attract more men than women.

The biggest problem with many of Dubai's bars is that the managers all seem to feel that a loud lounge singer is an essential part of any establishment. This usually means that your quiet conversation will be completely drowned out by a loud rendition of a Whitney Houston song. If nothing else it can demonstrate Dubai's multiculturalism. Here you are in the Middle East, sitting in a Texan theme bar, drinking a Dutch beer, listening to a half-Goan half-Filipino band playing a Jamaican reggae version of an Elvis tune.

Irish Village *(Map 3, #15;* ☎ *282 4750; Dubai Tennis Stadium, off Al-Garhoud Rd, Deira)*, behind the Aviation Club, is the best of the Irish pubs. It's very popular with British expats in Dubai and is a good, casual watering hole. It is expensive though – Dh18 for a pint and Dh9 for a soft drink. The pub has a large outdoor area with wooden tables and chairs and serves good, honest pub grub.

Harry's Place (Map 5, #4; ☎ 262 5555; Renaissance Dubai Hotel, Salahuddin Rd, Rigga) is a shrine to Hollywood in a most unusual way – the walls are covered in framed mug shots of Hollywood celebrities. From Jane Fonda to Robert Downey Jr, no-one is spared exposure. This is a sophisticated place with experienced and friendly bar staff and a great menu. Tucked away in a little room off to the side is the Cigar Room, adorned with leather couches.

Legends Bar (Map 7, #10; ☎ 398 2222; Rydges Plaza Hotel, Satwa) was Dubai's first Australian bar. Its pride and joy is the TV pumping out Aussie Rules football and cricket. The bar is decorated with sports memorabilia and its bistro offers moderately priced, modern pub grub.

Dubliners (Map 3, #10; ☎ 282 4040; behind Le Meridien Dubai, Al-Garhoud) is a cheerfully smoky and boozy Irish bar, open until 3am daily.

Barasti Bar (Map 2, #8; ☎ 399 3333; Le Meridien Mina Seyahi Beach Resort & Marina; Al-Sufouh Rd) is a seaside bar in the beach hotel strip. The big night here is Friday night, when a resident DJ and band pull in a big crowd. Other nights of the week it's still a nice place to smoke a *sheesha* (traditional pipe) and watch the waves roll in.

Jules Bar (Map 3, #10; behind Le Meridien Dubai, Al-Garhoud), near the airport, has a southern USA theme with a rather weird but quite cool Filipino band. The menu here features Cajun, Tex-Mex, Filipino and Mediterranean meals. It attracts a very mixed crowd; gay and straight Westerners, Gulf Arabs and businesswomen from the former Soviet Union – Dubai nightlife in a nutshell.

Carters (Map 3, #32; ☎ 324 0000; Wafi Pyramids) is a bar and restaurant with a colonial Egyptian theme. The terrace is a lovely place to sit and relax with a drink. The menu is mostly Continental with a few Asian dishes; mains cost around Dh40. A band usually plays after 10pm.

Sevilles (Map 3, #32; ☎ 324 4777; Wafi Pyramids) is another bar-cum-restaurant in the Wafi Pyramids part of the Wafi City complex, with an outdoor terrace overlooking an amazing swimming pool. There's a pair of highly skilled Spanish guitarists to entertain you.

Long's Bar (Map 3, #56; ☎ 312 2202; Tower Rotana Hotel, Sheikh Zayed Rd) is one of Dubai's more active music venues, with an ever-changing list of bands and DJs and a small dance floor. It tends to attract a crowd in their late 20s to early 30s. It also has a restaurant and is open until 3am.

Henry J Beans (Map 7, #1; ☎ 345 8350; Capitol Hotel, Al-Mina Rd, Satwa) is an American-theme bar and nightclub, popular with American expatriates. There's a band most nights.

Uptown (Map 2, #20; ☎ 348 0000; 24th floor, Jumeira Beach Hotel, Jumeira Rd) is where you can sit outside on the terrace and enjoy spectacular views across to the Burj al-Arab and along the coast towards the centre of Dubai. As with everything else in this hotel, the prices are on the high side.

Vu's Bar (Map 3, #51; ☎ 330 0000; 51st floor, Emirates Towers, Sheikh Zayed Rd) is 220m above Dubai, with amazing views over the city. The drinks have equally amazing prices, but the stylish decor helps to compensate. Dress to impress.

Rock Bottom Café (Map 6, #24; ☎ 396 3888; Regent Palace Hotel, Sheikh Khalifa bin Zayed Rd, Bur Dubai; open 10am-3am daily) is the bar/nightclub people end up at when common sense would tell them to go home. It's open until 3am and has a *shwarma* (grilled meat) stall for late-night feeds. It's well known for being a pick-up joint.

Henry Africa's (The Bunker) (Map 3, #58; ☎ 343 0501; behind Dusit Dubai, Sheikh Zayed Rd; open 10am-midnight Sat-Thur, 10am-1am Fri) is a long-established bar with a light-hearted African theme. It's a friendly place, popular with veteran expatriates.

Sho Chos (Map 7, #27; ☎ 346 1111; Dubai Marine Beach Resort & Spa, Jumeira Rd; open 7.30pm-12.30am Sat-Wed, 7.30pm-2.30am Thur-Fri) is a very groovy neo-Tokyo theme bar, with in-house DJ and too-sexy-for-my-shirt barmen. Definitely a place to dress up for.

Up on the Tenth (Map 4, #60; ☎ 205 7333; Dubai Inter-Continental Hotel; open noon-3am daily) is a piano bar with superb views

The Al-Dhiyafah Scene

Come Thursday and Friday night, this palm-lined boulevard of shops and cafés hums with Dubai's hottest wheels. Al-Dhiyafah Rd (Map 7) – the stretch between Al-Mina and Al-Mankhool Rds – is where the wealthy Emirati young bucks cruise the block, à la *American Graffiti*. Anyone can relax in a café with a *sheesha* pipe or an ice cream, and watch the world's finest automobiles drive by. A mere Lexus or Audi won't bring a second glance – to be noticed takes a Lamborghini, Porsche or Ferrari, preferably with impenetrably dark windows and an earthshaking set of sub-woofer speakers. The street gets so busy on a weekend evening that the sports cars slow to a crawl. At this pace you can appreciate them, rather than the usual fleeting glimpse on Sheikh Zayed Rd when they're doing 200km/h (no exaggeration). This automotive plumage display is mostly for the benefit of the people in the restaurants, sidewalk cafés and *sheesha* joints. It's a bit like a cross between Naples and Beverley Hills, set in Arabia – check it out, but don't bother bringing the rented hatchback.

over the Creek. As with all bars at five-star hotels, the prices are outrageous, but it's worth dropping in for an after-dinner drink.

NIGHTCLUBS

Dubai's nightclubs tend to be segregated into Arabic, Western, Filipino and Indian clubs. This is just the way people socialise in Dubai – apart. Wednesday, Thursday and Friday nights are the biggies, with music pumping until 3am or 4am.

Atlantis (Map 2, #12; ☎ 399 2222; Hard Rock Café, Sheikh Zayed Rd) is a long way from the centre, past Interchange No 4, but if you're staying at the beach hotels it's only a two-minute taxi ride. Atlantis is a modern nightclub with a thumping sound system that pumps out techno and trance music. The club sometimes has live entertainment, such as dancing girls, and sometimes hosts one-off events. It tends to attract an ethnically mixed, young crowd.

Maharlika (Map 6, #31; ☎ 334 6565; President Hotel, Sheikh Khalifa bin Zayed Rd, Karama) is a popular Filipino nightclub. Non-Filipinos pay Dh25 to get in, which includes a free drink. The main attraction is the vibrant floor show, which included the world's shortest Elvis impersonator when we were there. Cheesy but fun.

Planetarium (Map 3, #33; ☎ 324 4777; Planet Hollywood, Wafi City) is the nightclub attached to the franchised bar-restaurant Planet Hollywood. It hosts special appearances by international DJs and club acts. Dress to impress.

Dubai Water Sports Association (Map 3, #39; ☎ 324 1031), behind Jaddaf shipyard, hosts Friday-night house music and funk sessions in a more casual setting than some of the more zealously fashionable venues around town.

Scarlett's (Map 3, #51; ☎ 330 0000; Emirates Towers, Sheikh Zayed Rd; open 12.30pm-3am daily) is a trendy bar, restaurant and nightclub with a vaguely Dixieland theme and one of Dubai's better resident bands. It attracts an affluent, young (early 20s) clientele. It pays to dress up if you want to enjoy the place.

Kasbar (Map 2, #9; ☎ 399 9999; Royal Mirage, Al-Sufouh Rd; admission Dh50; open 9.30pm-3am Mon-Sat) is a Moroccan-theme nightclub in this lavish hotel complex. The admission fee entitles you to one free drink. The decor alone is worth the admission fee. The club is built on three levels, overlooking the dance floor; the uppermost is the most exclusive. The music is a mix of popular dance hits and techno-Arabic. If you want to meet a wealthy young sheikh, this would be the place.

SHEESHA CAFÉS

When in Dubai you should try one of the city's traditional pastimes; *sheesha* smoking. A *sheesha* (also known as a hubbly bubbly) is a long-stemmed, glass-bottomed smoking implement that's about 50cm high. They are common in various forms in much of the Middle East; the ones used in Dubai are similar to those found in Lebanon and Egypt.

ENTERTAINMENT

*Sheesha*s are packed with apple-flavoured tobacco, unless you ask for something different, such as strawberry, coffee, liquorice or tropical. The going rate for a *sheesha* is Dh10 to Dh15. *Sheesha* cafés are open until around midnight.

Fatafeet Café *(Map 4, #51;* ☎ *397 9222; Al-Seef Rd, Bur Dubai)* is the nicest place to enjoy a *sheesha* in Dubai. You also get great views across the water to Deira. The best time to go is at sunset when the glass and steel buildings on the opposite side of the Creek reflect the water and the whole city takes on a golden glow.

Al-Areesh Restaurant *(Map 3, #37;* ☎ *324 3000; Al-Boom Tourist Village)* offers a peaceful setting on the lawn under palm trees overlooking the eastern end of the Creek.

Tche Tche *(Map 4, #47,* ☎ *355 7575; Khalid bin al-Waleed Rd)* is a popular neighbourhood *sheesha* café in the middle of a strip of strikingly modern architecture – very Dubai.

Kanzaman *(Map 4, #2;* ☎ *393 9914; Heritage & Diving Village, Shindagha)* is more of a restaurant than simply a *sheesha* joint (see the Places to Eat chapter for more details), but its creekside location, size and popularity with Emiratis make it worthy of mention. The waterfront seats are the most popular.

CINEMAS

You can catch relatively recent Western films at a number of cinemas around town. The films shown are all mainstream Hollywood movies, with an emphasis on action. There are also quite a few cinemas catering to the large Asian population. These cinemas have a dual-pricing policy; families sit up in the more expensive balcony seats, while the cheaper seats on the floor tend to have a rowdier all-male audience. If you've never seen an Indian movie (also called Bollywood films, a cross between Bombay and Hollywood), they're quite fun. They are usually more than 2½ hours long, and packed with songs, dance routines, melodrama, romance and violence. The plots are rarely so complicated that you can't understand the film even if you don't know the language.

Films are subject to censorship and, as sex and romance are prime ingredients of most Hollywood recipes, films (subtitled in Arabic) are often cut to shreds. Cinemas are comfortable and clean; the biggest complex, Cinestar, has 11 cinemas. Programmes are published in the Tabloid section of the *Gulf News* and in the entertainment section of the *Khaleej Times*.

Al-Nasr (Map 3, #26; ☎ 337 4353) Off Oud Metha Rd, near Rashid Hospital; tickets Dh15-20. This cinema shows mostly South Indian movies (Tamil, Malayali, Telugu) and some Hindi movies. South Indian movies are much the same as Hindi movies, except the lead actors tend to be pudgy little guys with moustaches.

Almassa (Map 2, #28; ☎ 343 8383) Sheikh Zayed Rd; tickets Dh25. This eight-screen cinema complex is older than the other multiscreen cinemas. It shows English-language fare. It's next to the Metropolitan Hotel, at Interchange No 2.

Cinestar (Map 3, #21; ☎ 294 9000) Deira City Centre, Deira; tickets Dh20 before 6pm, Dh30 after 6pm. This 11-screen complex is Dubai's classiest movie venue, showing a range of Hollywood hits and some more intelligent American, British and European fare as well.

Deira (Map 5, #31; ☎ 222 3551) Omar ibn al-Khattab Rd, Deira; tickets Dh15-20. This is an old-fashioned movie house, screening South Indian movies.

Grand Cineplex (Map 3, #35; ☎ 324 2000) Al-Qataiyat Rd, near Wafi City; tickets Dh25-30. This is a new 10-screen complex showing English-language movies.

Hyatt Galleria (Map 3, #1; ☎ 209 6469) Al-Khaleej Rd, Deira; tickets Dh20. In the Hyatt Galleria shopping centre, attached to the Hyatt Regency Hotel, this is a smallish, two-screen cinema showing English-language pictures.

Lamcy (Map 3, #28; ☎ 336 8808) Lamcy Plaza, Al-Qataiyat Rd, Bur Dubai; tickets Dh20. A two-screen cinema showing Indian 'Bollywood' fare; it's newer than most of the cinemas showing Indian movies.

Rex Drive-In (Map 2, #37; ☎ 288 6447) Al-Khawaneej Rd, Mirdif; tickets Dh15. Dubai's only drive-in cinema is big enough for 150 cars, and shows Indian blockbusters.

Strand (Map 6, #22; ☎ 396 1644) Khalid bin al-Waleed Rd, Bur Dubai; tickets Dh15-20. An ageing landmark cinema, the Strand screens similar movies to the other Indian film houses.

CONCERTS

They just can't get enough 1970s and 1980s music in Dubai. If it's not enough that the English-language radio stations are stuck in the past, every winter there are visits from bands that have long since departed the scene in other parts of the world. Kool & The Gang, Gloria Gaynor and Roger Waters (ex-Pink Floyd) toured while we were in town, and Sting and Bryan Adams have been regular visitors. If the original band can't be resurrected, promoters will settle for a covers band. Thus New Year's Eve 2001 shook to the sounds of not just a Meatloaf imitator but a Freddie Mercury tribute, too. Almost every month you can see this sort of international act. These concerts are usually held in the large hotels or at the Dubai Tennis Stadium (Map 3, #14), behind the Aviation Club. Check the papers for details.

While the oldies are rattling their jewellery at Sting concerts, Dubai is also having some success attracting cutting-edge dance acts. A DJ with a box of discs is obviously easier to bring out than the Bee Gees. DJs such as Tall Paul, Artful Dodger and franchised club events such as Ministry of Sound have all been visitors. Atlantis (Map 2, #12) and Planetarium (Map 3, #33) are the usual venues, though occasionally special one-off events are staged somewhere unusual like the agricultural area of Al-Awir.

THEATRE

There isn't much in the way of live theatre in Dubai. The British Airways Playhouse visits every so often, usually to perform a 'rollicking' comedy. The British Touring Shakespeare Company has also toured. The Laughter Factory also comes here every few months; it features two or three British comedians on the same bill. All these usually perform in one of the major hotels such as the Hyatt Regency Dubai. There is always plenty of publicity for these events so watch the papers. Tickets cost around Dh80.

SPECTATOR SPORTS
Camel Racing

Since camels are the most common animal in the UAE, it's not surprising that camel

---

The Ubiquitous Camel

As a symbol of Arabia, a symbol of the desert and a symbol of the Bedouin, camels are very important creatures in the UAE. However, unless they are for eating or racing, camels don't seem to be of much use any more. They just wander around, and when they wander onto the road, they can get hit. As you can imagine, a road accident involving a camel is not a pretty sight, and human fatalities are quite high in such accidents. If you hit a camel (and survive) you must pay the owner for its loss, as well as the damage to your car. If you hit a camel and just injure it, chances are it will become your responsibility. We heard a story about an expat doctor who got himself into just such a situation. He had to load the camel onto the back of a pick-up and keep it in his backyard until he could find someone to take it off his hands.

---

racing is the main spectator sport. While it sounds fun, it isn't for the faint-hearted. Since the races begin on a 4km straight, the moment the gun sounds, dozens of Emiratis go screaming down the side of the track in their 4WDs, paying far more attention to the camels than to where they are going. It would be *very* easy to get run over in these circumstances, so be careful. The jockeys themselves are also at risk from these unwieldy ships of the desert. Due to allegations of child abuse, a decree was issued in 1993 prohibiting children from racing camels. In keeping with the international standards set for horse jockeys, the decree stated that all jockeys must weigh at least 45kg, though it is unclear whether this ruling has been fully embraced by the operators of the industry. In the past, boys from India and Bangladesh as young as five were stuck in the saddle with Velcro!

Races take place early on Thursday and Friday mornings and on public holidays during winter and spring at the **Dubai Camel Racecourse** *(Map 2; ☎ 338 2324; admission free)*, south of the centre off Oud Metha Rd on the Bur Dubai side. The races usually start around 7am and continue until about 9am. If you miss out on a race meeting you can usually catch training sessions each morning at about the same time or at around 5.30pm.

Desert Rallies
Although it's not quite the Paris-Dakar, the Desert Challenge is still a high-profile international driving event that attracts top rally drivers from all over the world. It is held in the first week of November as a part of the World Cup in Cross Country Rallying, starting in Abu Dhabi and finishing in Dubai. There are a number of smaller rally events during February and March, including the Drakkar Noir 1000 Dunes Rally, the Federation Rally and the Spring Desert Rally, which are all 4WD events. Contact the **Emirates Motor Sports Federation** (☎ 282 7111; e emsf@emirates.net.ae) for details.

Golf
It's not surprising that the Dubai Desert Classic (W www.dubaidesertclassic.com) attracts some of the wealthiest golfers in the world. It's the world's richest golf tournament, with prize money of US$1.4 million. In recent years it has been shared between the **Emirates Golf Club** (Map 2; ☎ 347 3222; Interchange No 5, Sheikh Zayed Rd) and the **Dubai Creek Golf & Yacht Club** (Map 3, #19; ☎ 295 6000; Al-Garhoud Rd). The four-day tournament is held annually in February or March. To watch it costs Dh130 per day for adults or Dh450 for the whole tournament (juniors pay half price). Throughout the year there are small amateur tournaments at the golf clubs in Dubai. Details are usually given in the daily newspapers.

Tennis
The Dubai Tennis Open, held in February, is a part of the ATP world series tour and total prize money is just over US$1 million. It is held at the **Dubai Tennis Stadium** (Map 3, #14; ☎ 206 2425; Al-Garhoud). Tickets get more expensive as the tournament progresses. It's about Dh100 for the first few matches and goes up to Dh250 for the finals. Tickets for the whole tournament, with food and drinks included, cost Dh2000 per person.

Cricket
To see international cricket you will have to go to nearby Sharjah (see the Excursions chapter), which hosts matches in October, November, March and April at the **Sharjah Cricket Stadium** (☎ 06-532 2991; 2nd Industrial Rd, Industrial Area 5, Sharjah; admission Dh20-150). The Sharjah Cup is held in March or April. Participating teams change every year, but there are three competing nations each time, one of which is India or Pakistan. These are usually 'day-night' matches, starting at 2.30pm and finishing under lights at around 10.15pm. Sharjah Cricket Stadium has held more one-day matches than any other venue in the world, and in 2001 it held its first test series (between Pakistan and the West Indies). Tickets go on sale at the stadium, which can hold 22,000 spectators. Matches between India and Pakistan are war by other means, and bring out fanatical support from resident fans.

Rugby
The Dubai Rugby Sevens tournament (see W www.dubiarugby7s.com for details) has the reputation of being Dubai's booziest sporting event, at least for the spectators. The competition attracts teams from rugby powerhouses such as New Zealand, France, Tonga and Fiji to the **Dubai Exiles Rugby Club** (Map 2, #38; ☎ 333 1198; Ras al-Khor Rd) near Dubai Country Club. The two-day contest also includes a team of expats banded together as the Arabian Gulf team. This very popular event usually falls in the first weekend of December, though the dates are shifted around to avoid coinciding with Ramadan. In 2001 the final between New Zealand and Fiji attracted 14,000 people. A season ticket costs Dh120, which includes entry to the rock concert after the final.

Horse Racing & Polo
A love of horses runs deep in Arab blood, and a number of sheikhs run stables with some of the finest horses in the world. Sheikh Mohammed, Dubai's crown prince, is somewhat of a racing celebrity and well known in the international racing community. The Dubai World Cup (W www.dubai

worldcup.com), held in March, is renowned for being the world's richest horse race with prize money of (gulp) US$6 million. It's held at the **Nad al-Sheba Club** *(Map 2, #32; ☎ 336 3666; general admission free, admission to member's stand Dh60)* 5km south-east of Dubai. To get there, head south down Oud Metha Rd until you get to a large roundabout with signs for Al-Ain and Hatta and you will see the sign for Nad al-Sheba. It is also signposted from Sheikh Zayed Rd.

The racing season lasts from November to March. Races are held at night from about 7pm (9pm during Ramadan). The members' stand is licensed. Call the club for the exact dates of race meetings throughout the year. It's a great opportunity for people-watching.

There are also dozens of desert endurance races during the winter. Stunning Arabian horses compete in these events as they are most suited to this kind of terrain. The most prestigious of these races is the Emirates Championship Cup, which is run over 130km. Many sheikhs enter these races and they usually seem to win.

Horse racing and polo matches are held at **Ghantoot Racing & Polo Club** (see Ghantoot in the Excursions chapter). The Dubai Polo & Equestrian Club is very exclusive and unless you're a member, you're unlikely to be allowed in to watch. Horse races are also held at the small **Jebel Ali Racecourse** *(Map 2; ☎ 347 5914; admission free)*;

the course is behind the Emirates Golf Club, off Sheikh Zayed Rd.

The **Emirates Racing Association** *(☎ 331 3311)* has a useful website with details of all race meets at W www.emiratesracing.com.

Marine Events

If fast boats give you a bit of a thrill you should come to Dubai in late October or early November when the city hosts the Class One World Offshore Championship powerboat races. These are held at the **Dubai International Marine Club** *(DIMC; Map 2, #7; ☎ 399 4111; Al-Sufouh Rd)* in Al-Mina al-Seyahi. Admission is free and entertainment is provided for kids.

It's hard to imagine it but they do race those big dhows. Up to 50 of them take part in a race. When they're all lined up with their sails hoisted, ready to begin, it's a spectacular sight. Races take place every weekend from October to May at the DIMC. Admission is free, but you won't really see much from the club as the races take place 8km off the coast. Many people watch from boats just beyond the breakwater.

The **President's Cup Dubai-Muscat Sailing Regatta** is held every year in March. It begins in Dubai at the DIMC and finishes in Muscat at the Marina Bandar al-Rowdha.

Call the Race Department of the DIMC for more information and the exact dates of any of these events.

Shopping

Dubai is a marvellous place for shopping. The lack of duty and taxes, in addition to the relatively cheap shipping costs, mean that travelling here for a shopping expedition is well worthwhile. The Dubai Shopping Festival, held every March, is promoted aggressively and brings in hundreds of tourists, especially from other Arab countries and the former Soviet Union.

The major shopping districts in Dubai are Karama (Map 6), Al-Rigga Rd in Rigga (Map 5), Al-Dhiyafah Rd and Al-Satwa Rd in Satwa (Map 7) and the various souqs in Deira (Map 4). The best of Dubai's shopping, though, is contained within the many shopping centres. These are scattered around the city, located on main roads and easy to reach by bus. The people of Dubai love to browse round the shops, so the centres are great places for people-watching. The number of upmarket boutiques and jewellery stores is staggering. Nearly all the centres are air-conditioned, which makes them even more popular in the sultry summer months.

WHAT TO BUY
Gold

Dubai has earned itself a well-deserved reputation as the City of Gold. Even seasoned veterans of Middle Eastern gold markets are likely to be blown away by the sheer scale of Dubai's Gold Souq and the Gold & Diamond Park.

Just about every conceivable kind of gold jewellery is on offer here. There are earrings, rings, pendants, necklaces and bracelets. Designs can be traditional or modern, bold or conservative, chunky or delicate. Different shades of gold are also available. The artisans can alter the composition of alloys in the gold to create pink, white, yellow or green hues in the one piece of jewellery. Items can have a dull or shiny polish applied to them. It's not just jewellery – you can buy coins or even ingots.

In most Gulf countries, a bride has to be laden with gold jewellery on her wedding day. Antique or second-hand gold passed down from previous generations is not considered good enough as a gift. Gold presented to a bride must be new, so this keeps a constant flow of customers coming to Dubai's Gold Souq. It also means that a lot of gold is recycled. Much of the new gold comes from Australia or South Africa; it is sent to Italy or Turkey for refining, then crafted in India and, finally, sold in the gold shops of Dubai.

There are very strict laws involving authenticity: gold traders are quickly put out of business if they try to dupe a customer. If a shop attendant tells you that a particular piece of jewellery is 22 carat (meaning that 22 of the 24 parts of the alloy are gold, the rest being zinc, copper and silver) you can be confident that it is.

Gold is sold by weight and prices fluctuate almost daily. There is room to bargain so don't accept the first price, and be sure to shop around. Prices also vary depending on whether the piece was made by a machine or an artisan.

A 22-carat machine-made gold bracelet costs around Dh300, while an intricately handcrafted one costs around Dh500, depending on your bargaining skills. A necklace can cost as much as Dh1500. Small items, such as simple earrings or a pendant, can be purchased for under Dh150 in lower grades of gold and can go up to Dh500 for 21- or 22-carat gold.

Carpets

Persian carpets, Turkish and Kurdish kilims, Turkmen 'Bukhara' rugs, and Kashmiri and Afghan rugs are widely available. Whenever you buy a rug you will be given a certificate of authentication, which is guaranteed by the Dubai Chamber of Commerce & Industry, so you can be sure that the Turkmen rug you're about to spend Dh4000 on is actually a Turkmen rug.

For more useful information on the history of Persian carpets, how they are made and what to look for when buying one, see the boxed text 'The Art of Carpet Buying' or read *Oriental Carpets: A Buyer's Guide* by Essie Sakhai.

For the best range of carpets, you need to go to the Central Market in the neighbouring emirate of Sharjah, a 10-minute drive from Dubai (see the Excursions chapter for more information). The only problem is that each year the prices seem to creep up as more and more tourists come here to shop. There is room to bargain, though, and if you're having trouble getting the price you want, just go to the next shop – there are dozens of them. Be aware that the carpet sellers here are not exclusively retailers, there are a few wholesalers as well. If you can seek out these shops you'll get much better prices.

If you can't make it to Sharjah, one of the best carpet shops in Dubai is **Red Sea Exhibitions** *(Map 3, #45; Beach Centre, Jumeira Rd)*. It has an excellent selection of oriental carpets, including many antiques, at very reasonable prices.

All the shopping centres listed later in this chapter have carpet shops. **Deira City Centre** *(Map 3, #21; Al-Garhoud Rd)* has the greatest number of rug shops. One of the best here is Pride of Kashmir, which has the largest range and very good prices.

In Deira try the **Deira Tower** *(Map 4, #70)* and **Dubai Tower** *(Map 4, #71)* on Baniyas Square, both of which have lots of small carpet boutiques. **Khyber Carpets** *(Map 3, #1; Hyatt Galleria, off Al Khaleej Rd)* has an enormous selection of high-quality carpets from Iran. They are expensive, however, and the vendors do not seem very interested in bargaining.

If you are interested in Afghan carpets in particular, you'll find the greatest selection at **Afghan Carpet Palace** *(Map 5, #11; Hamarain Centre, Abu Baker al-Siddiq Rd)*. If you've only got eyes for Persian carpets, go to **Sadaf Carpet** *(Map 5, #35; Al-Maktoum Rd, Rigga)*, next to the restaurant of the same name. It has rugs from Iran, both silk and wool, as well as a number of antiques. The prices are very reasonable here and they won't try to sweet-talk you.

The Art of Carpet Buying

Buying carpets without getting taken in requires great skill and patience. And it involves an understanding of the intricacies of the trade. These tips might help you navigate your way through the rigours of the purchasing process:

- Do not feel embarrassed or obliged to buy just because the shop attendant has unrolled 40 carpets for you; this is part of the ritual.
- Ask a lot of questions and bargain hard over a long period of time (preferably two to three visits).
- Remember that rugs from Iran or Turkmenistan are generally more valuable than those from Kashmir or Turkey. Silk rugs are more valuable than wool ones.
- The more knots there are per square inch, the more valuable the rug (flip the corner of a rug over and have a look at the back).
- Look closely at the detail in the design of the carpet and compare it with others. Often the value of a carpet is raised by the name of the family who made it.
- Natural dyes are more expensive than artificial dyes. Antique rugs are always naturally dyed. A naturally dyed rug will appear to be slightly faded, but this is not considered a flaw. The settling down of natural dyes creates a carpet that is well balanced in colour and tone.
- If you are buying an artificially coloured carpet check that the colours have not bled. Artificial dyes are used widely now and can be just as attractive as the natural dyes. Unless you are a real purist it really doesn't matter.

Arabian Souvenirs & Bedouin Jewellery

Most of the 'Arabian' souvenirs are actually made in India. Typical souvenirs include copper coffeepots (*dalla* in Arabic), which cost from Dh50 for small ones (about 8cm high) to Dh500 for large ones (about 50cm high). Antique *dalla*s cost from Dh300 to Dh1000, depending upon their condition. Decorated metal food platters, used for special occasions such as wedding banquets, can cost Dh150.

Carved wooden or leather stuffed camels are also a common souvenir; they cost anything from Dh30 to Dh350. Wooden Quran holders come in various sizes and fold up flat so they're not too bulky in your luggage. Most of them come from India and cost from Dh30 to Dh50.

Woollen camel bags, which are slung over a camel's back and have a large pocket on either side, mainly come from Afghanistan and cost anything from Dh250 to Dh500, depending on their size and quality. You can buy these, along with camel rugs, at a market attached to the Dubai Camel Racecourse (Map 2). The camel rugs and cloths are made of heavy cotton in a wide range of designs and colours. A camel rug measuring 1m by 1.5m costs about Dh35, while a thinner, lighter camel cloth of the same size costs about Dh20.

*Sheesha*s (water pipes) are nice Middle Eastern souvenirs, but they are not very practical to transport. Large *sheesha*s with a hose cost from Dh120 to Dh150. Some cost as little as Dh75, but they might not work very well. Always check that air flows well through a *sheesha* before you buy it. If you intend to smoke through your *sheesha* (rather than using it purely for decoration) there are a number of accessories you'll need (ask the shopkeeper), but they cost only a few dirhams each.

Sheesha pipes are available from tobacconists, shopping centres, hotel souvenir shops and some of the small grocery stores. One of the cheapest places is the tobacconist shop on the south side of Baniyas Square.

Most of the Bedouin jewellery you'll find comes from Oman. If you are travelling on to either Oman or Saudi Arabia, this sort of jewellery is much cheaper in those countries and the selection tends to be better. If you decide to make an excursion to Al-Ain you can cross to Buraimi on the Omani side of the border (without a visa) and shop for Omani jewellery, though the selection there tends to be pretty limited.

Some of the beautiful things you can buy are *khanjars* (daggers), gunpowder horns

and silver bracelets and necklaces. Look closely at the workmanship before you buy. Is the work detailed and intricate? Do the movable parts come on or off or slide around easily? Is the item dented or split?

As a rule any *khanjar* under Dh500 tends to be pretty nasty, but you should not invest more than Dh1200. Many shops sell *khanjar*s and jewellery in a display box so if you don't want to pay the extra price for this make it known.

Silver bracelets and necklaces from Oman are sold by weight, but often the shopkeeper has a fixed price for these items. The going rate is Dh1.80 per gram. For a simple studded

Khanjars

Worn mainly by Omani men, *khanjars* (daggers) are also worn by Emirati men in the rural east and north of the country. Traditionally the handles of these daggers were made from rhino horn, though today they are almost always made from either plastic or wood. *Khanjars* come in two basic designs: regular *khanjars* are identified by two rings where a belt is attached; Sayidi *khanjars* have five rings.

Regular *khanjars* are decorated entirely, or nearly entirely, with thin silver wire. The intricacy of the thread pattern, and the skill with which it is executed, are among the main determinants of value. Sayidi *khanjars* are often covered entirely in silver sheet and little or no wire is used.

The most important things to look for in assessing a *khanjar*'s quality are weight and the workmanship on the scabbard. A *khanjar* is a substantial item and ought to feel like one when you pick it up.

Some *khanjars* have a second knife inserted in a small scabbard attached to the back of the main scabbard. Don't pay too much of a premium for one of these – the knives in question are often cheap steak knives that have a bit of silver wrapped around the handle.

Do not believe anything anyone tells you regarding the age of individual pieces. Few *khanjars* will be more than 20 to 40 years old, and quality of workmanship, not age, should be the prime criterion.

Enjoy the air-conditioned splendour of the Bur Juman Centre, one of Dubai's many opulent malls

For a real taste of traditional Dubai, take a walk through the Spice Souq in Deira

CLINT LUCAS

CHRIS MELLOR

GUY MOBERLY

CHRIS MELLOR

NEIL SETCHFIELD

Shopping Dubai-style: fireworks during the Dubai Shopping Festival (top left); terracotta pots (top right); a 24-carat gold waistcoat (middle); gold bangles (bottom left); the Gold Souq at night (bottom right)

bracelet you will pay around Dh200 after bargaining. For larger and more ornate items, such as a bride's chest and head piece, you will probably be quoted around Dh1500. Make sure you ask for a discount, or for their best price before you agree to purchase. Larger silver prayer holders (about 20cm to 25cm in length) and gunpowder horns will cost around Dh350, but you could pay as much as Dh500 for really well-crafted items in good condition. Quality prayer holders made of white metal are not as valuable as the silver ones, but they still make a nice, and much more affordable, souvenir. You can get a small one for around Dh25.

In Dubai you can buy Omani jewellery at **Al-Kananah** *(Map 3, #1; Hyatt Galleria, off Al-Khaleej Rd)* in Deira. It also has some of the nicest *khanjar*s available in Dubai, for Dh500 to Dh1500, as well as various Arabic objects and souvenirs at a range of different prices depending on the quality.

Abu Ahmed Antiques *(Map 7, #15; Al-Dhiyafah Rd)* in Satwa has *khanjar*s and Bedouin jewellery from Oman as well as wooden chests, coffeepots and some very nice silver from Italy. The prices are very high, though, so it's worth shopping around a bit first.

If you have the time, the best place to shop for old Arabian souvenirs is actually in Sharjah at **Al-Arsah Souq** (see the Excursions chapter for more information). All the shopping centres mentioned later in this chapter have shops selling souvenirs. Sometimes you will have to wade through the merchandise from India, Africa and Thailand to be able to find any genuine Arabian bits and pieces.

You can also try the shops in the **Heritage Village** *(Map 4, #4; Al Shindagha Rd)*. As this is a touristy place, prices tend to be on the high side and bargaining doesn't bring them down much.

Most five-star hotels have shops selling good-quality souvenirs, jewellery and carpets, although prices are high. **Art & Culture** *(Map 4, #60; Dubai Inter-Continental Hotel)*, a crowded shop in the hotel lobby, has high-quality souvenirs and Bedouin jewellery. It also has very well-made *kandouras* (a Gulf version of a kaftan) and robes.

Perfume & Incense

When you pass black-cloaked Emirati women on the street you may catch a hint of an intense perfume. Arabic perfumes *(attar)* are very strong and spicy, unlike Western perfumes, which tend to be flowery and light. For centuries, Arab women have smothered themselves in perfumes. When there was no air-conditioning, and precious little water in the deserts of Arabia to wash bodies and clothes, people needed something to cover up the smell of perspiration.

You'll find perfume shops in all the shopping centres in Dubai, but the best place to look is the **Perfume Souq** *(Map 4)* on Sikkat al-Khail St in Deira, just east of the Gold Souq. Shopkeepers will want to daub you senseless with various perfumes, but a word of warning – the Arabic perfumes are oil-based and once on your clothes they can leave a stain. You can buy perfumes in bottles ranging from 12ml to 36ml. It is sold by the *tolah* (12ml or 12g) and prices vary, depending on the perfume. The cheapest is about Dh10 per *tolah* while the most expensive is an incredible Dh1500 per *tolah*. This expensive stuff, made from agar wood from Malaysia, is extremely concentrated. In fact, it's so concentrated that you will probably find it rancid and quite disgusting when you smell it in the perfume shop. When it settles down, though, it has a lovely, spicy fragrance and one drop is enough to last the whole day.

The perfume shops also sell an enormous range of incense. It can be in the form of compressed powder, crystals, rock or wood. Frankincense *(luban* in Arabic) is probably the most common form of incense. The quality varies – frankincense from Japan is not as valuable as the stuff from Iran or from the Dhofar region of southern Oman. The cheaper frankincense is about Dh20 per kilogram and the more expensive stuff is about Dh50. The wooden incense *(somok* in Arabic) is the nicest and most valuable of all incenses and comes from Malaysian agar wood. When burnt it gives off a sweet, rich log-fire smell. Agar wood ranges in price, depending on quality, from Dh10 per *tolah* to Dh30.

To burn incense you can either buy an electric incense burner, which has a metal plate that heats up, or you can buy a box of heat beads. The heat beads need to be set alight, then when they have settled down to a glow, then you put your piece of incense on top. You should consider, however, that travelling on a plane with these in your luggage is illegal as they are flammable. One option is to contact a church supplier when you get home – most Christian churches use special heat beads to burn frankincense.

Electronics

The UAE is the cheapest place in the Middle East to buy electrical goods. If it plugs into the wall you can buy it here, but the selection tends to be limited. Most shops stock the same three or four varieties of something (say, laptop or DVD player) at pretty much the same prices. You'll also discover that the shop attendants are not very knowledgeable about their stock so it helps to have a good idea of what you want before setting off on a shopping expedition. It is also a good idea, and it is accepted practice in the UAE, to plug your new gadget in at the shop to make sure that it works properly.

If you are looking for cheap electronics, try Al-Fahidi St in Bur Dubai (Map 4). Another place to look is the **Electronics Souq** *(Map 4)*, which covers an area around the corner of Al-Sabkha and Al-Maktoum Hospital Rds, near Baniyas Square. A medium-sized CD stereo with detachable speakers costs around Dh550; a 50cm TV costs about Dh600. Basic, multisystem videos should cost from about Dh250 to Dh350. More high-tech items such as laptops, DVD players and digital cameras tend to be similar in price to what you'd pay at home.

For software, go to Khalid bin al-Waleed Rd (Map 4) in Bur Dubai between Al-Mankhool Rd and the Falcon Roundabout. Taxi drivers still call this area Computer St.

Fabrics

The best place to buy fabrics is the **Dubai Souq** *(Map 4)* and along Al-Fahidi St (Map 4) in Bur Dubai. In fact, that's practically all you can buy here. All kinds and qualities of fabrics from India, Indonesia, Thailand, Japan and Korea are available here at very cheap prices. Cotton fabrics, depending on the weave, cost anywhere from 30 fils to Dh5 per metre. Silk costs around Dh8 per metre and linen about Dh7 per metre.

There are also plenty of tailors around here, all of whom are very good at what they do. They work very quickly so if you only have a few days in Dubai you'll still have time to have something made. A simple woman's skirt may cost about Dh30, while a more complicated skirt, blouse or trousers will cost from Dh40 to Dh50 to make. A man's shirt costs about Dh25, while you can get a suit made for about Dh150.

Miscellaneous

Dubai is probably the cheapest place outside Iran to buy Iranian caviar; it's sold in supermarket delicatessens and five-star hotels. There are speciality caviar shops at the airport, in Markaz al-Jumeira (Map 7, #31) on Jumeira Rd and at the Jumeira Beach Hotel (Map 2, #20).

Honey from Oman is another special product sold in Dubai. You'll find it in the odd grocery store or spice shop around the souq areas of Bur Dubai and Deira (Map 4). It ranges in colour from light golden to almost black, and is usually packaged in old Vimto bottles. Believe it or not it sells for anything between Dh100 and Dh700 a bottle. Though it seems to taste just like ordinary honey, the reason it is so expensive is that it is collected by hand from remote areas in the mountains and deserts of Oman.

The less flashy shopping areas, such as Karama (Map 6) and Al-Satwa Rd (Map 7), used to openly sell 'imitation' brand-name goods such as watches, sunglasses and handbags, not to mention CDs, DVDs, software and videos. The authorities have cracked down on shops openly selling this merchandise, but it's said that some shopkeepers in these areas still keep imitation stuff under the counter.

Kitsch Souvenirs

If you're looking for the ultimate kitsch souvenir from the UAE, it has to be the tacky mosque clock, which belts out the azan (the call to prayer). It costs Dh20, and if it doesn't get you out of bed in the morning, then you must be dead! You can buy it from just about anywhere, but try the shops around the Deira and Dubai souqs (Map 4) first. Another version of this clock comes in the form of the Quran.

Then there's the camel lighter – press its hump and it spits fire – which is available from some of the trinket shops on 67 St, near Deira Covered Souq (Map 4). Or the little camel toy which sings in Arabic – only Dh20 from the Karama Centre (Map 6, #32). Some of the imitation perfumes and aftershaves have real kitsch value too – Tonny Hilfiger and Oponi (in Opium packaging), for example.

Kitschy, though not cheap, are the little silver Emirati objects in frames, available from souvenir shops in shopping centres. These little objects include dhows, dallas, incense burners, camels and khanjars. They cost about Dh80 for the smallest ones and up to Dh500 for large ones.

WHERE TO SHOP
Shopping Centres
Shining marble floors, fountains and bracing air-conditioning can all be found in Dubai's many shopping malls. These palaces of retail commerce together contain thousands of shops. Nightlife for many families seems to consist of strolling around these malls. If you're really serious about engaging in retail therapy you could get the *Dubai Shopping Centre Directory*, which is available in bookshops and most upmarket hotel rooms. Included here is a selection of the major centres.

Deira City Centre *(Map 3, #21; Al-Garhoud Rd; bus Nos 3, 4, 6, 11, 15, 23 & 33; open 10am-11pm daily)*, near the Dubai Creek Golf & Yacht Club, is Dubai's biggest and most popular shopping centre, especially with teenagers and young families. It has the greatest range of shops in Dubai, including department stores, a Virgin Megastore and the biggest supermarket in the city, and a section devoted to gold and jewellery with about 20 specialist stores.

Bur Juman Centre *(Map 6, #25; cnr Sheikh Khalifa bin Zayed & Khalid bin al-Waleed Rds; bus Nos 3, 5, 21, 23, 33, 44, 61 & 90; open 10am-10pm Sat-Thur, 2pm-10pm Fri)* is popular because of its central location. It has mainly men's and women's international clothes shops, sports shops and shops selling home wares. At the time of writing it was undergoing a massive expansion, which will double its size.

Wafi City Shopping Centre *(Map 3, #34; Al-Qataiyat Rd; bus Nos 14, 16 & 44; open 10am-10pm Sat-Thur, 2pm-10pm Fri)*, near Al-Garhoud Bridge on the Bur Dubai side of the Creek, is an enormous shopping centre with lots of exclusive, upmarket shops. One of its big attractions is its Encounter Zone playground, which provides entertainment for children of all ages (for more details, see Dubai for Children in the Facts for the Visitor chapter).

Lamcy Plaza *(Map 3, #28; Al-Qataiyat Rd, Za'abeel; bus No 44; open 10am-10pm daily)*, near the corner of Za'abeel Rd, offers lower prices than most other big shopping centres and attracts Indo-Pakistani shoppers mainly. The replica of the London Bridge over the main entrance is truly weird. It has a couple of good department stores, a large CD shop and a cinema complex.

Al-Ghurair Centre *(Map 5, #27; cnr Al-Rigga & Omar ibn al-Khattab Rds, Deira; bus Nos 5, 6, 13, 19 & 20; open 9am-1pm & 5pm-10pm Sat-Thur, 5pm-10pm Fri)* was Dubai's first shopping centre and has recently been expanded to include more than 400 shops. It features some very impressive fabric and jewellery shops on the 1st floor.

Markaz al-Jumeira *(Map 7, #31; Jumeira Rd, Jumeira; bus No 8; open 9am-1pm & 4pm-9pm daily)* is a small shopping centre with a number of speciality shops, including designer home ware, art, framing and jewellery, caviar and cakes.

Karama Centre *(Map 6, #32; Kuwait St, Karama; bus Nos 5, 6, 23, 33 & 44; open 9am-1pm & 4pm-9pm daily)*, between Sheikh Khalifa bin Zayed and Za'abeel Rds, caters mainly to Indian clientele. The rest of the shops in the area are very cheap, selling copies of label jeans, watches and jewellery.

There are also a few shops selling musical instruments.

Twin Towers Shopping Centre (Map 4, #64; Baniyas Rd, Deira; bus Nos 4, 5, 8 & 11; open 10am-9pm daily) is a quiet, upmarket shopping centre with lots of designer shops.

Palm Strip Shopping Centre (Map 7, #26; Jumeira Rd, Jumeira; bus No 8; open 10am-1pm & 4.30pm-10pm Sat-Thur, 4.30pm-10pm Fri) is a small, very upmarket shopping centre, unusual for not being in an air-con building. The shops here include exclusive clothing stores such as Armani Jeans, as well as a Tower Records store.

Gold & Diamond Park (Map 2, #16; Sheikh Zayed Rd; open 10am-10pm Sat-Thur, 4pm-10pm Fri), near Intersection No 4, is a new development with 30 retailers and about 120 manufacturers. The shopping section is a handsome building designed along traditional lines, and has air-conditioning and a café. There is some traditional jewellery on display here, and the shops sell oddities such as purple gold and black pearls. Bus Nos 90 and 91 run along Sheikh Zayed Rd, but as you'd have to cross this busy freeway to get to the park, it would be better to catch a taxi.

Souqs

Even if you have no plans to buy anything, it is worth a visit to the **Gold Souq** (Map 4) in Deira simply to take in the atmosphere, and to ogle at the size of some of the jewellery on offer. The main drag of the Gold Souq runs along Sikkat al-Khail St, between Suq Deira and Old Baladiya Sts. The other part of the souq runs along 45 St, which comes off Sikkat al-Khail St to form a T-shape. Wooden lattice archways and roofs cover the entire area. The souq is aggressively promoted during the Dubai Shopping Festival and Dubai Summer Surprises, both of which send gold sales into orbit.

The **Spice Souq** (Map 4), also known as Deira Old Souq (since it doesn't just sell spices), is one place you must wander around for a real taste of traditional Dubai. The spices are mainly found at the souq's eastern end, in the area closest to the Creek. Sacks overflow with frankincense, dried lemons, ginger root, cardamom, dried fruit, nuts and pulses. For a few dirhams you can take home a bag of whatever exotic ingredients you want. Other shops in this souq sell tacky trinkets, kitchenwares, rugs, glassware and textiles, all at very low prices (though you will be expected to haggle a little). The alleyways here are narrow and intricate and there is no set route that you should take.

Deira Covered Souq (Map 4) is enclosed in the square between Al-Sabkha Rd and 67 St, and Naif Rd and Al-Maktoum Hospital Rd. The most interesting area is right in the middle, just west of the Al-Sabkha Rd bus station. The goods here are predominantly from India. You will find textiles, spices, kitchenware, walking sticks, *sheesha* pipes, clothes and a lifetime's supply of henna. Attractively patterned muslin headscarves and shawls cost about Dh10, with bargaining. A small box of henna costs Dh5. The prices of textiles here are the same as in the Dubai Souq (see Textiles under What to Buy earlier in this chapter).

Henna

Henna decoration is a Middle Eastern tradition dating back to Neolithic times. The leaves of the henna shrub (lawsonia inermis) have been dried, ground into powder and then turned into paste for at least 6000 years. In central Turkey in 4000 BC women painted their hands in homage to the Mother Goddess. This tradition spread through the eastern Mediterranean region where the henna shrub grows wild. The paste is applied and left to stain the skin any autumn colour from brown to red. Women decorate their hands, nails and feet, usually for a special event, such as a wedding, and it stays on for about six weeks. In the more conservative and traditional areas of Dubai Emirate, such as Hatta, most Emirati women will have some form of henna decoration on their hands and feet. There are many beauty salons in Dubai that do henna decorations for clients; just look for signs with painted hands on them. You'll find a number of such shops around the Deira souqs (Map 4) and in Karama (Map 6).

Dubai Souq *(Map 4)*, on the Creek waterfront in Bur Dubai, offers little in the way of Arabian antiques or souvenirs, but has a wide variety of textiles. If you want to have a sari made, this is the place to come. There are dozens of shops selling all kinds of materials from India, Thailand, Indonesia and Korea. They are broken up only by the odd tailor shop. You can also buy shoes and Indian snacks here. Note that the Dubai Souq is a little slow to get going in the morning and does not open up until 9am or 9.30am.

Al-Karama Shopping Centre *(Map 6)* is a souq by any other name; it lies either side of 18B St in the heart of the bustling Karama district. It offers cheap clothing, toys, accessories, Asian pop music in various languages and furniture, as well fake luxury goods or so they say. There are also grocery shops and cheap Indo-Pakistani and Filipino restaurants and cafés. Bargaining is the order of the day, and the shopkeepers are always touting for business.

Satwa *(Map 7)*, the area along Al-Satwa Rd between Al-Dhiyafah Rd and Al-Hudheiba Rd, is the place to buy shoes, textiles, cheap bags and suitcases. There are also a number of electronic spare-parts shops and lots of sweet shops. If you don't have time to visit this souq you won't be missing out on much, but if you are in the area it is worth a wander for the buzz. Neighbouring **Al-Dhiyafah Rd** *(Map 7)* is a more upmarket strip, a mix of restaurants, cafés, antiques and home-ware shops, as well as the smallish **Dune Centre** *(Map 7, #5)* shopping arcade. Shopping and eating on both streets continues until midnight every day.

Bookshops

One of Dubai's best bookshops is **Magrudy Books** *(Map 7, #30; Magrudy's Shopping Centre, Jumeira Rd; open 8.30am-1pm & 5pm-8pm Sat-Tues, 8.30am-8pm Wed & Thur)*. A rival for the title of Dubai's best bookshop is the branch of **Book Corner** *(Map 3, #21; Deira City Centre)*, which has ample space for browsing. Book Corner also has branches at the Dune Centre *(Map 7, #5; Al-Dhiyafah Rd, Satwa)*, Al-Khaleej Shopping Centre *(Map 4, #40; Al-Mankhool Rd)*; and Jumeira Plaza *(Map 7, #32; Jumeira Rd)*. **Books Gallery** *(Map 5, #27; Al-Ghurair Centre, cnr Omar Ibn al-Khattab & Al-Rigga Rds)* is another possibility. Most of the larger hotels have small selections in their bookshops. **House of Prose** *(Map 7, #32; Jumeira Plaza, Jumeira Rd)* is an excellent second-hand bookshop. Another place to look for second-hand books is **Bookzone** *(Map 6, #1; Al-Rais Centre, Al-Mankhool Rd)*.

Dar al-Hikma *(World of Wisdom; Map 7, #16; Al-Dhiyafah Rd, Satwa)* is a newsagency and bookshop with a relatively small but well-chosen selection of books in English. Along with the **Al-Jabre Bookshop** *(Map 6, #25; Bur Juman Centre)*, it's a good place to hunt for books on Islamic topics.

Excursions

If you are going to be in Dubai for more than a couple of days it's well worth making a day trip or overnight visit to some of the surrounding emirates (Map 1). Sharjah offers some terrific cultural attractions and a magnificent wildlife park. Deep in the rugged Hajar Mountains is the scenic town of Hatta, an enclave of Dubai Emirate. Between Dubai and the Hajars there are great, red-tinged dune fields and, further south, the oasis city of Al-Ain. Over the mountains lie the fine beaches and rocky headlands of the east coast, host to a string of dive sites, fishing villages, rugged wadis, sturdy forts and the busy ports of Khor Fakkan and Fujairah. All of this is accessible by a state-of-the-art road network and you're never more than a three-hour drive from Dubai.

All the trips mentioned here can be arranged with any tour company in Dubai (see Organised Tours in the Getting Around chapter earlier in this guide) but we suggest you just hire a car or catch a minibus to your destination and do it on your own. You'll get much better value for money and you won't be as rushed.

JEBEL ALI
☎ 09

If you want to get away from it all, the beach at Jebel Ali is like a desert island getaway, as long as you can ignore the industrial skyline of Jebel Ali Port in the distance. Currently designated a conservation area, this 15km-long stretch of sand is the last undeveloped coastal stretch in Dubai Emirate. The beach is long, wide and, generally, very clean. There are *barasti* (palm-leaf) shelters and showers at intervals along the beach, though you will have to get there early to nab one for yourself. You might see a few campers along here as it's a popular overnight getaway for Dubai residents. The further you get from Jebel Ali Hotel, the fewer people there are. There are patrols along the beach on weekends, so don't forget that drinking alcohol in public is illegal.

Insurance Warning

Bear in mind that unless you make other arrangements, the insurance on your rental car will only be valid inside the UAE. This means that if you go to Hatta, which involves passing through about 20km of Omani territory or you decide to visit Buraimi (in Oman) while on an excursion to Al-Ain – both of which can be done without an Omani visa – you had better not have even a minor accident while you are on the Omani side of the border. It is possible to add Oman to a rented car's insurance (if, say, you want to rent a car in Dubai and drive to Muscat), but the insurance will go up by Dh10 or Dh20 per day and the cost of renting the car itself may double.

Jebel Ali Hotel & Golf Resort (☎ 883 6000; e hoteluae@emirates.net.ae, w www .jebelalihotel.com; singles/doubles Dh1400/ 1550, villas from Dh1870) is the only place to stay if you don't have camping gear. This pricey resort extends over a large area and includes a nine-hole golf course, stables, marina, shooting range, tennis courts, a long private beachfront, wooded gardens (complete with wandering peacocks) and two swimming pools. The main building looks like an East German office block but there are some very pleasant new villas, with gardens and ocean views. There are often special weekend package deals that include a round of golf. The hotel provides a free shopping shuttle to Deira (though the shuttle does not go to the airport and will not let you take luggage).

It takes 25 minutes to drive to Jebel Ali from the centre of Dubai and it costs about Dh60 in a metered taxi or just Dh7 in a shared taxi, which you can catch from the Bur Dubai bus station. If you're headed for the beach, it's better to have your own transport otherwise getting back to Dubai means walking to the Jebel Ali Hotel and calling a taxi from there. To get to the beach, follow the signs for the Jebel Ali Hotel from the main Dubai–Jebel Ali highway. Instead of pulling into the hotel's main entrance, continue along a sandy path that follows the coast. You'll see dozens of tracks leading off to the beach on your right. Most saloon cars can make it, but if the track looks too sandy, just leave your car on the path and walk across the dunes.

GHANTOOT
☎ 02

Just across the 'border', in the oil-rich emirate of Abu Dhabi, lies the racecourse, polo club and resort hotel complex at Ghantoot. Once over the border you soon realise you're in an emirate with money to burn because of the vast forestry projects stretching along both sides of highway, where the trees are irrigated with hundreds of miles of black plastic tubing. Take a look around Ghantoot and the sense that money means little gets stronger. The **Ghantoot Racing & Polo Club** (☎ 562 9050) has an 1800m horse-racing track, a grandstand seating 2000, six polo fields and 200 polo ponies housed in its vast stables. The clubhouse has shops and a swimming pool as well as an Italian restaurant (open to nonmembers). The polo season runs from mid-October until mid-April, and spectators are welcome. In addition, three horse races are held here in November, December and January. Check the newspapers for details.

Sun Divers (☎ 562 9265, 050-653 7483; e sundiver@emirates.net.ae) is a German-run dive school based at the Jazira Hotel & Resort that offers SSI and PADI diving courses. It leads dives onto wrecks and coral in the Gulf. It will even arrange dives in the Hatta rock pools (see the entry Around Hatta later in this chapter). The price is Dh110 per dive for one to six dives, plus Dh70 for full equipment hire. Sun Divers is located at the western end of the chalet beach (turn left after the gate) at the resort. It's open year-round, and if the sea is too rough, lessons are held in the sea channel.

Between the chalets and the resort is a huge abandoned **palace** on the edge of the sea channel, never used because of faulty

construction. It remains fully furnished and utterly silent.

Jazira Hotel & Resort (☎ 562 9100; e jazbeach@emirates.net.ae; singles/doubles Dh335.50/427.60, bungalow Dh984) is Ghantoot's only hotel. This four-star resort is built in a style you might call futuristic Moroccan, although rooms were being refurbished when we visited. The resort offers a range of activities from tennis to squash and has a water frontage courtesy of its very own 7km-long sea channel, another extraordinary use of money. There is a small, private beach on the channel below the hotel. The best part of the hotel, however, is on the coast 7km away, where there are chalets (signposted on the road as bungalows) looking onto a glorious 900m-long stretch of pure white sand. The chalets (two bedrooms) are fiercely expensive, and at weekends prices rise by 50% on the rates we've listed. Nonguests can use the beach for Dh70 per day. The Dalma restaurant and bar is here, as well as the Sun Divers dive school.

Ghantoot lies about 65km from Dubai and the turn-off is clearly signposted. There's no public transport. A taxi from Dubai costs about Dh80.

SHARJAH
☎ 06 • pop 500,000

Dubai's neighbour Sharjah is the cultural capital of the UAE, with a proliferation of excellent museums and galleries. It also offers excellent shopping and nearby is a top-class wildlife park. Visitors to Dubai tend to miss out on Sharjah, but it's easy to get to and well worth a visit. The main sites can be covered in just half a day.

Sharjah is increasingly becoming a dormitory suburb for Dubai (rents are much lower here). During the first half of the 19th century, Sharjah was the most important port on the Arabian side of the lower Gulf, and during the latter half of the century its rulers vied with those of Abu Dhabi for the area's leading political role. However, this changed with Dubai's ascendancy, in terms of wealth and political power, in the 1980s. Today Sharjah is responsible for some 45% of the UAE's total industrial production.

The ruling Al-Qasimi family has close links with Saudi Arabia, and perhaps not coincidently Sharjah has the most culturally conservative laws in the UAE (see the boxed text 'Decency Laws' opposite for more details).

Orientation & Information

The centre of town is the area between the Corniche and Al-Zahra Rd, from the Central Market to Sheikh Sultan bin Saqr al-Qasimi Rd. It's not a huge area and it's pretty easy to get around on foot if the heat's not too debilitating.

Sharjah can be hellish to navigate when driving. Al-Wahda Rd, the main link with Dubai, is gridlocked during peak hours, especially at the King Faisal Square overpass. The proliferation of roundabouts, lengthy street names and the absence of directions to Ajman or Dubai make it easy to get lost. Street signs tend to be written in very small print and have similar-sounding names – Sheikh Mohammed bin Sultan al-Qasimi

Rd versus Sheikh Khalid bin Mohammed al-Qasimi Rd, for example.

The website **W** www.sharjah-welcome .com is a comprehensive resource aimed at tourists. Moneychangers and banks can be found on and around Burj Ave (also called Bank St). Also in the centre of town is the **main post office** (*Government House Square; open 8am-8pm Sat-Wed, 8am-6pm Thur*). The **Etisalat office** (*Kuwait Square; open 24 hrs*) offers telephone and fax services.

Al-Hisn Fort

This double-storey, three-towered fort (*Burj Ave; admission free; open 9am-1pm & 5pm-8pm Tues-Sun, 5pm-8pm Fri, women only Wed*) sits in the middle of Burj Ave. Originally built in 1820, it has been fully restored and houses a fascinating collection of photographs, artefacts and documents, many from the 1930s, showing members of the ruling Al-Qasimi family and the British Trucial Oman Scouts who were stationed

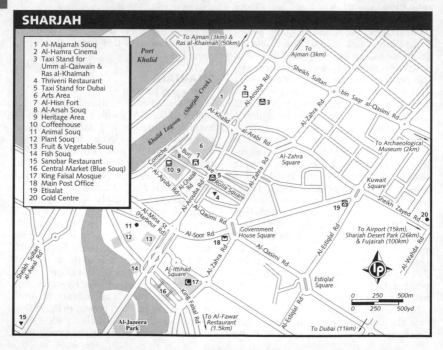

SHARJAH

1 Al-Majarrah Souq
2 Al-Hamra Cinema
3 Taxi Stand for Umm al-Qaiwain & Ras al-Khaimah
4 Thriveni Restaurant
5 Taxi Stand for Dubai
6 Arts Area
7 Al-Hisn Fort
8 Al-Arsah Souq
9 Heritage Area
10 Coffeehouse
11 Animal Souq
12 Plant Souq
13 Fruit & Vegetable Souq
14 Fish Souq
15 Sanobar Restaurant
16 Central Market (Blue Souq)
17 King Faisal Mosque
18 Main Post Office
19 Etisalat
20 Gold Centre

here at the time. As you enter the fort there is a room on your left showing footage of the first Imperial Airways flights from London, which landed here in 1932 on their way to India. The difference between Sharjah then and now is really incredible. Other rooms have displays of weapons (including a rifle called Abu Futilah, 'Father of Rifles', the first gun brought to the fort), jewellery, currency and items used in the pearl trade.

Heritage Area

All the buildings in this block, just inland from the Corniche, between Burj Ave and Al-Mina St, have been faithfully constructed incorporating traditional designs and materials such as sea rock and gypsum. Coming from Burj Ave, the first place you arrive at is **Literature Square**. At the **House of Poetry**, facing the square, public poetry readings are sometimes held. Across from here is **Bait al-Gharbi** *(admission free; open 8am-1pm & 5pm-8pm Tues-Sun, 5pm-8pm Fri, women only Wed)*, a house built around a courtyard with displays on traditional costumes, jewellery, ceramics, cooking utensils and furniture. The **Heritage Museum** *(admission free; open 8am-1pm & 5pm-8pm Tues-Sun, 5pm-8pm Fri, women only Wed)* displays much the same thing; it's worth exploring just for the traditional architecture of the building.

Next door is the **Islamic Museum** *(admission free; open 8am-1pm & 5pm-8pm Tues-Sun, 5pm-8pm Fri, women only Wed)*, which should definitely not be missed. It includes a large collection of coins from all over the Islamic world and a number of handwritten Qurans and writing implements. There are ceramics from Turkey, Syria and Afghanistan, as well as a display on the covering of the Kaaba stone at Mecca, the most holy sacred shrine for Muslims, including a copy of the embroidered cloth. Next to the cloth is the original holy key bag, which once held the key to the Kaaba. There's also a remarkable map of the region made 1200 years ago, which is quite accurate, once you realise that south is at the top.

At the museums, it seems you are obliged to sign each and every visitor's book. There are more restored old buildings north of the

Decency Laws

In 2001 Sharjah's government introduced new laws on 'decency and public conduct'. These are the strictest laws governing dress in the UAE, and along with Sharjah's ban on alcohol they represent a deepening conservatism in the emirate. For men, the new laws mean no bare chests or 'short' shorts in public or in commercial or public offices. Knee-length shorts are OK, if not exactly acclaimed. For women, the laws forbid clothing that exposes the stomach and back, clothing above the knee, and 'tight and transparent clothing that describes the body'. Obviously then, swimwear can't be worn in the streets, and only 'conservative' swimwear can be worn on Sharjah's public beaches.

The new laws also forbid 'a man and woman who are not connected by a legally acceptable relationship to be alone in public places or in suspicious times or circumstances'. No-one quite knows how widely this law applies. It doesn't seem to include looking around, say, the Arts Area with someone who isn't your sibling, parent or spouse, but you certainly could not share a hotel room with an unrelated member of the opposite sex. The interpretation of the laws is up to Sharjah's police and courts. The police, government employees, security officers and building guards have been charged to enforce the laws. These regulations apply to all of Sharjah territories, including Khor Fakkan, Dibba and Kalba on the east coast.

Heritage Museum, towards the Corniche; admission is free and they keep the same hours as the Heritage Museum. The **Majlis of Ibrahim Mohammed al-Midfa** is known for having the only round wind tower in the Gulf. The main **Al-Midfa House** across from the majlis has an elephant engraved on its door.

Arts Area

Tucked away on the other (north) side of Burj Ave from the Heritage Area is the Arts Area, where there is an imposing **Art Museum** *(admission free; open 9am-1pm & 5pm-8pm Sat-Thur, 5pm-8pm Fri)* exhibiting modern art from local and foreign artists. It's the finest art gallery in the UAE. Of the 72 different small galleries, eight hold a permanent collection of 19th-century European paintings and lithographs from Sheikh Sultan bin Mohammed al-Qasimi's own collection.

Bait Obeid al-Shamsi next to the Art Museum is a restored house that is now used as artists' studios. It is a lovely building featuring intricate pillars on the upper level. The **Arts Café** on the main square serves traditional drinks such as hot milk with ginger (delicious) for about Dh1. Next to the Arts Café is the **Very Special Arts Centre**, which is both a workshop and a gallery for disabled artists, and the **Emirates Fine Arts Society**, which also displays the works of local artists.

Archaeological Museum

This museum (*Al-Hizam al-Akhdar Rd; admission free; open 9am-1pm & 5pm-8pm Mon-Sat, 5pm-8pm Fri, men only Sat, women only Mon*), near Cultural Square, covers the earliest archaeological finds in the emirate (dating from 5000 BC) up to the beginning of the Islamic era. It uses lots of video and sound gadgetry to avoid the crushingly dull experience often associated with archaeological museums. The first hall has an interesting display on the science of archaeology, while the other five galleries cover different eras: fishermen, hunters and herders (5000–3000 BC); farmers, traders and craftspeople (3000–1000 BC); Wadi Suq (2000–1300 BC); oasis dwellers (1300–300 BC); and greater Arabia (300 BC–AD 600). Displays include reconstructions of tombs and houses, as well as weapons, pottery, tools, coins and jewellery. The café has sandboxes where kids can dig for 'artefacts'.

Souqs

Just in from the Corniche on the south side of Burj Ave is **Al-Arsah Souq**. It was restored by the government after large sections of it fell to pieces during the 1970s and '80s. The *areesh* (palm frond) roof and wooden pillars give it a traditional feel and it's a lovely place to wander around and look for Arabic and Bedouin souvenirs. Despite the efforts to recreate a traditional

atmosphere you can buy all kinds of non-Arabic souvenirs here too. There is also a traditional **coffeehouse and restaurant**.

The **Central Market** (also called the Blue Souq), on the Corniche near the King Faisal Mosque, has the best selection of oriental carpets in the country, and also hundreds of shops selling souvenirs and antiques from Oman, India, Thailand and Iran. The gold-domed **Al-Majarrah Souq** on the Corniche has about 50 shops selling textiles, perfumes and clothes. The **Gold Centre** on the corner of Sheikh Zayed and Al-Wahda Rds has about 40 shops selling jewellery, diamonds, gold coins and everything else that glitters. The **Fruit & Vegetable Souq, Animal Souq, Plant Souq** and **Fish Souq** are worth a visit if you have time to spare.

Places to Eat

The **coffeehouse** in the Al-Arsah Souq is one place that you really must visit while in Sharjah. For Dh10 you not only get a fairly large biryani but also salad and a bowl of fresh dates for dessert. The restaurant is a traditional coffeehouse, with seating on high benches. Backgammon sets are available and sweet tea is served out of a huge urn.

Thriveni Restaurant (*Rolla Square; meals around Dh5*) is a cheap Indian eatery. The surroundings are pleasant and you get a nice view out onto the square.

Al-Fawar (☎ 559 4662; King Faisal Rd; mezzes Dh8-12, mains Dh20-40) is a popular, long-running Lebanese restaurant. It has a cheaper cafeteria-style section next door, which also offers takeaway.

Sanobar Restaurant (☎ 528 3501; Al-Khan Rd; mezzes Dh10, mains Dh15-40) is an excellent seafood restaurant close to Sheikh Sultan al-Awal Rd. The atmosphere is reminiscent of a Greek taverna, with prices far lower than what you find in Dubai. It also offers Lebanese dishes.

Getting There & Away

Sharjah is about a 10-minute drive from Dubai city unless you encounter traffic, in which case it could take you 40 minutes. Avoid peak hours (1pm to 2pm and 5pm to 7pm). Minibuses (Dh5) go from the Deira taxi and minibus stand (Map 5, #30) on Omar ibn al-Khattab Rd. A taxi will cost you about Dh25. You won't be able to get a minibus back to Dubai though. You'll have to get a taxi from the stand at the north end of Rolla Square. These cost Dh30 (engaged) or Dh5 (shared). If you're heading north, there's a shared-taxi stand on Al-Arouba Rd opposite the Al-Hamra Cinema – a ride to Ras al-Khaimah costs Dh75 (engaged) or Dh15 (shared).

Getting Around

Since Sharjah has no bus system, getting around without your own car means either taking taxis or walking. The taxis have no meters and trips around the centre should cost Dh5 to Dh10 (agree on the fare before you get in). Sharjah's Arts and Heritage Areas can be covered on foot quite easily.

AROUND SHARJAH

Not to be missed is the **Sharjah Desert Park** *(Sharjah–Al-Dhaid Rd; adult/family Dh15/30; open 9am-7pm Sat-Wed, 11am-7pm Thur, 2pm-7pm Fri)*, a remarkable complex housing what is probably the best zoo in the Middle East. The **Children's Farm** *(closed noon-4pm daily)* has farm animals such as goats, camels and ducks, which kids can feed, pony rides for Dh5 and even eggs and cheese on sale.

Nearby is the wonderful **Arabia's Wildlife Centre**. This modern, well laid-out centre is a breeding centre and zoo for many of the species found on the Arabian Peninsula. These include a rather active family of puff adders (safely behind glass), wispy sand snakes, desert monitor lizards and Jayakar's sand boa, which spends its life wriggling beneath the surface of the sand. There are also rooms for nasties such as scorpions and the nightmarish camel spider. One of the highlights is the massive indoor aviary, home to flamingos, Houbara bustards and Indian rollers. The aviary also houses rock hyraxes, rabbit-sized critters distantly related to elephants. The cave area has a host of Egyptian fruit bats. There's also a section with several species of indigenous rodents. Check out the gorgeous bandy-legged lesser

jerboa. Outdoor enclosures are home to sacred baboons, striped hyenas, Arabian wolves and the splendid Arabian leopard. Don't miss the **restaurant**, which looks out over a large open-range area with flamingos, Nubian ibex, Arabian oryx, ostriches and sand gazelles. They're fed food and water near the windows so they can watch the humans feeding behind glass inside.

The third segment of the park is the **Natural History Museum**, an interesting and well-planned museum. It covers the evolution of the planet and also features dioramas of Sharjah's various ecosystems and environments. The museum may appeal to kids more than adults, but the gardens are worth anyone's time. They include a botanical garden with more than 120 types of wildflower.

The complex is 26km out of Sharjah (past Intersection No 8) towards Fujairah. Unfortunately for budget travellers, there's no public transport. A taxi out here would cost about Dh250 – you'd be better off hiring a car for the day.

HATTA

☎ 04 • pop 8000

Hatta, an enclave of Dubai Emirate nestled in the Hajar Mountains, is a great weekend getaway spot. It is 105km from Dubai by road, about 20km of which runs through Omani territory. There is no customs check as you cross the border, but remember that if you are driving a rental car your insurance does not cover accidents in Oman. This mountain town was once an important source of tobacco, as well as a vital staging post on the trade route between Dubai and Oman. Today, Hatta's main attractions are its relatively cool, humidity-free climate and the dramatic mountain scenery. The magnificent rock pools near Hatta are one of the UAE's highlights (see Around Hatta later in this chapter). Hatta makes a good base for off-road trips through the mountains.

Hatta's main attraction is the **Heritage Village** *(admission free; open 8am-8pm Sat-Thur, 2.30pm-8pm Fri)*, a re-creation of a traditional mountain village. Opening hours can be a bit erratic. In the complex is a restored fort and traditional buildings dedicated to

EXCURSIONS

weaponry, local songs and dances, palm-tree products and social life, plus other exhibits on facets of the old village society and economics. Most buildings have videos and mannequins to explain their theme. Climb up some stairs to the top of the watchtower here for some great views over the valley. There is a functioning *falaj* (irrigation channel) watering small but lush agricultural plots just below the Heritage Village. The traditional handicrafts building is across the road from the main complex, and features displays on weaving, cosmetics and perfumes, and traditional dress. The turn-off for the village is signposted to the left off the main street, about 3km from the Fort Roundabout and 500m from the bus stop.

With your own 4WD you can bump up the wadi to a **dam** above Hatta village. The turn-off is just after the mosque near the Heritage Village. The road soon deteriorates into a steep graded track. Don't try to get a saloon car up this road; the rental company won't thank you for it. The dam lies 2km up the rugged wadi.

Places to Stay & Eat

Hatta Fort Hotel (☎ 852 3211; ℮ hfhhotel@ emirates.net.ae; rooms Dh524/780 Sat-Wed/ Thur & Fri) is the only place to stay in Hatta. Built in 1986, the hotel is renowned for its lovely green gardens. Bird-watchers flock here to look for Indian rollers and other species. Accommodation is in chalets, which are comfortable but not cheap.

The **coffee shop** (mains about Dh30) at the hotel is a popular lunch stop. The setting and service are good, but the food is overpriced; a limp vegetarian pasta costs Dh28, a bland chicken Alexander will set you back Dh35. The hotel also has the highly regarded **Jeema Restaurant** (meals Dh200-300), which serves French cuisine and, although pricey, rivals anything in Dubai. The hotel also offers extensive sports facilities, including a modest nine-hole golf course.

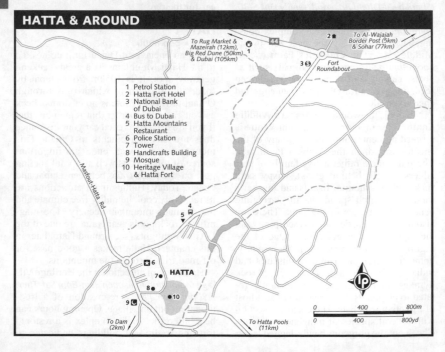

HATTA & AROUND

To Rug Market & Mazeirah (12km), Big Red Dune (50km) & Dubai (105km)

To Al-Wajajah Border Post (5km) & Sohar (77km)

Fort Roundabout

1 Petrol Station
2 Hatta Fort Hotel
3 National Bank of Dubai
4 Bus to Dubai
5 Hatta Mountains Restaurant
6 Police Station
7 Tower
8 Handicrafts Building
9 Mosque
10 Heritage Village & Hatta Fort

Masfout-Hatta Rd

HATTA

To Dam (2km)

To Hatta Pools (11km)

0   400   800m
0   400   800yd

There isn't much choice when it comes to eating in Hatta village, but for a great omelette sandwich for around Dh5, try the **Hatta Mountains Restaurant**, which is on the main street, near the bus stop.

Getting There & Away

From Dubai buses leave every hour for Hatta from 6.10am to 9pm (Dh10, one hour). In Dubai they leave from the Deira bus station (Map 4, #101). In Hatta, the buses depart from the red bus shelter near the Hatta Mountains Restaurant. Buy tickets from the driver. Buses leave Hatta for Dubai every hour from 6am to 9pm. Shared/engaged taxis leave from Bur Dubai bus station (Map 4, #23) in Bur Dubai and cost Dh25/100.

AROUND HATTA
Rock Pools

Most people come to Hatta to visit the rock pools, which are about 20km south of Hatta town. They are actually across the border in Oman, but access is from Hatta. This intricately carved miniature canyon has water year-round, and it's an amazing experience to swim through these narrow rock corridors and play at the waterfalls. The area gets busy at weekends, and unfortunately there's some litter and graffiti scattered around.

You don't need a 4WD to get to the rock pools from Hatta, but if you want to continue past the pools and on to Al-Ain you will need one. To get to the rock pools, turn right at the fort roundabout on the edge of town and head into the centre. After 2.7km take the turn-off to the left for the Heritage Village. Then turn left when you get to the T-junction at the mosque, 50m past the entrance to the Heritage Village. Follow this road for 900m as it bends around to the left. At this point take the turn-off onto the tarmac road to the right. This will take you past a row of identical houses, along a stretch with lots of speed bumps. Continue along this road for 6.5km until the tarmac road ends. At this point there is a turn-off to the right onto a graded track. There is a stop sign here as well. Follow the graded track for 6km, passing blue-and-white road signs to the Omani villages of A'Tuwayah, Al-

Karbi al-Gharbiyah, Al-Qarbi a'Sharqiyah and Al-Bon. Along this road is some wonderful scenery, particularly the striking layers of folded sedimentary rock on the hillsides. Watch out for oncoming traffic, though. After the sign to Al-Bon the road goes over a steep hill. The track to the parking area to the pools is a sharp left at the bottom of the hill. It leads to a parking area about 600m away, at the edge of a *falaj*. The pools are a short walk from here.

If you don't have your own transport, the Hatta Fort Hotel (see Hatta earlier in this chapter) offers a 4WD safari to the rock pools. A three-hour trip for six people costs Dh600, including soft drinks and towels. A seven-hour trip for six people costs Dh1400 and includes a picnic lunch.

Mazeirah Rug Market

There is a huge rug market at the village of Mazeirah, about 12km west of Hatta on the main highway. This is the only other large country market apart from the one at Masafi (see East Coast later in this chapter). If you're looking for rugs, it's worth a stop as you can pick up great bargains.

Big Red

Midway between Dubai and Hatta is the 100m-high dune known as Big Red. The highway cuts right between the towering peach-coloured dune system. This is a hugely popular spot for local 4WD fanatics to let down their tyres and tackle the slopes. On weekends, dozens of vehicles crawl up and down the soft sands. On the Hatta side of the road, **Al-Badayer Motors** (☎ 050-655 5447) hires out 150cc quad bikes from Dh40 for 30 minutes (it's worth bargaining), so you can tear up the dunes on one of these offensively noisy vehicles. Presumably any wildlife here has long since fled or been squashed. On the Dubai side of the road, **Al-Ramool Motors** (☎ 050-452 5855) hires out 150cc quad bikes for the same price. Both are open from 8am until sunset daily. Assuming you don't get run over by quad bikes and 4WDs, it takes about 20 minutes to walk from the highway to the top of the dunes.

EAST COAST

The east coast is one of the most beautiful parts of the UAE. The Hajar Mountains provide a stunning backdrop to the waters of the Gulf of Oman. It's very green here as the run-off from the mountains provides irrigation for most of the year. There are wadis to explore in the mountains, and water holes that are full year-round. The area north of Khor Fakkan is well known for diving and snorkelling. South of Khor Fakkan the sea is less inviting. The port at Fujairah is the second-busiest bunkering (refuelling) port in the world, and at any time there are dozens if not hundreds of ships queued up offshore. The line of ships runs the entire length of the coast! It seems that some ships illegally empty out their holds before they head into the Gulf to pick up another load of oil. The degree of pollution varies according to the currents, but most days you're likely to pick up a sticky sheen. The effects on local fisheries and wildlife can be imagined.

Fujairah
☎ 09 • pop 45,000

This prosperous little city is the capital of the emirate of the same name. There isn't a great deal to see in Fujairah itself, but it only takes 1¼ hours to get here from Dubai and it makes a good base for exploring the rest of the east coast.

The main business strip is Hamad bin Abdullah Rd, between the Fujairah Trade Centre and the coast. Along this road, just west of the Trade Centre, is the Etisalat office, the 48-storey Fujairah Tower, banks and, at the intersection with the coast road, the Central Market. The main post office is on Al-Sharqi Rd, just off Hamad bin Abdullah Rd.

The **old town** is best described as spooky. Of interest is the cemetery and a 300-year-old fort (under restoration) which overlooks the ruins of old Fujairah. There is a shanty settlement here whose residents don't especially like tourists walking around.

The **Fujairah Museum** (admission Dh1; open 8.30am-1.30pm, 4.30pm-6.30pm Sun-Thur, 2pm-6.30pm Fri) has exhibits on maritime activities, archaeological finds from around the emirate (such as items from tombs near Qidfa dating from 1500 BC), displays of heritage jewellery and a collection of photographs showing local life in the pre-oil era.

Ain al-Madhab Garden (admission with/without swim Dh2/5; gardens open 10am-10pm daily, swimming pools open 10am-7pm

Bullfighting

Every Friday, at around 4.30pm, Fujairah's special brand of bullfighting gets under way at a site next to the road to Kalba, near Al-Rughailat Bridge. There are no prancing matadors; this contest is bull against bull. The horns of the opponents are blunted, and bloodshed is rare. The bulls lower their heads almost to the ground and mostly head-butt and shove each other around. Sooner or later one bull forces another out of the ring, or else one tires of the struggle and walks away. Usually there are four or five contests, after which the competitors are led into pick-up trucks and driven home.

One tradition has it that the Portuguese introduced bullfighting to Fujairah, though other sources say that the bullfights predate the arrival of Islam. A more colourful legend holds that long ago two young men came into conflict over their desire to marry the same woman, so their families decided to let battling bulls settle the matter.

The beasts are descended from Brahmin bulls brought from India to turn waterwheels. Camels, which are common in the other emirates, are rare on the east coast. Today pumps do the job but Fujairah's landowners still keep bulls to fight against each other. Prize fighters are said to be pampered with a diet of dates, honey and butter, costing up to Dh2000 a month. There's no gambling on the result; victory simply confers honour on the bull's owners. A champion bull can be worth as much as Dh50,000. Fujairah's bullfights won't please animal rights activists but it's hugely popular with locals, and visitors are very welcome to watch the spectacle.

Sun-Fri) on the edge of town is nothing special, but the swimming pools here are clean, cool and segregated into men's and women's sections. There is a small **Heritage Village** *(admission free; open 9am-6pm daily)* across from the garden, fenced with palm fronds. Here you'll find a reconstructed coastal desert village, complete with a real cow.

Places to Stay & Eat Off Al-Faseel Rd near the sports club, **Fujairah Youth Hostel** *(☎ 222 2347, 050-458 4044; dorm beds Dh15/30 for HI members/nonmembers)* will only accommodate women if it is empty

enough to segregate them from men. Considering there are only six rooms (24 beds in total), a single woman stands a fairly high chance of being turned away on weekends.

Ritz Plaza Hotel *(☎ 222 2202; e ritzplza@ emirates.net.ae; rooms Dh288)* is a mid-range hotel offering small but comfortable rooms.

Fujairah Hilton *(☎ 222 2411; e shjhitwrm@ hilton.com; Al-Faseel Rd; singles/doubles Dh747.50/805)* is closer to the centre. This low-rise complex has pleasant gardens and a beachfront bar. We were offered a 40% discount rather promptly.

EXCURSIONS

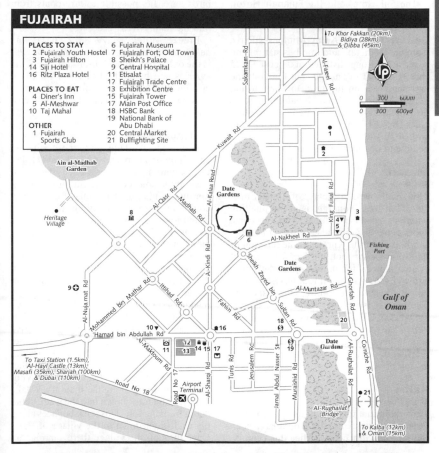

FUJAIRAH

PLACES TO STAY
2 Fujairah Youth Hostel
3 Fujairah Hilton
14 Siji Hotel
16 Ritz Plaza Hotel

PLACES TO EAT
4 Diner's Inn
5 Al-Meshwar
10 Taj Mahal

OTHER
1 Fujairah
  Sports Club

6 Fujairah Museum
7 Fujairah Fort; Old Town
8 Sheikh's Palace
9 Central Hospital
11 Etisalat
12 Fujairah Trade Centre
13 Exhibition Centre
15 Fujairah Tower
17 Main Post Office
18 HSBC Bank
19 National Bank of
   Abu Dhabi
20 Central Market
21 Bullfighting Site

Ain al-Madhab Garden

Heritage Village

To Khor Fakkan (20km); Bidiya (28km) & Dibba (45km)

Date Gardens

Fishing Port

Gulf of Oman

Date Gardens

Date Gardens

Al-Rughailat Bridge

To Taxi Station (1.5km), Al-Hayl Castle (13km), Masafi (35km), Sharjah (100km) & Dubai (110km)

Airport Terminal

To Kalba (12km) & Oman (15km)

Taj Mahal *(☎ 222 5225; Hamad bin Ab-dullah Rd; mains from Dh10)* serves excellent Indian and Chinese food. It is also clean, cool, comfortable and the service is good. It is at the back of the building opposite the Etisalat office.

Diner's Inn *(☎ 222 6351; Al-Faseel Rd; meals from Dh8)*, across from the Hilton, has good cheap Indian and Chinese food served in reasonably large helpings.

Al-Meshwar *(☎ 222 9255; King Faisal Rd; mezzes Dh7-12, mains Dh12-25)* is a more upmarket, medium-priced Lebanese restaurant. It's in the block behind the Diner's Inn.

The **Siji Hotel** and the **Fujairah Hilton** have upmarket multicuisine restaurants.

Getting There & Away Minibuses leave from the Deira taxi and minibus station and cost Dh25. Long-distance taxis cost Dh25 shared or Dh150 engaged. In Fujairah the taxi station is on the road to Sharjah and Dubai. Minibuses from Dubai continue as far as Khor Fakkan. A shared/engaged taxi costs Dh5/20 from Fujairah to Khor Fakkan and Dh20/100 to Dibba, though you should be able to negotiate a discount.

Masafi
☎ 09

This small town, an enclave of Ajman Emirate 35km from Fujairah, is at the junction where the road from Dubai to the east coast splits into two and heads north to Dibba and south to Fujairah. Known as the location of the Masafi water-bottling factory, the town is also famous for its **Friday market**, confirmed by the number of tour buses that stop here on their way to and from the east coast. The market is actually open every day of the week and has an enormous range of carpets, plants and souvenirs for sale. You are sure to get a bargain here, but you have to work at it – aim to pay 40% to 50% of the asking price.

Kalba
☎ 09

This traditional fishing village, just south of Fujairah, shows what life would have been like on the Gulf coast earlier this century.

Shasha, small, canoe-shaped fishing boats made from stripped palm fronds, and crayfish baskets line the beach, and fishermen can be seen setting out each morning and pulling in their nets each evening.

Kalba is part of Sharjah Emirate. The *khor* (inlet), just south of town, is part of a conservation reserve, the Khor Kalba Conservation Reserve, and the site of the oldest mangrove forest in Arabia. Birdlife is particularly abundant in the reserve, which is the only place in the world that the Khor Kalba white-collared kingfisher is found. There are reported to be 44 pairs of the birds here. It's possible to hire boats from the local fishermen and paddle up the inlets into the mangroves.

Breeze Motel *(☎ 277 8877,* e *jasmine dela_cruz@hotmail.com; rooms from Dh125)* is the only hotel. It's a bit run-down, but the aviaries and bougainvillea cheer the place up. Check a few rooms before choosing.

A taxi from Fujairah to Kalba should cost you about Dh10 to Dh12.

Al-Hayl Castle

You'll need a 4WD to get to these ruins set among mountain peaks in Wadi Hayl, 13km from Fujairah. They were once the site of the summer palace of the ruling Al-Sharqi family of Fujairah. The ruins of the palace, complete with freestanding pillars and watch towers, look stunning set against the mountains. The cultivated valley floor is a pleasant place to wander.

Coming from Fujairah towards Dubai, the signposted turn-off for Al-Hayl Castle is on the left about 2km past the main roundabout on the outskirts of town. Follow the tarmac road for 4km, then turn left towards the quarries. The turn-off is 700m past the first roundabout. Take a right after 1km and drive up the wadi. The paved road runs out after 3km; take the main graded track straight ahead. The castle lies a bumpy 3km further on. There's a much rougher route back to Fujairah. Returning along the main track, take the left-hand route down into the wadi, about 800m from the fort. This track bounces along the wadi floor down to the village of Hayl. Once through the village there's tarmac all

Off-road safaris are a great way to experience the rugged terrain of the Hajar Mountains east of Dubai

The abundance of reef life makes the east coast of the UAE popular with scuba divers and snorkellers

A hilltop fort in Hatta, a great weekend getaway spot in the Hajar Mountains

The ancient Round Structure at Hili, near Al-Ain

The spectacular gateway to the gardens at Hili

The magnificent rock pools at Hatta

the way back to Fujairah. Allow half a day for a trip here from Fujairah.

Khor Fakkan
☎ 09

One of Sharjah Emirate's enclaves, and the largest town on the east coast after Fujairah, Khor Fakkan sits on the prettiest bay in the UAE. While the port has proved to be a roaring success, the development of tourism has been somewhat held back by Sharjah's ban on alcohol.

The sweeping Corniche is bounded by the port and fish market at the southern end and the luxurious Oceanic Hotel to the north, with a nice beach between. The beach is fronted by a leafy strip of parkland, ideal for strolling. **Sharq Island**, at the entrance to Khor Fakkan's bay, is a popular diving spot – contact any of the diving operators in Dubai to arrange a diving excursion (see Diving in the Things to See & Do chapter for details). The name doesn't refer to *Jaws*; *sharq* means 'east' in Arabic.

If you have your own transport it's worth a drive to **Rifaisa Dam**, in the mountains above the town. This mountain lake is supposed to have a village submerged beneath it, which you can see when the water is clear (it wasn't when we visited). It's a very peaceful spot. To get to the dam, turn inland from the main street at the Emarat petrol station, then go left at the T-intersection (there should be a red-and-white radio tower on your left), then turn right onto the graded track after the mosque but before the bridge. The track divides after 300m or so; stick to the right. Follow this road up the valley for 4.7km to the dam. You'll notice a couple of ruined watchtowers atop hills along the way.

Accommodation options in Khor Fakkan are fairly limited.

Khor Fakkan Youth Hostel *(☎ 237 0886; dorm beds Dh25/40 for HI members/nonmembers)* is on the traffic circle just north of Oceanic Circle. It's new and clean, but there are only six rooms, and given that Khor Fakkan is part of Sharjah it's unlikely women can stay here (see the boxed text 'Decency Laws' under Sharjah earlier in this chapter for more information).

Oceanic Hotel *(☎ 238 5111; e oceanic2@ emirates.net.ae; singles/doubles Dh460/575)* is a comfortable establishment at the northern end of the Corniche. The hotel has a groovy 1970s nautical theme, especially the top-floor restaurant. The beach in front is clean and secluded.

Lebanon Cafeteria *(☎ 238 5631; mains Dh20)* on the Corniche is a good option for a meal, with a range of grills and Lebanese mezze as well as the usual Indian fare of biryanis and tikka dishes.

Taj Khorfakkan Restaurant *(☎ 222 5995; mains Dh10-15)* is a nicely decorated restaurant with reasonably priced food, mostly Indian with some Chinese dishes. It's just inland from the Central Market, across from the Saheel Market shop.

Minibuses to Khor Fakkan cost Dh30 and leave from the Deira minibus and taxi station (Map 5, #30). An engaged taxi to or from Dubai will cost about Dh250, with a little bargaining.

Bidiya
☎ 09

The charming fishing village of Bidiya, 8km north of Khor Fakkan, is one of the oldest towns in the Gulf. Archaeological digs have shown that the site of the town has been settled more or less continuously since the 3rd millennium BC. Today it is best known for its **mosque**, a small whitewashed structure of stone, mud brick and gypsum, which is still in use. It is said to have been built around AD 640, although other sources date it to AD 1449, and is the oldest mosque in the UAE. It was closed for restoration when we last visited. It is built into a low hillside along the main road just north of the village, and on the hillside above and behind it are several ruined **watchtowers**.

There are two dive schools in or near Bidiya. **Scuba 2000** *(☎ 238 8477; e scuba uae@emirates.net.ae)* is in Bidiya. Snorkelling equipment costs Dh50 per day; a one-dive trip with full equipment costs Dh130; a two-dive trip costs Dh200. Owner Hassan also arranges diving trip on the east coast of the Musandam Peninsula (Oman) for Dh310 with full equipment. An introductory diving course costs Dh250. It has a cheerful compound with accommodation for divers and snorkellers right on Bidiya's lovely beach. There are two simple but clean double rooms with attached bathrooms for Dh150. To get to the dive school, look for the sign about 300m north of the mosque. Turn right at the T-intersection, then continue along the beach about 300m past the fishing boats until you see the blue-and-yellow compound. Alternatively, the dive school offers transport to and from Dubai for Dh260.

Sandy Beach Diving Centre (☎ 244 5050; e sbdiving@emirates.net.ae, w www.alboom marine.com) is a branch of an established Dubai dive school, based at the Sandy Beach Motel about 6km north of Bidiya. A single supervised dive trip with full equipment costs Dh250, while a 'discover scuba diving' course costs Dh300. It also arranges diving trips along the east coast of the Musandam Peninsula for Dh515 per person (minimum 10 people). Snoopy Island, just offshore from the hotel, is a popular diving and snorkelling spot. There are stonefish around the island, so wear shoes while paddling around. Don't be alarmed by the family of reef sharks here; they're friendly. Access to the hotel's beach and Snoopy Island costs Dh25 per day.

Bidiya Beach Villa (☎ 244 5050; e sbdiv ing@emirates.net.ae; dorm beds Dh50) offers backpacker-style accommodation in this delightfully rustic seaside village. Close to Scuba 2000, this old, walled villa has eight bunk beds in two rooms (with shared toilet facilities). You have to book first by phone, then drop by the Sandy Beach Diving Centre at the Sandy Beach Motel to collect the key. Someone from the dive centre then takes you to the villa by truck. Cooking facilities are available, and the local market is a 10-minute walk away.

Near the village market is a **restaurant**, where wholesome, basic curries cost Dh5.

Sandy Beach Motel (☎ 244 5555; e sandy bm@emirates.net.ae, w www.sandybm.com; singles/doubles Dh302.50/385, chalets Dh418) is outside Bidiya, near the village of Aqqa.

Thanks to the lovely beach, lush gardens and relaxed atmosphere, guests tend to forgive the high prices, average food and rooms in definite need of renovation. With the restaurant, stick to simple dishes the cooks know, such as the mixed grill (Dh40). Western dishes are usually awful.

The stretch of beach just south of the hotel is a popular unofficial **camp site**. About a kilometre north of the hotel, a multistorey **Le Meridien** is being built. Expect five-star facilities and prices.

To get to Khor Fakkan, you could engage a taxi in Dubai for Dh250 to Dh300 to take you here, or you could take a bus to Fujairah and bargain with a taxi driver there for the last leg (about Dh80 to Dh100). Otherwise there's really no public transport.

AL-AIN & BURAIMI
☎ 03 & 00968

These two towns lie within the Buraimi Oasis. The border between the UAE and Oman wriggles through this collection of interconnected oases. In the days before the oil boom, the oasis was a five-day overland journey by camel from Abu Dhabi. Today the trip takes 1½ hours on a tree-lined freeway. In barely 30 years Al-Ain (in Abu Dhabi Emirate on the UAE side of the border) has been transformed from a series of rustic villages into a suburbanised garden city. It's best to make an overnight trip, but if you are really pressed for time you could get there, zip around the sites and get back to Dubai in a day, as long as you get an early start. Once in the oasis, you can cross freely between the UAE and Oman – the official frontier post to enter Oman is 50km east of Buraimi. UAE currency is accepted in Buraimi at a standard rate (at the time of writing) of OR1 = Dh10.

One of Al-Ain's main attractions during summer is its dry air, which is a welcome change from the humidity of the coast. The temperate climate has ensured that many sheikhs from around the Emirates have their summer palaces here. The cool and quiet date-palm oases all over town are pleasant to wander through at any time of the year.

Orientation & Information

The main streets in Al-Ain are Khalifa bin Zayed St and Zayed bin Sultan St. The main north–south streets are Abu Bakr al-Siddiq St, which extends into Buraimi, and Al-Ain St. Two useful landmarks for navigational purposes are the Clock Tower and Coffeepot Roundabouts. Distances in both Al-Ain and Buraimi are large, but taxis are abundant and cheap. It's fairly easy to find most of the things worth seeing in Al-Ain by following the big, purple tourist signs.

There are lots of banks in Al-Ain near the Clock Tower Roundabout; the area around the Grand Mosque has several money-changers. In Al-Ain the post office is on the Clock Tower Roundabout and the Etisalat office is nearby.

Eastern Fort & Al-Ain Museum

The museum (☎ 764 1595; Sultan bin Zayed St; admission 50 fils; open 8am-1pm & 3.30pm-5.30pm Mon-Thur, 9am-11.30am Fri, 8am-1pm Sat Nov-Apr; 8am-1pm & 4.30pm-6.30pm Mon-Thur, 9am-11.30am Fri, 8am-1pm Sat May-Oct) and fort are in the same compound, south-east of the overpass near the Coffeepot Roundabout. This is one of the

EXCURSIONS

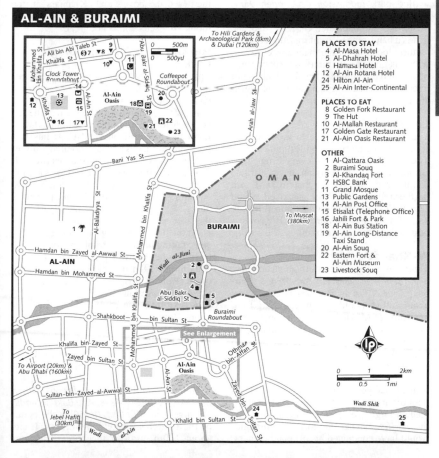

AL-AIN & BURAIMI

To Hili Gardens & Archaeological Park (8km) & Dubai (120km)

To Muscat (380km)

OMAN

BURAIMI

AL-AIN

To Airport (20km) & Abu Dhabi (160km)

To Jebel Hafit (30km)

Buraimi Roundabout

See Enlargement

Wadi Shik

Wadi al-Ain

PLACES TO STAY
4 Al-Masa Hotel
5 Al-Dhahrah Hotel
6 Hamasa Hotel
12 Al-Ain Rotana Hotel
24 Hilton Al-Ain
25 Al-Ain Inter-Continental

PLACES TO EAT
8 Golden Fork Restaurant
9 The Hut
10 Al-Mallah Restaurant
17 Golden Gate Restaurant
21 Al-Ain Oasis Restaurant

OTHER
1 Al-Qattara Oasis
2 Buraimi Souq
3 Al-Khandaq Fort
7 HSBC Bank
11 Grand Mosque
13 Public Gardens
14 Al-Ain Post Office
15 Etisalat (Telephone Office)
16 Jahili Fort & Park
18 Al-Ain Bus Station
19 Al-Ain Long-Distance Taxi Stand
20 Al-Ain Souq
22 Eastern Fort & Al-Ain Museum
23 Livestock Souq

best museums in the country and is a highlight of a visit to Al-Ain. The fort was the birthplace of the UAE's president, Sheikh Zayed. As you enter the museum, take a look at the *majlis* (formal meeting room) and be sure to see the display of photographs of Al-Ain in the 1960s – it's unrecognisable. Other exhibits cover traditional education, flora, fauna, weapons and Bedouin life. A large portion of the museum is dedicated to the archaeology of the area.

Jahili Fort & Park

This beautifully restored fort is set inside a walled park *(admission Dh1; open 9am-10pm daily)*, next to the public gardens, near the Al-Ain Rotana Hotel. Built in 1898, the fort is a handsome piece of traditional architecture; look out for the main corner tower, which is graced with three concentric rings of serrated battlements. The fort itself is not open but you can wander round the pleasant gardens.

Livestock Souq

You can see the entrance to the livestock souq from the museum and fort parking lot. The souq, which sells everything from Brahmin cows to Persian cats, attracts people from all over the eastern UAE and northern Oman. Don't be surprised if you see an Emirati loading goats into the back seat of a late-model Mercedes. The souq is best before 9am, when trading is heaviest.

Al-Khandaq Fort

This thoroughly restored fort *(admission free; open 8am-6pm Sat-Wed, 8am-1pm & 4pm-6pm Thur & Fri)* in Buraimi is said to be about 400 years old. If you're coming from the centre of Al-Ain you'll see it about 200m off the road to your left, about 750m past the border, near Buraimi Souq. Be sure to climb one of the battlements for a view of the surrounding oasis. Unusually for an Omani fort, there are both inner and outer defence walls. Once you get into the courtyard head directly across it and slightly to the left to reach a large, well-restored room. This was the *majlis*, where the fort's commander would have conducted his official business.

The large enclosed yard just east of the fort is Buraimi's **Eid prayer ground**, where people gather to pray during the holidays marking the end of Ramadan and the end of the pilgrimage season.

Buraimi Souq

Buraimi's main souq is housed in the large brown building at the Horse Roundabout and sells fruit, vegetables, meat and household goods. The enclosed (concrete) part of the souq includes a few shops that sell Omani silver jewellery and *khanjars*, the ornate daggers worn by many Omani and some Emirati men (see the boxed text 'Khanjars' in the Shopping chapter for more information), though the selection is not great.

Hili Gardens & Archaeological Park

This combined public park and archaeological site *(admission Dh1; open 9am-10pm daily)* is about 8km north of the centre of Al-Ain, off the Dubai road. The main attraction is the **Round Structure**, a building dating from the 3rd millennium BC. It has two porthole entrances and is decorated with relief carvings of animals and people. Although this structure is referred to as a tomb locally, it may not have been a tomb at all. No bones were ever found here, just remnants of pottery, and there are suggestions that it may have been a temple.

At the time of writing further excavations were taking place on a **tomb** that dates back to somewhere between 2300 and 2000 BC. This tomb is 8m in length and adjoins the older Round Structure. More than 250 skeletons were found here.

A taxi from the centre of Al-Ain costs about Dh6.

Places to Stay

If you're on a budget you'll want to stay in Buraimi. None of the hotels in Buraimi serve alcohol.

Hamasa Hotel *(☎ 651 200, fax 651 210, in the UAE ☎ 050-619 4248; Abu Bakr al-Siddiq St; singles/doubles Dh120/150)* is the better of the two cheap hotels in Buraimi. It sits about 100m north of the border, on your right as you enter Buraimi from Al-Ain. The rooms are larger than at the nearby Al-Dhahrah Hotel, though not quite as clean.

Al-Dhahrah Hotel (☎ 650 492; e sirshirt@ omantel.net.om; Abu Bakr al-Siddiq St; singles/doubles Dh130/160) is a few doors north of the Hamasa Hotel. The rooms were clean and the bathrooms spotless, but the beds seemed rather hard.

Al-Masa Hotel (☎ 653 007, fax 653 008; Abu Bakr al-Siddiq St; singles/doubles Dh200/300) is a new mid-range hotel about 500m from the border, on the left as you enter Buraimi from Al-Ain. All rooms have satellite TV and a small balcony.

Back in the UAE, there are three five-star hotels.

Al-Ain Inter-Continental (☎ 768 6686; e alain@interconti.com; Khalid bin Sultan St; singles/doubles Dh671/700) has spacious gardens, lots of sports facilities and Al-Ain's most popular expat bar, the Horse & Jockey.

Al-Ain Rotana Hotel (☎ 751 5111; e alain.hotel@rotana.com; Mohammed bin Khalifa St; singles/doubles Dh760/814) is probably the second-best of the three; it's bland but fairly new (it opened in 1999).

Hilton Al-Ain (☎ 768 6666; e alhilton@ emirates.net.ae; Khalid bin Sultan St; singles/doubles Dh600/670) is the oldest of the three, and while perfectly comfortable it doesn't quite match up to its rivals.

Places to Eat

You won't have any trouble finding cheap eats in the centre of Al-Ain. In Buraimi your options are limited to the standard cheap fare of a helping of biryani for about Dh10 at any of the places along the main street or around the market.

Golden Fork (☎ 766 9033; Khalifa St; mains Dh7-15) is a branch of the popular Filipino restaurant chain, offering noodle dishes and mixed grills.

Golden Gate Restaurant (☎ 766 2467; Al-Ain St; mains Dh15-25) is a little more up-market and serves very good Chinese and Filipino food.

Al-Mallah (☎ 766 9928; Khalifa St; mains Dh20-40) serves generous portions of Leb-anese cuisine. Mezzes cost around Dh7, shish tawouq (grilled, skewered chicken pieces) Dh20, but fish and prawn dishes can cost up to Dh40.

The Hut (☎ 751 6526; Khalifa St) is a Western-style coffee shop. It offers good cappuccino and other coffees as well as a wide selection of cakes, pastries and sandwiches. At Dh5 for a cappuccino the prices are a bit high, but the comfortable surroundings make up for it.

Al-Ain Oasis Restaurant (☎ 766 5340; Al-Ain Oasis; mains Dh15-30) is in a beautiful setting in the heart of the oasis. It's about a 500m walk from the Al-Ain Museum. The menu includes mixed grills and fish biryani (recommended).

The three five-star hotels all have bars and several restaurants each. You can get a good buffet lunch at all of them for about Dh70.

Getting There & Away

Minibuses (Dh30, 1½ hours) to Al-Ain leave from the main bus station (Map 4, #23) in Bur Dubai. A shared/engaged taxi from the Bur Dubai bus station costs Dh30/150. To return to Dubai you'll need to catch a shared taxi (the taxi stand is next to the bus station), as the minibuses don't take passengers in the other direction. Shared taxis take four to seven passengers to Dubai (Dh30); an engaged taxi will cost about Dh130 to Dh150, depending on your negotiating skills.

Getting Around

All Al-Ain's buses run roughly on the half-hour from 6am to midnight. Most fares are Dh1. There are no local buses in Buraimi. Almost everyone travels by taxi in Al-Ain as they are so cheap. Most trips around the centre will only cost you Dh3. It's better to use the gold-and-white Al-Ain taxis than the orange-and-white Buraimi ones, which don't have meters.

AROUND AL-AIN & BURAIMI

South of Al-Ain is **Jebel Hafit**, a jagged 1160m-high limestone mountain that rears out of the plain. The views from the top of this mountain and on the winding drive up are well worth the effort of getting here. The summit is about 30km by road from the centre of Al-Ain. At the time of writing a luxury hotel about 3km from the summit had not yet opened.

To get there, head south from the Clock Tower Roundabout and turn right at Khalid bin Sultan St. From there follow the purple tourist signs. There are no buses to Jebel Hafit. A taxi will cost around Dh50 for the round trip.

Language

English is widely spoken throughout the UAE, but a few words of Arabic can do a lot to ease your passage through the country.

There are several different varieties of Arabic. Classical Arabic, the language of the Quran (Koran), is the root of all of today's dialects of spoken and written Arabic. A modernised and somewhat simplified form of classical Arabic is the common language of the educated classes in the Middle East. This language, generally known as Modern Standard Arabic (MSA), is used in newspapers and by TV and radio newsreaders. It's also used as a medium of conversation by well-educated Arabs from different parts of the region. Such a written language is necessary because the dialects of spoken colloquial Arabic differ to the point where a few of them are mutually unintelligible. Mercifully, the words and phrases a traveller is most likely to use are fairly standard throughout the Gulf. The words and phrases in this chapter should be understood anywhere in the region.

Transliteration

It's worth noting here that transliterating from Arabic script into English is at best an approximate science. The presence of sounds unknown in European languages, and the fact that the script is 'incomplete'

The Transliteration Dilemma

TE Lawrence, when asked by his publishers to clarify 'inconsistencies in the spelling of proper names' in *Seven Pillars of Wisdom* – his account of the Arab Revolt in WWI – wrote back:

Arabic names won't go into English. There are some 'scientific systems' of transliteration, helpful to people who know enough Arabic not to need helping, but a washout for the world. I spell my names anyhow, to show what rot the systems are.

(most vowels are not written), combine to make it nearly impossible to settle on one method of transliteration. A wide variety of spellings is therefore possible for words when they appear in roman script – and that goes for places and people's names as well.

The matter is further complicated by the wide variety of dialects and the imaginative ideas Arabs themselves often have on appropriate spelling in, say, English: words spelt one way in Dubai may look very different in Syria, heavily influenced by French (not even the most venerable of western Arabists have been able to come up with an ideal solution).

Pronunciation

Pronunciation of Arabic can be tongue-tying for someone unfamiliar with the intonation and combination of sounds. Pronounce the transliterated words slowly and clearly.

This language guide should help, but bear in mind that the myriad rules governing pronunciation and vowel use are too extensive to be covered here.

Vowels

a	as in 'had'
e	as in 'bet'
i	as in 'hit'
o	as in 'hot'
u	as in 'put'

A macron over a vowel indicates that the vowel has a long sound:

ā	as the 'a' in 'father'
ē	as in 'ten', but lengthened
ī	as the 'e' in 'ear', only softer
ō	as in 'for'
ū	as the 'oo' in 'food'

You may also see long vowels transliterated as double vowels, eg, 'aa' (ā), 'ee' (ī) and 'oo' (ū).

LANGUAGE

The Arabic Alphabet

final	medial	initial	alone	transliteration	pronunciation
ﺎ			ا	ā	as the 'a' in 'father'
ﺐ	ﺒ	ﺑ	ب	b	as in 'bet'
ﺖ	ﺘ	ﺗ	ت	t	as in 'ten' (but the tongue touches the teeth)
ﺚ	ﺜ	ﺛ	ث	th	as in 'thin'; also as 's' or 't'
ﺞ	ﺠ	ﺟ	ج	j	as in 'jet'; often also as the 's' in 'measure'
ﺢ	ﺤ	ﺣ	ح	H	a strongly whispered 'h', almost like a sigh of relief
ﺦ	ﺨ	ﺧ	خ	kh	a rougher sound than the 'ch' in Scottish *loch*
ﺪ			د	d	as in 'den' (but the tongue touches the teeth)
ﺬ			ذ	dh	as the 'th' in 'this'; also as 'd' or 'z'
ﺮ			ر	r	a rolled 'r', as in the Spanish word *caro*
ﺰ			ز	z	as in 'zip'
ﺲ	ﺴ	ﺳ	س	s	as in 'so', never as in 'wisdom'
ﺶ	ﺸ	ﺷ	ش	sh	as in 'ship'
ﺺ	ﺼ	ﺻ	ص	ṣ	emphatic 's' *
ﺾ	ﻀ	ﺿ	ض	ḍ	emphatic 'd' *
ﻂ	ﻄ	ﻃ	ط	ṭ	emphatic 't' *
ﻆ	ﻈ	ﻇ	ظ	ẓ	emphatic 'z' *
ﻊ	ﻌ		ع	'	the Arabic letter 'ayn; pronounce as a glottal stop – like the closing of the throat when saying 'Oh oh!' (see Other Sounds opposite)
ﻎ	ﻐ	ﻏ	غ	gh	a guttural sound like Parisian 'r'
ﻒ	ﻔ	ﻓ	ف	f	as in 'far'
ﻖ	ﻘ	ﻗ	ق	q	a strongly guttural 'k' sound; often pronounced as a glottal stop
ﻚ	ﻜ	ﻛ	ك	k	as in 'king'
ﻞ	ﻠ	ﻟ	ل	l	as in 'lamb'
ﻢ	ﻤ	ﻣ	م	m	as in 'me'
ﻦ	ﻨ	ﻧ	ن	n	as in 'name'
ﻪ	ﻬ	ﻫ	ه	h	as in 'ham'
ﻮ			و	w	as in 'wet'; or
				ū	long, as the 'oo' on 'food'; or
				aw	as the 'ow' in 'how'
ﻲ	ﻴ	ﻳ	ي	y	as in 'yes'; or
				ī	as the 'e' in 'ear', only softer; or
				ay	as the 'y' in 'by' or as the 'ay' in 'way'

Vowels Not all Arabic vowel sounds are represented in the alphabet. See Pronunciation on p151.

*Emphatic Consonants Emphatic consonants are similar to their nonemphatic counterparts but are pronounced with greater tension in the tongue and throat.

Consonants

Pronunciation for all Arabic consonants is covered in the alphabet table on the preceding page. Note that when double consonants occur in transliterations, both are pronounced. For example, *al-Hammam* (toilet/bath), is pronounced 'al-ham-mam'.

Other Sounds

Arabic has two sounds that are very tricky for non-Arabs to produce: the 'ayn and the glottal stop. The letter 'ayn represents a sound with no English equivalent that comes even close. It is similar to the glottal stop (which is not actually represented in the alphabet) but the muscles at the back of the throat are gagged more forcefully – it has been described as the sound of someone being strangled. In many transliteration systems, 'ayn is represented by an opening quotation mark, and the glottal stop by a closing quotation mark. To make the transliterations in this language guide (and throughout the rest of the book) easier to use, we have not distinguished between the glottal stop and the 'ayn, using the closing quotation mark to represent both sounds (as in the suburb Za'abeel). You'll find that Arabic speakers will still understand you.

Pronouns

I	*ānē*
you (sg)	*inta/inti* (m/f)
he	*huwa*
she	*hiya*
we	*nahnu*
you (pl)	*untum/inti* (m/f)
they	*uhum*

Greetings & Civilities

Hello.	*as-salāma alaykum*
Hello. (response)	*wa alaykum e-salām*
Goodbye. (person leaving)	*ma'al salāma*
Goodbye. (person staying)	*alla ysalmak* (to a man) *alla ysalmich* (to a woman) *alla ysallimkum* (to a group)

Goodbye.	*Hayyākallah* (to a man) *Hayyachallah* (to a woman) *Hayyakumallah* (to a group)
Goodbye. (response)	*fi aman ullah* or *alla yHai'īk* (to a man) *alla yHai'īch* (to a woman) *alla yHai'īkum* (to a group)
Good morning.	*sabaH al-kheir*
Good morning. (response)	*sabaH an-nur*
Good afternoon/evening.	*masa' al-kheir*
Good afternoon/evening. (response)	*masa' an-nur*
Good night.	*tisbaH ala-kheir* (to a man) *tisbiHin ala-kheir* (to a woman) *tisbuHun ala-kheir* (to a group)
Good night. (response)	*wa inta min ahlil-kheir* (to a man) *wa inti min ahlil-kheir* (to a woman) *wa intu min ahlil-kheir* (to a group)
Welcome.	*ahlan wa sahlan* or *marHaba*
Welcome to you.	*ahlan fik* (to a man) *ahlan fich* (to a woman) *ahlan fikum* (to a group)
Pleased to meet you. (also said on leaving)	*fursa sa'ida*
Pleased to meet you. (response)	*wa ana as'ad* (by an individual) *wa iHna as'ad* (by a group)

Basics

Yes.	*aiwa/na'am*
No.	*lā*
Maybe.	*mumkin*

LANGUAGE

Please.	*min fadhlik* or *lō tsimaH* (to a man) *min fadhlich* or *lō tsimiHīn* (to a woman) *min fadhelkum* or *lō tsimiHūn* (to a group)
Thank you.	*shukran* or *mashkur* (to a man) *mashkura* (to a woman) *mashkurin* (to a group)
You're welcome.	*afwan/al-afu*
Excuse me.	*lō tsimaH* (to a man) *lō tsimiHīn* (to a woman) *lō tsimiHūn* (to a group)
I'm sorry/ Forgive me.	*ānē āsef*
After you.	*atfaddal* or *min badik* (to a man) *min badak* (to a woman)
OK.	*zein/kwayyis/tayib*
No problem.	*mafī mushkila*
Impossible.	*mish mumkin*
It doesn't matter/ I don't mind.	*ma'alish*

Small Talk

How are you?	*kef Halak?* (to a man) *kef Halik?* (to a woman) *kef Halkum?* (to a group)
Fine, thanks.	*(zein) al-Hamdulillah* (by a man) *(zeina) al-Hamdulillah* (by a woman) *(zeinin) al-Hamdulillah* (by a group)

What's your name?	*shismak?* (to a man) *shismich?* (to a woman) *shisimkum?* (to a group)
My name is ...	*ismi ...*
Do you like ...?	*tahabi ...?*
I like ...	*ahib ...*
I don't like ...	*la ahib ...*
God willing.	*inshallah*

I'm from ...	*ana min ...*
Australia	*usturālyē*
Canada	*kanadē*
Europe	*ōrobba*
France	*faransa*
Germany	*almania*
Netherlands	*holanda*
New Zealand	*nyūzilande*
South Africa	*jinūb afrīqye*
Switzerland	*swissra*
UK	*britania*
USA	*amrika*

Language Difficulties

I understand.	*ana fahim* (by a man) *ana fahma* (by a woman)
We understand.	*iHna fahmīn*
I don't understand.	*ana afHām*
We don't understand.	*iHna nafHām*
Please repeat that.	*lō simaHt ti'id hādtha*

I speak ...	*ana atkallam ...*
Do you speak ...?	*titkallam ...?*
English	*inglīzi*
French	*fransawi*
German	*almāni*

I don't speak Arabic.	*ma-atkallam arabi*
I speak a little Arabic.	*atkallam arabi shwayē*
What does this mean?	*shu ya'ani?*
How do you say ... in Arabic?	*kef igūl ... bila'arabi?*

I want an interpreter.	*urīd mutarjem*

Getting Around

I want to go to ...	*abga arouH li ...*
When does the ... leave?	*mata yamshi il ...?*
When does the ... arrive?	*mata tosal il ...?*
What is the fare to ...?	*cham il tadhkara li ...?*
Which bus/taxi goes to ...?	*ai bas/tax yrouH il ...?*
Does this bus/taxi go to ...?	*Hadhal bas yrouH il ...?*
How many buses go to ...?	*cham bas yrouH li ...?*
Please tell me when we arrive at ...	*lau samaHtit goul li mata nosal li ...*
May I sit here?	*mumkin ag'id hina?*
May we sit here?	*mumkin nag'id hina?*
Stop here, please.	*'ogaf hina, law samaHt*
Please wait for me.	*law samaHt, intidherni*

Where is the ...?	*wein al ...?*
How far is the ...?	*cham yibe'id ...?*
airport	*al-matār*
bus stop	*mokaf al-bas*
bus station	*maHattat al-bas*
taxi stand	*maHattat taks/ maHattat ajara*
train station	*maHattat al-qatar*

boat	*markub*
bus	*bas*
camel	*jamal*
car	*sayyara*
donkey	*Hmār*
horse	*Hsan*
taxi	*taks/ajara*

daily	*kil yōm*
ticket office	*maktab al-tadhāker*
ticket	*tadhkara/bitāq*
1st class	*daraje ūlā*
2nd class	*daraje thānye*
crowded	*zaHme/matrūs*

Signs

Entry	مدخل
dukhūl	
Exit	خروج
khurūj	
Toilets (Men)	حمام للرجال
Hammam lirrijal	
Toilets (Women)	حمام للنساء
Hammam linnisa'a	
Hospityl	مستشفى
mustashfa	
Police	الشرطة
shurta	
Prohibited	ممنوع
mamnu'u	

Where can I rent a ...?	*min wein agdar asta'ajir ...?*
bicycle	*saikel*
motorcycle	*motorsaikel*

Directions

Where is the ...?	*wein al ...?*
Is it near?	*uhwe girīb?*
Is it far?	*uhwe bi'īb?*
How many kilometres?	*kam kilometer?*
Can you show me the way to ...?	*mumkin tdallini mukān ...?*

address	*onwān*
street	*shāri'*
number	*raqam*
city	*madina*
village	*qaria*

here	*hnī*
there	*hnāk*
next to	*yam*
opposite	*gbāl/mgābel*
behind	*warā/khaif*
to	*min*
from	*ıle*
left	*yasār*
right	*yimīn*
straight	*sīda*
north	*shimāl*
south	*jinūb*
east	*sharq*
west	*gharub*

Around Town

I'm looking for the ...	*ga'ed adawwēr ala ...*
Where is the ...?	*wein al ...?*
bank	*al-bank*
barber	*al-Hallaq*
beach	*il-shatt/il-shāt'i*
city centre	*wasat al-balād*
customs	*aljamarek*
embassy	*al-safara*
mosque	*al-masjid*
museum	*al-matHaf*
old city	*al-madina il-qadima*
palace	*al-qasr*
passport & immigration office	*markaz aljawazat welhijrā*
police station	*al-makhfar*
post office	*maktab al-barīd*
telephone	*al-telefon/al-hataf*
telephone centre	*maqsam al-hatef*
toilet	*al-Hammam*
tourist office	*isti'ilāmāt al-suyyaH*
university	*il-jam'a*
zoo	*Hadiqat il-Haywan*
What time does it open?	*mita tiftaH?*
What time does it close?	*mita tsaker?*
I'd like to make a telephone call.	*abgyi attisel telefōn/ abi akhaber*
I want to change money.	*abga asrif flūs*
I want to change travellers cheques.	*abga asrif sheikat syaHīa*

Accommodation

Where is the hotel?	*wein al-funduq/el-ōtel?*
I'd like to book a ...	*abgyi aHjiz ...*
bed	*sarīr/frāsh*
cheap room	*ghurfa rikhīsa*
single room	*ghurfa mifred*
double room	*ghurfa mijwīz*
room with a bathroom	*ghurfa ma'Hammam*
room with air-conditioning	*ghurfa mukhayyafa*
for one night	*la leila wiHdē*
for two nights	*la leiltein thintein*

May I see the room?	*mumkin ashuf al-ghurfah?*
May I see other rooms?	*mumkin ashuf ghuraf dhānia?*
How much is this room per night?	*cham ujrat hādhil ghurfah fil-leila?*
How much is it per person?	*shtiswa ala eshshakhs al-āhed?*
Do you have any cheaper rooms?	*fih ghuraf arkhas?*
This is fine.	*hadha zein.*
This is very ...	*hādhi wāhed ...*
noisy	*muzi'ije*
dirty	*waskha*
expensive	*ghalye*
address	*al-unw*
blanket	*battaniyye*
camp site	*emakan al-mukhayyam*
electricity	*kahruba*
hotel	*funduq/ōtel*
hot water	*māi Hār*
key	*miftaH*
manager	*al-mudīr*
shower	*al-dūsh*
soap	*sābūn*
toilet	*Hammam*

Food

I'm hungry.	*āne jūda'ān*
I'm thirsty.	*āne atshān*
I'd like ...	*aHib/abghi ...*
Is service included in the bill?	*al-fatūra fihā qīmat al-khidma?*
What is this?	*shinū hādhe*
Another one, please.	*ba'ad wiHde min fadhlik?*
breakfast	*riyūg/ftūr*
lunch	*al-ghade*
dinner	*al-ashe*
restaurant	*mata'ām*
set menu	*qa'imat al-akel muHaddada*
bread	*khubz*
chicken	*dajaj/tawouq*
coffee	*qahwa*
fish	*samak*

meat	*laHma*
milk	*laban/halīb*
pepper	*felfel*
potatoes	*batatas*
rice	*roz*
salt	*sel/melaH*
sugar	*suker*
tea	*chai*
water	*mayya*

Shopping

I want ...	*abga ...*
Do you have ...?	*indik ...?* (to a man)
	indich ...? (to a woman)
Where can I buy ...?	*wein agdar ashtiri ...?*
How much is this?	*kam hadha?*
How much is that?	*kam hadhak?*
How much are those?	*kam hadhol?*
How much ...?	*kam ...?*
It costs too much.	*ghalia wai'd*
bookshop	*al-maktaba*
chemist/pharmacy	*saydaliyya*
laundry	*masbagha*
market	*souq*
newsagents/ stationers	*maktabet-al-qurtāsiyye*
big	*chibīr*
bigger	*akbar*
small	*sighīr*
smaller	*asghar*
cheap	*rikhīs*
cheaper	*arkhas*
expensive	*ghali*
open	*āmaftūH*
closed	*msakkar/mughlaq*
money	*flūs*

Health

I need a doctor.	*abi tabīb*
My friend is ill.	*sidiji marīd/ayyān*
headache	*wija' rās*
hospital	*mustashfa*
pharmacy	*saydaliyye*
prescription	*wasfa tibbiyā*
stomachache	*wija' batun*
tampons	*fuwat siHiyya lalHarīm*

Numbers

Arabic numerals are simple to learn and, unlike the written language, run from left to right. Note the order of the words in numbers from 21 to 99.

0	٠	*sifir*
1	١	*waHid*
2	٢	*idhnīn*
3	٣	*dhaladha*
4	٤	*arba'a*
5	٥	*khamsa*
6	٦	*sitta*
7	٧	*sab'a*
8	٨	*dhimania*
9	٩	*tis'a*
10	١٠	*ashra*
11	١١	*Hda'ash*
12	١٢	*dhna'ash*
13	١٣	*dhaladhta'ash*
14	١٤	*arba'ata'ash*
15	١٥	*khamista'ash*
16	١٦	*sitta'ash*
17	١٧	*sabi'ta'ashr*
18	١٨	*dhimanta'ash*
19	١٩	*tisi'ta'ash*
20	٢٠	*'ishrīn*
21	٢١	*waHid wa 'ishrīn*
22	٢٢	*idhnīn wa 'ishrīn*
30	٣٠	*dhaladhīn*
40	٤٠	*arbi'īn*
50	٥٠	*khamsīn*
60	٦٠	*sittīn*
70	٧٠	*saba'īn*
80	٨٠	*dhimanīn*
90	٩٠	*tis'īn*
100	١٠٠	*imia*
101	١٠١	*imia wa-waHid*
200	٢٠٠	*imiatayn*
300	٣٠٠	*dhaladha imia*
1000	١٠٠٠	*alf*
2000	٢٠٠٠	*alfayn*
3000	٣٠٠٠	*dhaladha-alaf*

Ordinal Numbers

first	*awwal*
second	*dhānī*
third	*dhālidh*
fourth	*rābi'*
fifth	*khāmis*

Emergencies

Help me!	sā'idūnī!
I'm sick.	ana marīd (m)/
	ana marīda (f)
Call the police!	ittuṣil bil bolīṣ!
doctor	duktūr/tabīb
hospital	al-mustash-fa
police	ash-shurta/al-bolīṣ
Go away!	rouh min hūn!
Shame on you!	istiHi a'la Hālak!
(said by woman)	

Time & Dates

What time is it?	as-sa'a kam?
It is ...	as-sa'a ...
one o'clock	waHda
1.15	waHda wa rob'
1.20	waHda wa tilt
1.30	waHda wa nus
1.45	idhnīn illa rob' (lit:
	'quarter to two')
When?	mita?
now	alHīn

after	ba'ad
daily	kil yom
today	al-yom
yesterday	ams
tomorrow	bukra
morning	es-subāH
afternoon	ba'ad ezzuhur/
	edhuhur
evening	al-masa
day	nahār
night	leil
week	esbū'u
month	shahar
year	sine
early	mbach'ir/badri
late	mit'akhir
on time	alwaqit
Monday	yom al-idhnīn
Tuesday	yom al-dhaladh
Wednesday	yom al-arbā'
Thursday	yom al-khamis
Friday	yom al-jama'a
Saturday	yom as-sabt
Sunday	yom al-Had

خروج

Glossary

abeyya – woman's full-length black robe
abra – small, flat-decked motorboat
azan – call to prayer

bait – house
barasti – traditional method of building palm-leaf houses and the name of the house itself
Bedouin – also Bedu; desert dweller of Arabia
biryani – very common Indo-Pakistani dish consisting of spiced meat with rice
burj – tower

dalla – traditional copper coffeepot
dhow – traditional sailing vessel of the Gulf
dishdasha – name of man's shirt-dress worn in the UAE

falaj – traditional irrigation system used in the Gulf States
felafel – deep-fried balls of mashed chickpeas with spices, served in a piece of flat bread with salad
fuul – dish made from stewed broad beans

GCC – Gulf Cooperation Council: membership includes Saudi Arabia, Kuwait, Bahrain, Qatar, Oman and the UAE; Yemen holds partial membership

haj – annual Muslim pilgrimage to Mecca
halal – religiously acceptable or permitted (usually refers to meat)
hamour – common species of fish found in Gulf waters
haram – forbidden by Islam; religiously unacceptable

imam – prayer leader, Muslim cleric

jebel – hill, mountain

kandoura – casual shirt-dress worn by men and women
khanjar – traditional dagger in a curved scabbard
khor – inlet or creek

majlis – formal meeting room or reception area; also parliament
masjid – mosque
mihrab – niche in a mosque indicating the direction of Mecca
mina – port
minaret – the spire or tower of a mosque
minbar – pulpit used for sermons in a mosque
mosque – the Muslim place of worship
muezzin – person who sings the *azan* (call to prayer)

qibla – the direction of Mecca, indicated in a mosque by the *mihrab*
Quran – the holy book of Islam; also spelt Koran, the name comes from the root word for 'recite' and 'read'

Ramadan – the Muslim month of fasting

sheesha – tall, glass-bottomed smoking implement, also called a hubbly bubbly
sheikh – a venerated religious scholar, a tribal chief, a ruler, an elderly man worthy of respect; also spelt shaikh
sheikha – daughter of a sheikh
Shiite – sect of Islam which believes that the line of a caliph descends through the Prophet Mohammed's son-in-law, Ali; the majority sect in Iran, Iraq and Bahrain
shwarma – grilled meat sliced from a spit and served in pitta bread with salad
souq – market or shopping centre
Sunni – follower of the majority sect of Islam that holds that any Muslim who rules with justice and according to Islamic law can become a caliph

Trucial States – colonial era name for the United Arab Emirates

wadi – dried up river bed; seasonal river
wind tower – an architectural feature of traditional Gulf houses designed to keep the house cool
wusta – influence gained by way of connections in high places

LONELY PLANET

ON THE ROAD

Travel Guides explore cities, regions and countries, and supply information on transport, restaurants and accommodation, covering all budgets. They come with reliable, easy-to-use maps, practical advice, cultural and historical facts and a rundown on attractions both on and off the beaten track. There are over 200 titles in this classic series, covering nearly every country in the world.

 Lonely Planet Upgrades extend the shelf life of existing travel guides by detailing any changes that may affect travel in a region since a book has been published. Upgrades can be downloaded for free from **www.lonelyplanet.com/upgrades**

For travellers with more time than money, **Shoestring** guides offer dependable, first-hand information with hundreds of detailed maps, plus insider tips for stretching money as far as possible. Covering entire continents in most cases, the six-volume shoestring guides are known around the world as 'backpackers bibles'.

For the discerning short-term visitor, **Condensed** guides highlight the best a destination has to offer in a full-colour, pocket-sized format designed for quick access. They include everything from top sights and walking tours to opinionated reviews of where to eat, stay, shop and have fun.

CitySync lets travellers use their Palm™ or Visor™ hand-held computers to guide them through a city with handy tips on transport, history, cultural life, major sights, and shopping and entertainment options. It can also quickly search and sort hundreds of reviews of hotels, restaurants and attractions, and pinpoint their location on scrollable street maps. CitySync can be downloaded from **www.citysync.com**

MAPS & ATLASES

Lonely Planet's **City Maps** feature downtown and metropolitan maps, as well as transit routes and walking tours. The maps come complete with an index of streets, a listing of sights and a plastic coat for extra durability.

Road Atlases are an essential navigation tool for serious travellers. Cross-referenced with the guidebooks, they also feature distance and climate charts and a complete site index.

LONELY PLANET

ESSENTIALS

Read This First books help new travellers to hit the road with confidence. These invaluable predeparture guides give step-by-step advice on preparing for a trip, budgeting, arranging a visa, planning an itinerary and staying safe while still getting off the beaten track.

Healthy Travel pocket guides offer a regional rundown on disease hot spots and practical advice on predeparture health measures, staying well on the road and what to do in emergencies. The guides come with a user-friendly design and helpful diagrams and tables.

Lonely Planet's **Phrasebooks** cover the essential words and phrases travellers need when they're strangers in a strange land. They come in a pocket-sized format with colour tabs for quick reference, extensive vocabulary lists, easy-to-follow pronunciation keys and two-way dictionaries.

Miffed by blurry photos of the Taj Mahal? Tired of the classic 'top of the head cut off' shot? **Travel Photography: A Guide to Taking Better Pictures** will help you turn ordinary holiday snaps into striking images and give you the know-how to capture every scene, from frenetic festivals to peaceful beach sunrises.

Lonely Planet's **Travel Journal** is a lightweight but sturdy travel diary for jotting down all those on-the-road observations and significant travel moments. It comes with a handy time-zone wheel, a world map and useful travel information.

Lonely Planet's eKno is an all-in-one communication service developed especially for travellers. It offers low-cost international calls and free email and voicemail so that you can keep in touch while on the road. Check it out on **www.ekno.lonelyplanet.com**

FOOD & RESTAURANT GUIDES

Lonely Planet's **Out to Eat** guides recommend the brightest and best places to eat and drink in top international cities. These gourmet companions are arranged by neighbourhood, packed with dependable maps, garnished with scene-setting photos and served with quirky features.

For people who live to eat, drink and travel, **World Food** guides explore the culinary culture of each country. Entertaining and adventurous, each guide is packed with detail on staples and specialities, regional cuisine and local markets, as well as sumptuous recipes, comprehensive culinary dictionaries and lavish photos good enough to eat.

OUTDOOR GUIDES

For those who believe the best way to see the world is on foot, Lonely Planet's **Walking Guides** detail everything from family strolls to difficult treks, with 'when to go and how to do it' advice supplemented by reliable maps and essential travel information.

Cycling Guides map a destination's best bike tours, long and short, in day-by-day detail. They contain all the information a cyclist needs, including advice on bike maintenance, places to eat and stay, innovative maps with detailed cues to the rides, and elevation charts.

The **Watching Wildlife** series is perfect for travellers who want authoritative information but don't want to tote a heavy field guide. Packed with advice on where, when and how to view a region's wildlife, each title features photos of over 300 species and contains engaging comments on the local flora and fauna.

With underwater colour photos throughout, **Pisces Books** explore the world's best diving and snorkelling areas. Each book contains listings of diving services and dive resorts, detailed information on depth, visibility and difficulty of dives, and a roundup of the marine life you're likely to see through your mask.

OFF THE ROAD

Journeys, the travel literature series written by renowned travel authors, capture the spirit of a place or illuminate a culture with a journalist's attention to detail and a novelist's flair for words. These are tales to soak up while you're actually on the road or dip into as an at-home armchair indulgence.

The range of lavishly illustrated **Pictorial** books is just the ticket for both travellers and dreamers. Off-beat tales and vivid photographs bring the adventure of travel to your doorstep long before the journey begins and long after it is over.

Lonely Planet **Videos** encourage the same independent, tough-minded approach as the guidebooks. Currently airing throughout the world, this award-winning series features innovative footage and an original soundtrack.

Yes, we know, work is tough, so do a little bit of deskside dreaming with the spiral-bound Lonely Planet **Diary** or a Lonely Planet **Wall Calendar**, filled with great photos from around the world.

TRAVELLERS NETWORK

Lonely Planet Online. Lonely Planet's award-winning Web site has insider information on hundreds of destinations, from Amsterdam to Zimbabwe, complete with interactive maps and relevant links. The site also offers the latest travel news, recent reports from travellers on the road, guidebook upgrades, a travel links site, an online book-buying option and a lively travellers bulletin board. It can be viewed at **www.lonelyplanet.com** or AOL keyword: lp.

Planet Talk is a quarterly print newsletter, full of gossip, advice, anecdotes and author articles. It provides an antidote to the being-at-home blues and lets you plan and dream for the next trip. Contact the nearest Lonely Planet office for your free copy.

Comet, the free Lonely Planet newsletter, comes via email once a month. It's loaded with travel news, advice, dispatches from authors, travel competitions and letters from readers. To subscribe, click on the Comet subscription link on the front page of the Web site.

Lonely Planet Guides by Region

onely Planet is known worldwide for publishing practical, reliable and no-nonsense travel information in our guides and on our Web site. The Lonely Planet list covers just about every accessible part of the world. Currently there are 16 series: Travel guides, Shoestring guides, Condensed guides, Phrasebooks, Read This First, Healthy Travel, Walking guides, Cycling guides, Watching Wildlife guides, Pisces Diving & Snorkeling guides, City Maps, Road Atlases, Out to Eat, World Food, Journeys travel literature and Pictorials.

AFRICA Africa on a shoestring • Botswana • Cairo • Cairo City Map • Cape Town • Cape Town City Map • East Africa • Egypt • Egyptian Arabic phrasebook • Ethiopia, Eritrea & Djibouti • Ethiopian Amharic phrasebook • The Gambia & Senegal • Healthy Travel Africa • Kenya • Malawi • Morocco • Moroccan Arabic phrasebook • Mozambique • Namibia • Read This First: Africa • South Africa, Lesotho & Swaziland • Southern Africa • Southern Africa Road Atlas • Swahili phrasebook • Tanzania, Zanzibar & Pemba • Trekking in East Africa • Tunisia • Watching Wildlife East Africa • Watching Wildlife Southern Africa • West Africa • World Food Morocco • Zambia • Zimbabwe, Botswana & Namibia
Travel Literature: Mali Blues: Traveling to an African Beat • The Rainbird: A Central African Journey • Songs to an African Sunset: A Zimbabwean Story

AUSTRALIA & THE PACIFIC Aboriginal Australia & the Torres Strait Islands •Auckland • Australia • Australian phrasebook • Australia Road Atlas • Cycling Australia • Cycling New Zealand • Fiji • Fijian phrasebook • Healthy Travel Australia, NZ & the Pacific • Islands of Australia's Great Barrier Reef • Melbourne • Melbourne City Map • Micronesia • New Caledonia • New South Wales • New Zealand • Northern Territory • Outback Australia • Out to Eat – Melbourne • Out to Eat – Sydney • Papua New Guinea • Pidgin phrasebook • Queensland • Rarotonga & the Cook Islands • Samoa • Solomon Islands • South Australia • South Pacific • South Pacific phrasebook • Sydney • Sydney City Map • Sydney Condensed • Tahiti & French Polynesia • Tasmania • Tonga • Tramping in New Zealand • Vanuatu • Victoria • Walking in Australia • Watching Wildlife Australia • Western Australia
Travel Literature: Islands in the Clouds: Travels in the Highlands of New Guinea • Kiwi Tracks: A New Zealand Journey • Sean & David's Long Drive

CENTRAL AMERICA & THE CARIBBEAN Bahamas, Turks & Caicos • Baja California • Belize, Guatemala & Yucatán • Bermuda • Central America on a shoestring • Costa Rica • Costa Rica Spanish phrasebook • Cuba • Cycling Cuba • Dominican Republic & Haiti • Eastern Caribbean • Guatemala • Havana • Healthy Travel Central & South America • Jamaica • Mexico • Mexico City • Panama • Puerto Rico • Read This First: Central & South America • Virgin Islands • World Food Caribbean • World Food Mexico • Yucatán
Travel Literature: Green Dreams: Travels in Central America

EUROPE Amsterdam • Amsterdam City Map • Amsterdam Condensed • Andalucía • Athens • Austria • Baltic States phrasebook • Barcelona • Barcelona City Map • Belgium & Luxembourg • Berlin • Berlin City Map • Britain • British phrasebook • Brussels, Bruges & Antwerp • Brussels City Map • Budapest • Budapest City Map • Canary Islands • Catalunya & the Costa Brava • Central Europe • Central Europe phrasebook • Copenhagen • Corfu & the Ionians • Corsica • Crete • Crete Condensed • Croatia • Cycling Britain • Cycling France • Cyprus • Czech & Slovak Republics • Czech phrasebook • Denmark • Dublin • Dublin City Map • Dublin Condensed • Eastern Europe • Eastern Europe phrasebook • Edinburgh • Edinburgh City Map • England • Estonia, Latvia & Lithuania • Europe on a shoestring • Europe phrasebook • Finland • Florence • Florence City Map • France • Frankfurt City Map • Frankfurt Condensed • French phrasebook • Georgia, Armenia & Azerbaijan • Germany • German phrasebook • Greece • Greek Islands • Greek phrasebook • Hungary • Iceland, Greenland & the Faroe Islands • Ireland • Italian phrasebook • Italy • Kraków • Lisbon • The Loire • London • London City Map • London Condensed • Madrid • Madrid City Map • Malta • Mediterranean Europe • Milan, Turin & Genoa • Moscow • Munich • Netherlands • Normandy • Norway • Out to Eat – London • Out to Eat – Paris • Paris • Paris City Map • Paris Condensed • Poland • Polish phrasebook • Portugal • Portuguese phrasebook • Prague • Prague City Map • Provence & the Côte d'Azur • Read This First: Europe • Rhodes & the Dodecanese • Romania & Moldova • Rome • Rome City Map • Rome Condensed • Russia, Ukraine & Belarus • Russian phrasebook • Scandinavian & Baltic Europe • Scandinavian phrasebook • Scotland • Sicily • Slovenia • South-West France • Spain • Spanish phrasebook • Stockholm • St Petersburg • St Petersburg City Map • Sweden • Switzerland • Tuscany • Ukrainian phrasebook • Venice • Vienna • Wales • Walking in Britain • Walking in France • Walking in Ireland • Walking in Italy • Walking in Scotland • Walking in Spain • Walking in Switzerland • Western Europe • World Food France • World Food Greece • World Food Ireland • World Food Italy • World Food Spain **Travel Literature:** After Yugoslavia • Love and War in the Apennines • The Olive Grove: Travels in Greece • On the Shores of the Mediterranean • Round Ireland in Low Gear • A Small Place in Italy

Lonely Planet Mail Order

Lonely Planet products are distributed worldwide. They are also available by mail order from Lonely Planet, so if you have difficulty finding a title please write to us. North and South American residents should write to 150 Linden St, Oakland, CA 94607, USA; European and African residents should write to 10a Spring Place, London NW5 3BH, UK; and residents of other countries to Locked Bag 1, Footscray, Victoria 3011, Australia.

INDIAN SUBCONTINENT & THE INDIAN OCEAN Bangladesh • Bengali phrasebook • Bhutan • Delhi • Goa • Healthy Travel Asia & India • Hindi & Urdu phrasebook • India • India & Bangladesh City Map • Indian Himalaya • Karakoram Highway • Kathmandu City Map • Kerala • Madagascar • Maldives • Mauritius, Réunion & Seychelles • Mumbai (Bombay) • Nepal • Nepali phrasebook • North India • Pakistan • Rajasthan • Read This First: Asia & India • South India • Sri Lanka • Sri Lanka phrasebook • Tibet • Tibetan phrasebook • Trekking in the Indian Himalaya • Trekking in the Karakoram & Hindukush • Trekking in the Nepal Himalaya • World Food India **Travel Literature:** The Age of Kali: Indian Travels and Encounters • Hello Goodnight: A Life of Goa • In Rajasthan • Maverick in Madagascar • A Season in Heaven: True Tales from the Road to Kathmandu • Shopping for Buddhas • A Short Walk in the Hindu Kush • Slowly Down the Ganges

MIDDLE EAST & CENTRAL ASIA Bahrain, Kuwait & Qatar • Central Asia • Central Asia phrasebook • Dubai • Farsi (Persian) phrasebook • Hebrew phrasebook • Iran • Israel & the Palestinian Territories • Istanbul • Istanbul City Map • Istanbul to Cairo • Istanbul to Kathmandu • Jerusalem • Jerusalem City Map • Jordan • Lebanon • Middle East • Oman & the United Arab Emirates • Syria • Turkey • Turkish phrasebook • World Food Turkey • Yemen **Travel Literature:** Black on Black: Iran Revisited • Breaking Ranks: Turbulent Travels in the Promised Land • The Gates of Damascus • Kingdom of the Film Stars: Journey into Jordan

NORTH AMERICA Alaska • Boston • Boston City Map • Boston Condensed • British Columbia • California & Nevada • California Condensed • Canada • Chicago • Chicago City Map • Chicago Condensed • Florida • Georgia & the Carolinas • Great Lakes • Hawaii • Hiking in Alaska • Hiking in the USA • Honolulu & Oahu City Map • Las Vegas • Los Angeles • Los Angeles City Map • Louisiana & the Deep South • Miami • Miami City Map • Montreal • New England • New Orleans • New Orleans City Map • New York City • New York City City Map • New York City Condensed • New York, New Jersey & Pennsylvania • Oahu • Out to Eat – San Francisco • Pacific Northwest • Rocky Mountains • San Diego & Tijuana • San Francisco • San Francisco City Map • Seattle • Seattle City Map • Southwest • Texas • Toronto • USA • USA phrasebook • Vancouver • Vancouver City Map • Virginia & the Capital Region • Washington, DC • Washington, DC City Map • World Food New Orleans **Travel Literature**: Caught Inside: A Surfer's Year on the California Coast • Drive Thru America

NORTH-EAST ASIA Beijing • Beijing City Map • Cantonese phrasebook • China • Hiking in Japan • Hong Kong & Macau • Hong Kong City Map • Hong Kong Condensed • Japan • Japanese phrasebook • Korea • Korean phrasebook • Kyoto • Mandarin phrasebook • Mongolia • Mongolian phrasebook • Seoul • Shanghai • South-West China • Taiwan • Tokyo • Tokyo Condensed • World Food Hong Kong • World Food Japan **Travel Literature:** In Xanadu: A Quest • Lost Japan

SOUTH AMERICA Argentina, Uruguay & Paraguay • Bolivia • Brazil • Brazilian phrasebook • Buenos Aires • Buenos Aires City Map • Chile & Easter Island • Colombia • Ecuador & the Galapagos Islands • Healthy Travel Central & South America • Latin American Spanish phrasebook • Peru • Quechua phrasebook • Read This First: Central & South America • Rio de Janeiro • Rio de Janeiro City Map • Santiago de Chile • South America on a shoestring • Trekking in the Patagonian Andes • Venezuela **Travel Literature**: Full Circle: A South American Journey

SOUTH-EAST ASIA Bali & Lombok • Bangkok • Bangkok City Map • Burmese phrasebook • Cambodia • Cycling Vietnam, Laos & Cambodia • East Timor phrasebook • Hanoi • Healthy Travel Asia & India • Hill Tribes phrasebook • Ho Chi Minh City (Saigon) • Indonesia • Indonesian phrasebook • Indonesia's Eastern Islands • Java • Lao phrasebook • Laos • Malay phrasebook • Malaysia, Singapore & Brunei • Myanmar (Burma) • Philippines • Pilipino (Tagalog) phrasebook • Read This First: Asia & India • Singapore • Singapore City Map • South-East Asia on a shoestring • South-East Asia phrasebook • Thailand • Thailand's Islands & Beaches • Thailand, Vietnam, Laos & Cambodia Road Atlas • Thai phrasebook • Vietnam • Vietnamese phrasebook • World Food Indonesia • World Food Thailand • World Food Vietnam

ALSO AVAILABLE: Antarctica • The Arctic • The Blue Man: Tales of Travel, Love and Coffee • Brief Encounters: Stories of Love, Sex & Travel • Buddhist Stupas in Asia: The Shape of Perfection • Chasing Rickshaws • The Last Grain Race • Lonely Planet ... On the Edge: Adventurous Escapades from Around the World • Lonely Planet Unpacked • Lonely Planet Unpacked Again • Not the Only Planet: Science Fiction Travel Stories • Ports of Call: A Journey by Sea • Sacred India • Travel Photography: A Guide to Taking Better Pictures • Travel with Children • Tuvalu: Portrait of an Island Nation

LONELY PLANET

You already know that Lonely Planet produces more than this one guidebook, but you might not be aware of the other products we have on this region. Here is a selection of titles that you may want to check out as well:

Oman & the United Emirates
ISBN 1 86450 130 8
US$15.99 • UK£9.99

Middle East
ISBN 1 86450 349 1
US$24.99 • UK£14.99

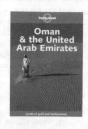

Egyptian Arabic phrasebook
ISBN 1 86450 183 9
US$7.99 • UK£4.50

Travel with Children
ISBN 0 86442 729 8
US$14.99 • UK£8.99

Travel Photography
ISBN 1 86450 207 X
US$16.99 • UK£9.99

Farsi (Persian) phrasebook
ISBN 1 86442 581 3
US$7.99 • UK£4.50

Diving & Snorkeling Red Sea
ISBN 1 86450 205 3
US$19.99 • UK£12.99

Travel Journal
ISBN 1 86450 343 2
US$12.99 • UK£7.99

Available wherever books are sold

Index

Text

Bold indicates maps.

Places to Stay

Places to Eat

Bold indicates maps.

Boxed Text

CHRIS MELLOR

TONY WHEELER

TONY WHEELER

CHRIS MELLOR

To orient yourself in Dubai (top), use landmarks such as the skyscrapers on Sheikh Zayed Rd (middle left) and the Clock Tower Roundabout (middle right); in Al-Ain, use the Coffeepot Roundabout (bottom).

Strait of Hormuz

Ras Sheikh Masud

Tumb Kubra

OMAN

Sham

Khor Khowair

Abu Musa

*ARABIAN
GULF*

Rams

Gulf of Oman

Ras al-Khaimah

Habab

**RAS
AL-KHAIMAH**

Al-Jazirah al-Hamra

Digdagga

Hamraniyah

ELEVATION

	600m
	300m
	150m
	75m
	0

Al-Rafaah
Ras al-Khaimah
International
Airport

Habab

Dibba

**Umm
al-Qaiwain**

FUJAIRAH

Hamriya

Dadna
Aqqa
Sharam
Bidiya

Az-Zora

**UMM
AL-QAIWAIN**

Al-Uyaynah

Biatah

Tayyibah

Rifaisa
Dam

SHARJAH

AJMAN

Hamadiyah

Nabbha

Manama

AJMAN

Khor Fakkan

Ajman

Al-Hilew

Masafi

OMAN

Sharjah

*Sharjah
International
Airport*

*Sharjah
Desert Park*

Al-Dhaid

Madha

Mirbah

MAP 2 GREATER DUBAI

SHARJAH

Siji

FUJAIRAH

DUBAI

Al-Awir

Mileiha

Bithnah

Al-Hayl
Castle

Fujairah
International
Airport

Fujairah

Jebel Ali Port

Bahuth
Ruwayyah

Al Haba

Fili

Kalba

SHARJAH

*Jebel Ali Hotel
& Golf Resort*

Jebel Ali Village

Al-Madam

Khor Kalba
Conservation
Reserve

*Ghantoot Racing
& Polo Club*

DUBAI

Al-Liseli

Big Red

Margham

Al-Ghirefah

Khatmat
Malahah

*Jazira Hotel
& Resort*

Muraqqab

*Al-Maha
Resort*

Mazeirah

**RAS AL-
KHAIMAH**

Wahlah

AJMAN

Masfout

DUBAI

**UNITED
ARAB
EMIRATES**

Ash-Shuayb

Hatta

Al-Wajajah

Al-Faqa

*Hatta
Pools*

Al-Samha

Sumayni

OMAN

Ajban

Fa'iyyah

Al-Juwayf

To Abu Dhabi
(30km)

Al-Haiyl

Zaymi

*To Abu Dhabi
International Airport
(5km)*

Sweihan

Sharm

Al-Hijr al-Gharbi

To Abu Dhabi
(30km)

Mahdah

Al-Ohab

*Al-Ain
International
Airport*

ABU DHABI

Al-Saad

Al-Ain

Buraimi

*Wadi
al-Jizzi*

Al-Khatam

Al-Khawrah

Al-Wasit

Al-Khaznah

Zakhir

Al-Zahir

Jebel Hafit

Hafit

MAP 2 – GREATER DUBAI

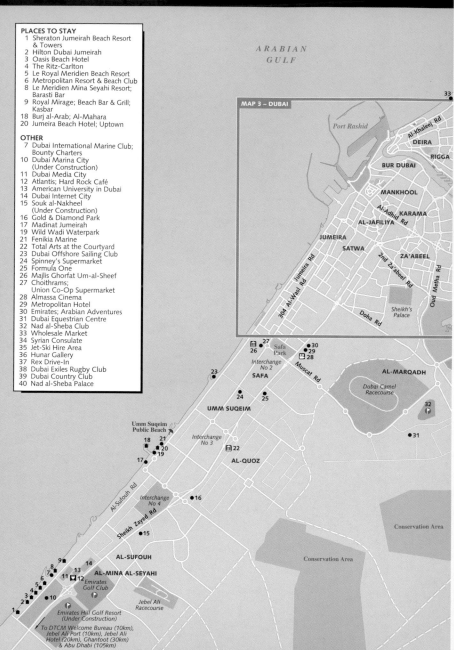

PLACES TO STAY

1 Sheraton Jumeirah Beach Resort & Towers
2 Hilton Dubai Jumeirah
3 Oasis Beach Hotel
4 The Ritz-Carlton
5 Le Royal Meridien Beach Resort
6 Metropolitan Resort & Beach Club
8 Le Meridien Mina Seyahi Resort; Barasti Bar
9 Royal Mirage; Beach Bar & Grill; Kasbar
18 Burj al-Arab; Al-Mahara
20 Jumeira Beach Hotel; Uptown

OTHER

7 Dubai International Marine Club; Bounty Charters
10 Dubai Marina City (Under Construction)
11 Dubai Media City
12 Atlantis; Hard Rock Café
13 American University in Dubai
14 Dubai Internet City
15 Souk al-Nakheel (Under Construction)
16 Gold & Diamond Park
17 Madinat Jumeirah
19 Wild Wadi Waterpark
21 Fenikia Marine
22 Total Arts at the Courtyard
23 Dubai Offshore Sailing Club
24 Spinney's Supermarket
25 Formula One
26 Majlis Ghorfat Um-al-Sheef
27 Choithrams; Union Co-Op Supermarket
28 Almassa Cinema
29 Metropolitan Hotel
30 Emirates; Arabian Adventures
31 Dubai Equestrian Centre
32 Nad al-Sheba Club
33 Wholesale Market
34 Syrian Consulate
35 Jet-Ski Hire Area
36 Hunar Gallery
37 Rex Drive-In
38 Dubai Exiles Rugby Club
39 Dubai Country Club
40 Nad al-Sheba Palace

ARABIAN GULF

MAP 3 – DUBAI

Port Rashid

Al-Khaleej Rd

DEIRA

RIGGA

BUR DUBAI

MANKHOOL

Al-Adhid Rd

KARAMA

AL-JAFILIYA

JUMEIRA

SATWA

ZA'ABEEL

2nd Za'abeel Rd

Oud Metha Rd

Sheikh's Palace

Doha Rd

Jumeira Rd

304 Al-Wasl Rd

Safa Park

AL-MARQADH

Muscat Rd

Dubai Camel Racecourse

SAFA

Interchange No 2

UMM SUQEIM

Umm Suqeim Public Beach

Interchange No 3

AL-QUOZ

Al-Sufouh Rd

Interchange No 4

Sheikh Zayed Rd

AL-SUFOUH

AL-MINA AL-SEYAHI

Emirates Golf Club

Conservation Area

Conservation Area

Jebel Ali Racecourse

Emirates Hill Golf Resort (Under Construction)

To DTCM Welcome Bureau (10km), Jebel Ali Port (10km), Jebel Ali Hotel (20km), Ghantoot (30km) & Abu Dhabi (105km)

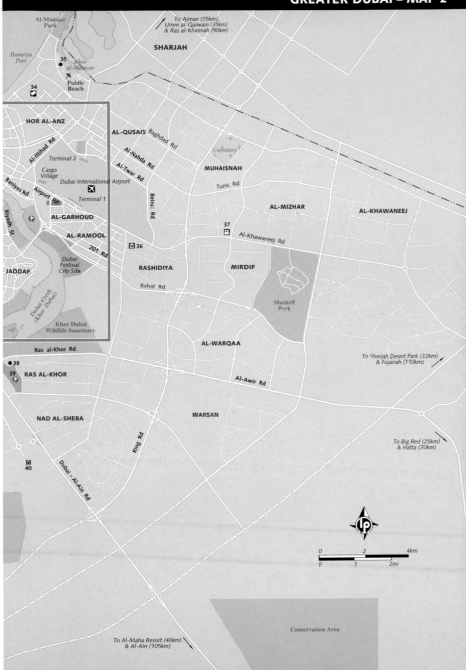

Al-Mamzar
Park

To Ajman (15km),
Umm al-Qaiwain (35km)
& Ras al-Khaimah (90km)

SHARJAH

Hamriya
Port

Khor
al-Mamzar

35

Public
Beach

34

HOR AL-ANZ

Al-Ittihad Rd

AL-QUSAIS

Baghdad Rd

Terminal 2

Al-Nahda Rd

Cargo
Village

Al-Twar Rd

Dubai International Airport

✈

Terminal 1

Airport Rd

Baniyas Rd

Beirut Rd

Cemetery

MUHAISNAH

Tunis Rd

AL-MIZHAR

AL-KHAWANEEJ

37

Al-Khawaneej Rd

Riyadh St

AL-GARHOUD

AL-RAMOOL

201 Rd

36

RASHIDIYA

MIRDIF

JADDAF

Dubai
Festival
City Site

Rahat Rd

Dubai Creek
(Khor Dubai)

Mushrif
Park

Khor Dubai
Wildlife Sanctuary

Ras al-Khor Rd

AL-WARQAA

38

To Sharjah Desert Park (32km)
& Fujairah (110km)

39

RAS AL-KHOR

Al-Awir Rd

WARSAN

NAD AL-SHEBA

Ring Rd

To Big Red (25km)
& Hatta (70km)

40

Dubai – Al-Ain Rd

0   2   4km

0   1   2mi

Conservation Area

To Al-Maha Resort (40km)
& Al-Ain (105km)

MAP 3 – DUBAI

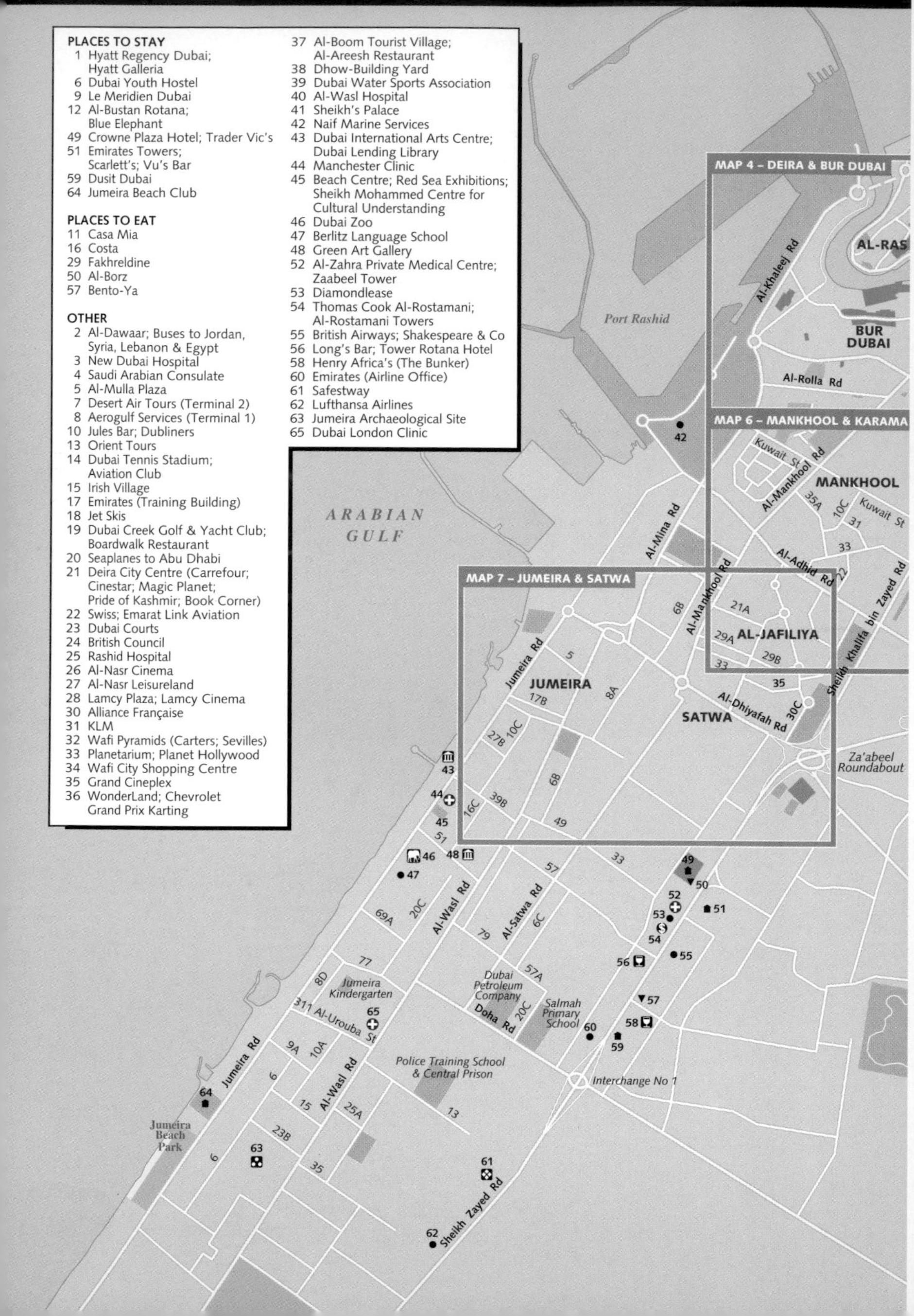

PLACES TO STAY
1 Hyatt Regency Dubai; Hyatt Galleria
6 Dubai Youth Hostel
9 Le Meridien Dubai
12 Al-Bustan Rotana; Blue Elephant
49 Crowne Plaza Hotel; Trader Vic's
51 Emirates Towers; Scarlett's; Vu's Bar
59 Dusit Dubai
64 Jumeira Beach Club
PLACES TO EAT
11 Casa Mia
16 Costa
29 Fakhreldine
50 Al-Borz
57 Bento-Ya
OTHER
2 Al-Dawaar; Buses to Jordan, Syria, Lebanon & Egypt
3 New Dubai Hospital
4 Saudi Arabian Consulate
5 Al-Mulla Plaza
7 Desert Air Tours (Terminal 2)
8 Aerogulf Services (Terminal 1)
10 Jules Bar; Dubliners
13 Orient Tours
14 Dubai Tennis Stadium; Aviation Club
15 Irish Village
17 Emirates (Training Building)
18 Jet Skis
19 Dubai Creek Golf & Yacht Club; Boardwalk Restaurant
20 Seaplanes to Abu Dhabi
21 Deira City Centre (Carrefour; Cinestar; Magic Planet; Pride of Kashmir; Book Corner)
22 Swiss; Emarat Link Aviation
23 Dubai Courts
24 British Council
25 Rashid Hospital
26 Al-Nasr Cinema
27 Al-Nasr Leisureland
28 Lamcy Plaza; Lamcy Cinema
30 Alliance Française
31 KLM
32 Wafi Pyramids (Carters; Sevilles)
33 Planetarium; Planet Hollywood
34 Wafi City Shopping Centre
35 Grand Cineplex
36 WonderLand; Chevrolet Grand Prix Karting
37 Al-Boom Tourist Village; Al-Areesh Restaurant
38 Dhow-Building Yard
39 Dubai Water Sports Association
40 Al-Wasl Hospital
41 Sheikh's Palace
42 Naif Marine Services
43 Dubai International Arts Centre; Dubai Lending Library
44 Manchester Clinic
45 Beach Centre; Red Sea Exhibitions; Sheikh Mohammed Centre for Cultural Understanding
46 Dubai Zoo
47 Berlitz Language School
48 Green Art Gallery
52 Al-Zahra Private Medical Centre; Zaabeel Tower
53 Diamondlease
54 Thomas Cook Al-Rostamani; Al-Rostamani Towers
55 British Airways; Shakespeare & Co
56 Long's Bar; Tower Rotana Hotel
58 Henry Africa's (The Bunker)
60 Emirates (Airline Office)
61 Safestway
62 Lufthansa Airlines
63 Jumeira Archaeological Site
65 Dubai London Clinic
MAP 4 – DEIRA & BUR DUBAI
MAP 6 – MANKHOOL & KARAMA
MAP 7 – JUMEIRA & SATWA
Port Rashid
ARABIAN GULF
AL-RAS
BUR DUBAI
MANKHOOL
AL-JAFILIYA
JUMEIRA
SATWA
Al-Khaleej Rd
Al-Rolla Rd
Kuwait St
Al-Mankhool Rd
Al-Mina Rd
Al-Adhid Rd
Sheikh Khalifa bin Zayed Rd
Jumeira Rd
Al-Dhiyafah Rd
Za'abeel Roundabout
Al-Wasl Rd
Al-Satwa Rd
Al-Urouba St
Doha Rd
Sheikh Zayed Rd
Interchange No 1
Jumeira Kindergarten
Dubai Petroleum Company
Salmah Primary School
Police Training School & Central Prison
Jumeira Beach Park

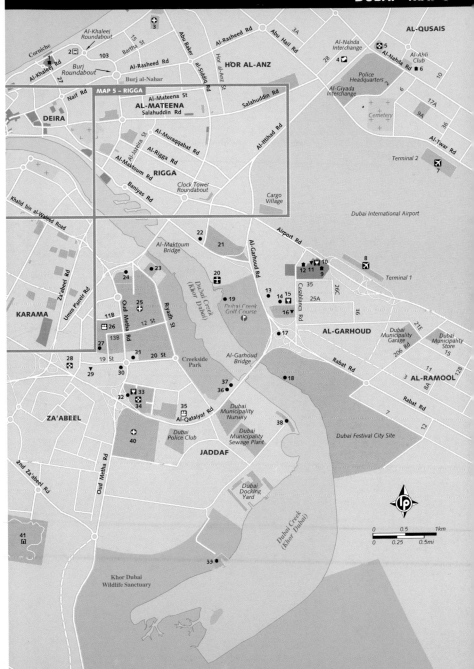

AL-QUSAIS

Al-Khaleej
Roundabout

Corniche

Al-Nahda
Interchange

5

Al-Ahli
Club

2

103

Al-Khaleej Rd

Burj
Roundabout

27

Bartha St

15

Abu Baker

al-Siddiq Rd

Al-Rasheed Rd

Abu Hail Rd

3A

4

6

Al-Nahda Rd

10

Naif Rd

Al-Rasheed Rd

Burj al-Nahar

HOR AL-ANZ

Hor Al-Anz St

Al-Giyada
Interchange

Police
Headquarters

2

6

17A

MAP 5 – RIGGA

DEIRA

Al-Mateena St

AL-MATEENA
Salahuddin Rd

Salahuddin Rd

Cemetery

9A

36

Al-Twar Rd

Al-Jazeira St

Al-Muraqqabat Rd

Al-Rigga Rd

Al-Maktoum Rd

RIGGA

Al-Ittihad Rd

Terminal 2

7

Khalid bin al-Waleed Road

Baniyas Rd

Clock Tower
Roundabout

Cargo
Village

Dubai International Airport

22

Al-Maktoum
Bridge

21

Airport Rd

KARAMA

Za'abeel Rd

Umm Hurair Rd

24

23

20

Al-Garhoud Rd

12 11 10

9

8

Terminal 1

Oud Metha Rd

25

Riyadh St

Dubai Creek
(Khor Dubai)

19

Dubai Creek
Golf Course

13

14 15

16

35

25A

26C

36

11B

26

13B

12 St

17

AL-GARHOUD

Casablanca Rd

Dubai
Municipality
Garage

206 Rd

21E

Dubai
Municipality
Store

75

27

19 St

31

20 St

Creekside
Park

Al-Garhoud
Bridge

Rabat Rd

11

AL-RAMOOL

28

29

30

18

8A

12B

32

33

34

37

36

Rabat Rd

12

ZA'ABEEL

35

Al-Qatalyat Rd

Dubai
Municipality
Nursery

38

7

Dubai Festival City Site

40

Dubai
Police Club

Dubai
Municipality
Sewage Plant

JADDAF

Oud Metha Rd

2nd Za'abeel Rd

Dubai
Docking
Yard

41

39

Khor Dubai
Wildlife Sanctuary

Dubai Creek
(Khor Dubai)

0   0.5   1km

0   0.25   0.5mi

MAP 4 – DEIRA & BUR DUBAI

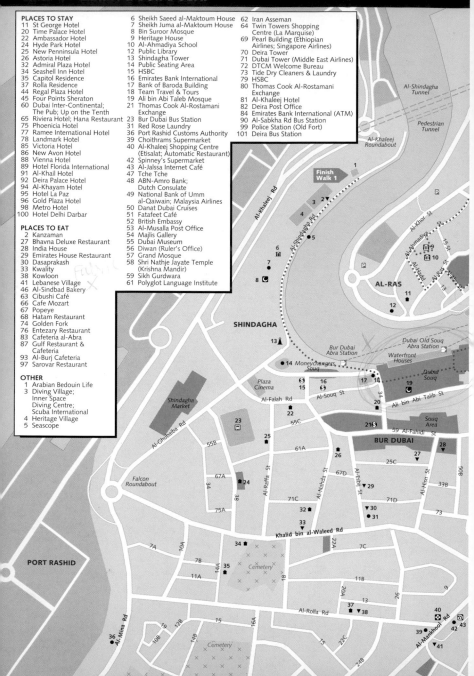

Deira Meat, Fish
Fruit & Vegetable
Market
Al-Khaleej Rd

101

57

12 Al-Daghaya St
28 St
20
75

4
10
15
11A
14A
21B
19B
27

Naif Rd

35
37

24

35A

Naif Rd

29B
29B
18D

DEIRA

100

Naif Rd

99

2A

9A

17

17A
2C

10A
12A
25

27A

Finish
Walk 2

Naif Park

Naif
Roundabout

Al-Musalla Rd

34B
29D

Perfume
Souq

98

Al-Soor St
38 St

Naif Rd

Naif
Souq

Al-Wasl
Souq

17B
19B
21C
23B
30 Al-Nakhal St
31
34A
38C

Gold Souq

97

Sikkat al-Khail

32

45

96
95
94
93
Sikkat al-Khail St
Sikkat al-Khail St

Bin Dalta

91

90
89
88
87

Deira
Covered Souq

Deira St
Al-Burj St

77

76
75
74

73
72

Al-Maktoum Hospital Rd

Cemetery

Old Bahadiya St

Al-Butleen St

12
97

86

Electronics
Souq

78

80
79

72

Baniyas
Square

70
71

Spice Souq
(Deira Old Souq)

20D St

Murshid Souq

Al-Suq al-Kabeer St

85

84
82

81

Road 14

69

Baniyas Rd

Start
Walk 2

68
67
66

83

65

62
63
64

61

Al-Maktoum Rd

15

Deira Old Souq
Abra Station

Dhow Wharfage

Sabkha
Abra Station

18 St

Baniyas Rd

Dubai Creek
(Khor Dubai)

59
58
57

56

Bastakia
Quarter

Dubai
Municipality
Headquarters

60

Al-Seef Rd

Al-Ittihad
Square

55

Start
Walk 1

54

Cemetery

53

Al-Fahidi
Roundabout

78A
83B
76

3

51

78B
74B
69D
71E

4A

13

52

50

Al-Musalla Rd

19
2C
6

9

15

8

16

45

Khalid bin al-Waleed Rd

44

46

47
48

49

21

Sheikh Khalifa bin Zayed Rd

3A

0   150   300m
0   150   300yd

MAP 5 – RIGGA

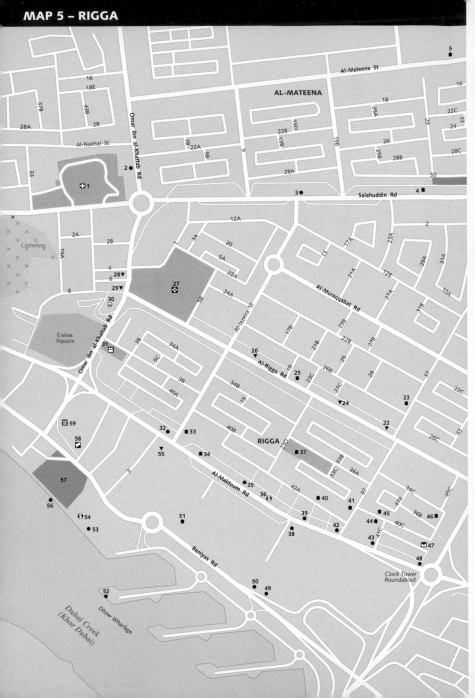

AL-MATEENA

Al-Mateena St

Al-Nakhal St

Omar ibn al-Khattab Rd

Salahuddin Rd

Cemetery

Union Square

Al-Muraqqabat Rd

Al-Jazeira St

Al-Rigga Rd

RIGGA

Al-Maktoum Rd

Baniyas Rd

Clock Tower Roundabout

Dhow Wharfage

Dubai Creek (Khor Dubai)

Toubritilah
Primary
School

HOR
AL-ANZ

PLACES TO STAY
4 Renaissance Dubai Hotel;
  Harry's Place
5 Sheraton Deira
10 JW Marriott Hotel;
   JW's Steakhouse
23 Holiday Inn Downtown
25 Quality Inn Horizon
33 Lords Hotel
34 Metropolitan Palace Hotel
37 Taj Palace Hotel; Topkapi
40 Mayfair Hotel
41 Sun and Sand Hotel
44 Nihal Hotel
45 Orchid Hotel
46 Avari Dubai Hotel
51 Hilton Dubai Creek; Verre;
   Glasshouse Brasserie
57 Sheraton Dubai

PLACES TO EAT
22 King Pastries
24 Automatic Restaurant
26 Harry Ramsden's
28 Barrio Fiesta
29 Iranian Sweets

55 Little Italy; Al-Khaleej
   Palace Hotel

OTHER
1 Al-Maktoum Hospital
2 Arabian Dream Tours
3 Gulf Air
6 Prolab
7 Spinney's Supermarket
8 Dubai Cinema
9 Juma al-Majid Cultural
  & Heritage Centre
11 Hamarain Centre (Afghan
   Carpet Palace, Inet)
12 Net Tours & Travels
13 The Travel Market
14 Thai Airways International
15 Cargo Village
16 Budget
17 Hertz
18 Air France;
   Cathay Pacific Airways
19 DNATA Airline Centre
   (DNATA Head Office;
   Emirates; SriLankan
   Airlines; Oman Transport)

20 Patriot Rent-A-Car
21 Mosque
27 Al-Ghurair Centre
   (Books Gallery; Gerard Café)
30 Deira Minibus & Taxi Station
31 Deira Cinema
32 Qatar Airways
35 Sadaf Carpet
36 Emirates Bank International
38 Air India
39 EgyptAir
42 Al-Ghaith & Al-Moosa
   Travel Agency;
   Czech Airlines
43 Avis
47 Al-Rigga Post Office
48 Saudi Arabian Airlines
49 Iran Air
50 Alitalia
52 Creek Cruises
53 Dubai Chamber of
   Commerce & Industry
54 National Bank of Dubai
56 Coastline Leisure
58 Kuwaiti Consulate
59 Etisalat (Headquaters)

Dubai
International
Airport

0   125   250m
0   125   250yd

MAP 6 – MANKHOOL & KARAMA

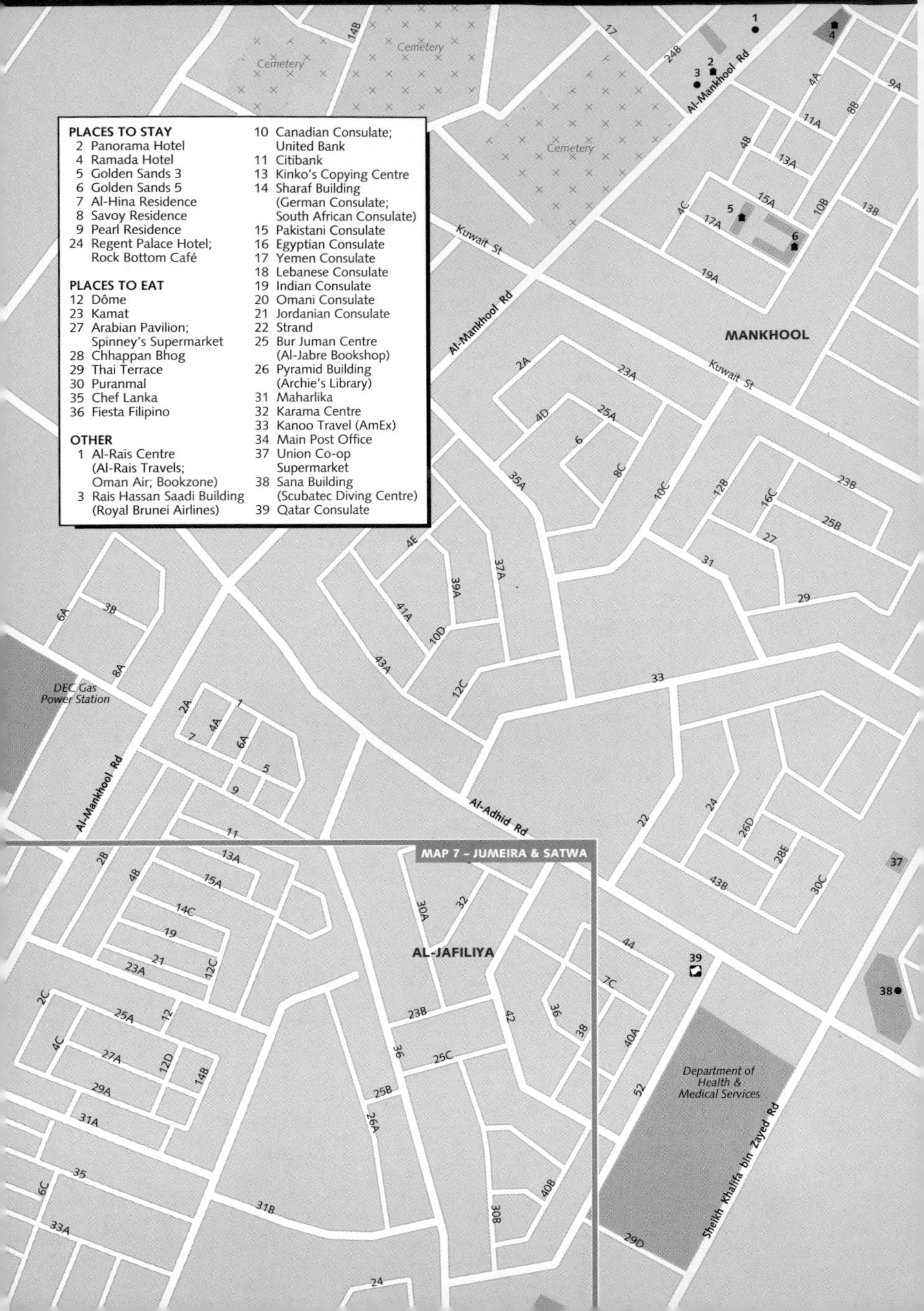

Cemetery

Cemetery

Cemetery

PLACES TO STAY
2 Panorama Hotel
4 Ramada Hotel
5 Golden Sands 3
6 Golden Sands 5
7 Al-Hina Residence
8 Savoy Residence
9 Pearl Residence
24 Regent Palace Hotel;
Rock Bottom Café

PLACES TO EAT
12 Dôme
23 Kamat
27 Arabian Pavilion;
Spinney's Supermarket
28 Chhappan Bhog
29 Thai Terrace
30 Puranmal
35 Chef Lanka
36 Fiesta Filipino

OTHER
1 Al-Rais Centre
(Al-Rais Travels;
Oman Air; Bookzone)
3 Rais Hassan Saadi Building
(Royal Brunei Airlines)

10 Canadian Consulate;
United Bank
11 Citibank
13 Kinko's Copying Centre
14 Sharaf Building
(German Consulate;
South African Consulate)
15 Pakistani Consulate
16 Egyptian Consulate
17 Yemen Consulate
18 Lebanese Consulate
19 Indian Consulate
20 Omani Consulate
21 Jordanian Consulate
22 Strand
25 Bur Juman Centre
(Al-Jabre Bookshop)
26 Pyramid Building
(Archie's Library)
31 Maharlika
32 Karama Centre
33 Kanoo Travel (AmEx)
34 Main Post Office
37 Union Co-op
Supermarket
38 Sana Building
(Scubatec Diving Centre)
39 Qatar Consulate

Al-Mankhool Rd

Kuwait St

Kuwait St

MANKHOOL

Al-Mankhool Rd

DEC Gas Power Station

Al-Mankhool Rd

Al-Adhid Rd

MAP 7 – JUMEIRA & SATWA

AL-JAFILIYA

Department of Health & Medical Services

Sheikh Khalifa bin Zayed Rd

10 11
13
18
6 7B
7 17 8
9 16 19
7 12 14 20
8 15 11 21
22A 26A 5B 24 23 7 Iranian 16A
GOLDEN SANDS 25 School

Khalid bin al-Waleed Rd

9A 2A
11B 4A
13C 16B
15B 26B 5 A'ishat
17B 28B 11 12A Intermediate
19B 27B 13 26 School Al-Karama Islamic
27 9A Kindergarten Studies
Ministry 3A College
28 of Health 10A 14A 7A
29 4B 13B
30 6A 8B 10B 13B
21 17A 12B Sheikha Latifa
10C 12C 18A 20A Bint Hamdan
School 24

31 Kuwait St 33
KARAMA 32 34
Al-Sae Divyat
International 27A
School
31 29A Karama Park 35
33A 29B
35
37B 15 20B
39 33B
41
45B Al-Karama
47A Shopping Centre 2
6 12E
Al-Adhid Rd 36
2D 45B
47B

Sheikh Khalifa bin Zayed Rd
Sheikh Khalifa bin Zayed Rd
Za'abeel Rd
Umm Hureir Rd

13A
47C
17A
4
10
15
12A

0 125 250m
0 125 250yd

MAP 7 – JUMEIRA & SATWA

ARABIAN
GULF

JUMEIRA

Public
Beach

PLACES TO STAY
1 Capitol Hotel; Henry J Beans
10 Rydges Plaza Hotel;
   Legends Bar
20 The World Trade Centre Hotel
21 Dubai World Trade Centre
   Apartments; Scuba Dubai
27 Dubai Marine Beach Resort & Spa;
   El Malecon; Capanna Nuova;
   Al-Qasr; Sho-Chos

PLACES TO EAT
6 Feras Sweets
8 Kitchen Restaurant
11 Pars Iranian Kitchen
12 Ravi Restaurant
14 Istanbouli Restaurant
17 Mini Chinese
28 Lime Tree Café

OTHER
2 Flagpole
3 Ruler's Guesthouse
4 Internet Café
5 Dune Centre (Book Corner;
   Voyagers Xtreme)
7 Adnan Ali Laundry
9 Al-Ghurair Exchange
13 Union Co-op Society
15 Abu Ahmed Antiques
16 Dar al-Hikma
18 Satwa Post Office
19 Dubai World Trade Centre
   (Australian Consulate; US Consulate;
   Turkish Consulate; Italian Consulate;
   Arabic Language Centre)
22 API World Tower
   (French Consulate)
23 Iranian Hospital
24 Iranian Mosque
25 Jumeira Mosque
26 Palm Strip Shopping Centre
   (Japengo; La Marquise;
   Formula One)
29 Spinney's Supermarket
30 Magrudy's Shopping Centre
   (Magrudy Books; General
   Medical Clinic; Gerard Café)
31 Markaz al-Jumeira
32 Jumeira Plaza
   (House of Prose; Book Corner)
33 Al-Boom Diving
34 Iranian Consulate

Al-Adhid Rd

Al-Mankhool Rd

7A

3

9

11A

13A

15A

19

2B

4B

21

23A

12C

3

30A

32

AL-JAFILIYA

44

7C

2B

4B

13

11

17

68

8C

15

19

6B

25A

12

2C

4C

27A

12D

14B

23B

25C

36

42

46

48

50A

29A

31A

68

33A

31B

25B

34

38B

50B

52

▼6

●7 ▼8

6C

MAP 6 – MANKHOOL & KARAMA

Al-Mankhool Rd

17▼

16●

3C

15▼

14

▲10 ▼11

57A

22

24A

24

39B

Satwa Roundabout

18A

16A

7D

45B

Department of Immigration & Naturalisation

36

13● 12
▼

2

6A

57B

57C

55B

54

Dubai Traffic

18 ✉

9

22A

Al-Dhiyafah Rd

SATWA

Al-Satwa Rd

Satwa Souq

13A

6C

8C

17

17B

14A

18B

20A

22B

11

Za'abeel Roundabout

1

28A

30A

7

19

8A

10B

19

21

26A

28A

5

22 ☑

19

21 ♦

20 ☗

14A

18A

20B

22B

32C

Sheikh Zayed Rd

Exhibition Halls

0   125   250m
0   125   250yd

UP

MAP LEGEND

CITY ROUTES

- Freeway .... Sealed Highway
- Highway .... Primary Road
- Road .... Secondary Road
- Street .... Street
- Lane .... Lane
- .... On/Off Ramp

- ==== .... Unsealed Road
- → .... One Way Street
- .... Pedestrian Street
- .... Stepped Street
-)= == .... Tunnel
- .... Footbridge

REGIONAL ROUTES

- .... Sealed Highway
- .... Primary Road
- .... Secondary Road
- ==== .... Unsealed Road

BOUNDARIES

- —·—·— .... International
- —·—· .... State
- — — — .... Disputed
- .... Fortified Wall

TRANSPORT ROUTES & STATIONS

- ●—— .... Train
- □ .... Ferry
- — — — .... Walking Trail

- · · · · · .... Walking Tour
- .... Path
- .... Pier/Jetty

HYDROGRAPHY

- .... River/Creek/Wadi
- .... Rapids
- ◉ .... Spring

- .... Lake
- .... Dry Lake
- .... Salt Lake

AREA FEATURES

- .... Building
- .... Park/Gardens

- .... Market
- .... Sports Ground

- ↗ .... Beach
- .... Campus

- x x x .... Cemetery
- .... Rock

POPULATION SYMBOLS

- ✪ **CAPITAL** .... National Capital
- ◉ **CAPITAL** .... State Capital

- ● **CITY** .... City
- ● **Town** .... Town

- ◉ Village .... Village
- .... Urban Area

MAP SYMBOLS

- ✈ Airfield/Airport
- ❸ Bank
- ⚲ Bird Sanctuary
- ⬡ Border Crossing
- Bus Station/Stop
- ⊞ Cinema
- ◳ Embassy/Consulate
- ▣ Fort
- ◔ Golf Course

- ⬓ Hindu Temple
- ✚ Hospital
- ▣ Internet Café
- ✳ Lookout
- ✖ Mine
- ⚑ Monument
- ◖ Mosque
- ▥ Museum/Gallery
- ⬓ National Park

- ▦ Oasis
- ▥ Palace
- ▣ Parking
- ◑ Petrol
- ▼ Place to Eat
- ■ Place to Stay
- ● Point of Interest
- ✪ Police Station
- ▭ Post Office

- ▣ Pub/Bar/Nightclub
- ▣ Ruins
- ▣ Sheesha Café
- ▣ Shopping Centre
- ▨ Sikh Temple
- ▣ Taxi Rank
- ☎ Telephone
- ❶ Tourist Information
- ▣ Zoo

Note: not all symbols displayed above appear in this book

LONELY PLANET OFFICES

Australia
Locked Bag 1, Footscray, Victoria 3011
☎ 03 8379 8000 fax 03 8379 8111
email: talk2us@lonelyplanet.com.au

USA
150 Linden St, Oakland, CA 94607
☎ 510 893 8555 TOLL FREE: 800 275 8555
fax 510 893 8572
email: info@lonelyplanet.com

UK
10a Spring Place, London NW5 3BH
☎ 020 7428 4800 fax 020 7428 4828
email: go@lonelyplanet.co.uk

France
1 rue du Dahomey, 75011 Paris
☎ 01 55 25 33 00 fax 01 55 25 33 01
email: bip@lonelyplanet.fr
www.lonelyplanet.fr

World Wide Web: www.lonelyplanet.com *or* AOL keyword: lp
Lonely Planet Images: www.lonelyplanetimages.com